AI Agents in Virtual Reality Worlds

Programming Intelligent VR in C++

Mark Watson

John Wiley & Sons, Inc.

New York • Chichester • Brisbane • Toronto • Singapore

Publisher: Katherine Schowalter

Senior Editor: Diane D. Cerra

Managing Editor: Micheline Frederick

Text Design & Composition: Integre Technical Publishing Co., Inc.

Designations used by companies to distinguish their products are often claimed as trademarks. In all instances where John Wiley & Sons, Inc. is aware of a claim, the product names appear in initial capital or all capital letters. Readers, however, should contact the appropriate companies for more complete information regarding trademarks and registration.

This text is printed on acid-free paper.

This publication is designed to provide accurate and authoritative information in regard to the subject matter covered. It is sold with the understanding that the publisher is not engaged in rendering legal, accounting, or other professional service. If legal advice or other expert assistance is required, the services of a competent professional person should be sought.

Library of Congress Cataloging-in-Publication Data:
Watson, Mark, 1951–
    AI agents in virtual reality worlds : programming intelligent VR
in C++ / Mark Watson.
        p.   cm.
    Includes index.
    ISBN 0-471-12708-6 (pbk. CD : alk. paper)
    1. C++ (Computer program language)   2. Virtual reality (Computer
science)   3. Artificial intelligence.   I. Title.
QA76.73.C153W395   1996
794.8'163—dc20   95-23675
                                                                      CIP

Printed in the United States of America

10 9 8 7 6 5 4 3 2 1

Contents

Acknowledgments

I would like to thank my wife Carol for her constant encouragement while I was writing this book. I would like to thank Mark V Systems for the use of its ObjectMaker CASE tool for writing the software in this book, and Borland for providing OS/2, Windows, and NT versions of its C++ development environments. I also used Microsoft Visual C++ 2.0, Symantec C++, and Watcom C++ 10.0 for compiling some of the example programs included in this book.

I would like to thank the following companies for allowing me to include their software in the CD-ROM that is included with this book:

- Mark V Systems, for a demonstration version of the ObjectMaker CASE tool.

- Criterion Software, for a demonstration program using its RenderWare 3D graphics API.

I would also like to thank Silicon Graphics and Microsoft for making the OpenGL library available as a standard feature in Windows NT 3.5.

I would like to thank Will Scarvie for discussions on Genetic Algorithms. I would like to thank my agent Matt Wagner at Waterside Productions; my acquisition editor at John Wiley, Diane Cerra; my production editor, Micheline Frederick; and my copy editor, Janice Borzendowski. I would like to thank Copy 'n Grafix in San Diego for their help in preparing the CD-ROM master.

Foreword

The market for games and virtual reality (VR) entertainment systems is enormous. In fact, today, the market for computer games is larger than the market for movies. There are many new VR books on the market, but most of them deal with the graphics and sound-generation techniques for constructing VR worlds, especially on low-cost personal computers. This book is targeted at developers of all levels of VR entertainment software, including:

- Home hobbyists who want to impress their friends and write shareware games.

- Professional game developers.

- Developers of location-based VR entertainment systems.

A visit to a computer store or a game arcade will illustrate how well graphics and sound combine to create entertaining game systems. However, these systems usually do not have interesting computer-controlled adversaries. Specifically, we do not usually experience computer agents with these behaviors:

- Changes in time in reaction to our behavior in a VR world or game.

- "Real world" knowledge or analytic skills to solve problems that occur uniquely in the VR environment because of our actions.

- Multiple behavior scripts that prevent repetitive experiences for the human participants in VR experiences.

This book concentrates on practical examples for creating realistic computer opponents and allies for VR worlds. An annotated bibliography provides the advanced reader with references for additional theory of artificial intelligence (AI) and VR world construction.

In order to test the C++ Class libraries for building the intelligent agents (IA) that are developed in this book, we will design and implement a space simulation (with 3D graphics) and a game (with 2D graphics) in which three types of player- or robot-controlled ships interact:

- A Processor ship that accepts Magnozate ore that the Player ship has collected from asteroids; it also barters with the player for energy conversion costs.

- Crogan ships are like mosquitoes. There are many of them, and they slowly steal energy from nearby Player or Processor ships. Crogan ships use genetic algorithms to continually evolve to become more dangerous opponents.

- A Player ship in which the player "stays alive" in the game by mining for Magnozate, bartering for energy conversion, and avoiding Crogans. The Player ship has an intelligent agent that can help the human player maneuver the ship and barter.

This game is divided into three code modules:

- Specific code for a particular platform (Windows, Windows with RenderWare, UNIX X Windows, OpenGL, and the Macintosh):

Main program.

Graphics window.

Graphics code for displaying game objects.

Event loop (checks for user input, simulates movement of physical objects, calls the agent manager, and displays the game world).

- Specific code for the behavior of AI agents:

World database.

Log manager for storing information from individual agents (such as inputs, reasons for taking actions, and so on).

Utility C++ classes for neural networks.

Utility C++ classes for genetic algorithms.

Utility C++ classes for Expert System construction.

Utility C++ classes for a Plan Manager.

- Example game code:

Data for training neural networks for sample game.

Expert System rule functions for sample game, which handle decisions based on only the current game situation.

Plan Manager rule functions, which handle situations in which decisions are made that require a series of actions executed in sequence.

Genetic algorithm fitness function to allow Crogan ships to evolve into better opponents during play.

The game is first implemented in text mode. Later chapters add a 3D graphics space simulation for RenderWare and OpenGL environments, and 2D graphics version of the simulation written as an interactive game for Microsoft Windows, UNIX X Windows, and the Macintosh.

Both text and graphics (2D and 3D) mode test programs are important tools for refining implementations of intelligent agents. As a creator of intelligent agent software, you can both study the text log output detailing the low-level decision-making process of the agents in a virtual environment, and you can watch a real-time graphic display (in two or three dimensions) of your agents in action.

A complete C++ source code implementation of a VR Agent Toolkit is provided in the book. The toolkit uses the following technologies:

- Neural networks.

- Genetic algorithms.

- Rule-based programming (Expert Systems) for decision-making based on only the current game situation.

- Plan Manager programming for identifying plans based on the current game situation, which require a series of actions over time.

These underlying technologies are explained with detailed examples. The reader will gain an understanding of when and how to apply these technologies. The provided C++ source code for the VR Agent Toolkit is documented in Chapters 2, 3, and 4. An annotated bibliography provides the interested reader with suggested reading material for a more detailed treatment of the theory.

What Is on the Disc

The CD-ROM contains all of the source code to the VR Agent Toolkit and the sample applications and demonstration programs provided by Mark V Systems and Criterion Software.

Recommended Computer Requirements

486 PC running Windows 95 or Windows NT, with either Microsoft Visual C++ version 2.0 or higher, Borland C++ version 4.5 or higher, or Watcom C++ version 10.0a or higher.

8 megabytes of memory for Windows 95, or 16 megabytes for Windows NT

15 megabytes of free disk space

Note: The Macintosh version of the VR Agent Toolkit was written and tested on a Macintosh II CX with 8 megabytes of memory using Symantec C++ version 6.0.

Note: The UNIX X Windows version of the VR Agent Toolkit was written and tested under Linux on a 486 machine with 20 megabytes of memory (12 megabytes is adequate). You will want about 10 megabytes of free disk space for development.

How to Use This Disc

The CD-ROM contains versions of the VR Agent Toolkit to run under a variety of operating systems and graphics APIs. The reader should choose an initial development environment and copy the required sub-directories from the directory SRC on the CD-ROM to their hard disk. The VR Agent Toolkit libraries are found in the sub-directory SRC, in the "sub-sub" directories:

AGENT
EXPERT
GENETIC
NN   (for neural network)
PLAN
UTILS

The text based demo simulation is found in:

SCR\TXT_GAME

A word to the wise: do not skip over the text based simulation. The directory SRC\TXT_GAME contains the implementation of agent code specific to all the graphics-based demonstration programs (both 2D and 3D) also.

ALL SOURCE CODE IN THE DIRECTORY SRC AND THE SUB-DIRECTORIES BELOW SRC CAN BE USED IN COMPILED FORM WITHOUT RESTRICTION. YOU ARE NOT PERMITTED

TO RE-DISTRIBUTE THE SOFTWARE IN SOURCE CODE FORM (for example, you can write games using the software, and distribute your games in compiled form without any restriction, but you are NOT ALLOWED to post the source code to any bulletin boards, the Internet, etc.)

The 3D simulation implemented in Open GL and Criterion Software's Renderware can be found in:

> SRC\OPENGL
> SRC\RW   (Windows version)
> SRC\RW_NT   (Windows NT version)

In order to use the RenderWare programs, set the environment variable RWSHAPEPATH to the directory containing the SCRIPTS and TEXTURES sub-directories in the directory RENDWARE.

The simple 2D space ship demo game is implemented for Windows 3.1, Apple Macintosh, and UNIX X Windows (there is a TAR file all set to go for LINUX) can be found in:

> SRC\WIN31
> SRC\MAC
> SRC\LINUX

PLEASE NOTE: You must have the data file NAV.NET in the current directory for all of the sample programs. This file can be re-created using the executable TXT_GAME\NAV_TRN.EXE (which can be re-built from the source files in TXT_GAME and NN).

The datafile CROGAN.DAT is a saved genetic algorithm data file containing a set of chromosomes which encode the control strategy for all Crogan ships in the example programs. You can delete CROGAN.DAT, and it will be re-created "on the fly"; it will take a minute or so of game play to evolve a new efficient population.

I use Mark V System's ObjectMaker CASE tool for my software development. You will see several Booch 94 Class diagrams and Harel state transition diagrams in the book that I created with ObjectMaker. The directory:

> MARK_V

contains a demo version of ObjectMaker. You can either run the demo version off of the CD-ROM, or follow the directions in the introduction of the book to install it on your hard disk. If you want to purchase ObjectMaker, there is a file MARK_V\README.TXT that contains product information. I thank Mark V Systems for allowing me to both use ObjectMaker for preparing the book diagrams, and also for including the demo version of ObjectMaker for the Booch 94 method on this CD-ROM.

You can install the demo version of ObjectMaker by running the SETUP.EXE program in the DISK_01 directory, then the SETUP.EXE program in the DISK_02 directory. NOTE: Since the CD-ROM program only contains the Booch setup files, the second SETUP.EXE program will terminate abnormally; please ignore any warning messages.

The demo version is also installed ready to run in the sub-directory OBJMAKR3. You can copy this entire sub-directory to your hard disk, instead of running the two SETUP.EXE programs (as mentioned in the last paragraph).

When running ObjectMaker: the demo version has the file load/save disabled, so you must specify the diagram file name that you want to view on either the command line (if you are running ObjectMaker from a Windows 95, or Windows NT console window), or as a command line argument if you are using the Windows Program Manager.

I would also like to thank Criterion Software for allowing me to use their RenderWare 3D graphics library for writing the 3D sample program in Chapter 6, and for also allowing me to include an executable version of my example program without license fees (usually, developers must pay a small per copy royalty for the use of RenderWare). I have also included a neat RenderWare demo "Cyber Street" in the directory:

RENDWARE\RWCYBER

There is also a read me file in RENDWARE\READ.ME with product information for RenderWare.

Contents of the CD-ROM

The following indented listing shows the directory structure on the CD-ROM included with this book:

BOOK
DIAGRAMS—Contains MarkV ObjectMaker Booch 94 C++ class diagrams
OBJMAKER—Contains a demonstration version of the MarkV ObjectMaker
                CASE tool
RENDWARE—Material from Criterion Software: RenderWare demo and
                data files
    SCRIPTS
    TEXTURES
SRC—All source code and executables for C++ class library and examples
    AGENT—Agent base class library
        AGENT.H
        AGENT.CPP
    EXPERT
        EXPERT.H
        EXPERT.CPP
        TEST_EXP.CPP
        EXPERT.IDE—Borland C++ 4.5 project file for test program
    GENETIC—C++ class for using genetic algorithms
        GENETIC.H
        GENETIC.CPP
        TEST_GEN.CPP
        TEST_GEN.PRJ—Borland C++ 4.5 project for test program
    LINUX —Version of the 2D demo game for UNIX X Windows
        MAKEFILE—Uses source files in AGENT, EXPERT, GENETIC, NN,
                PLAN, and TXT_GAME
        TEST_X.CPP
        TXT_GAME.CPP
        NAV.NET —Trained neural network data file for navigation
        VR_AGENT.TAR – UNIX tar file containing a makefile and all source code
    MAC—Contains a main program for an Apple Macintosh version of the 2D
                demo game
        GUI_MAC.CPP—Requires source files in AGENT, EXPERT, GENETIC,
                NN, PLAN, and TXT_GAME
        NAV.NET—Trained neural network data file for navigation
        VR_sit.hqx—BinHex file containing a StuffIt archive
    NN—C++ class for using neural networks
        NEURAL.H
        NEURAL.CPP

NN_TEST.CPP
TEST.NET—Sample saved neural network data file
OpenGL—Spaceship 3D simulation using OpenGL. Requires source files in
AGENT, EXPERT, GENETIC, NN, PLAN, and TXT_GAME
GLOS.H —OpenGL specific header file
NAV.NET—Trained neural network data file for navigation
TEST_GL.CPP —Main program for OpenGL 3D simulation
TEST_ZGL.MAK—Microsoft Visual C++ 2.0 makefile
MAKEFONT.CPP—Font creation function from Silicon Graphics/
Microsoft
WinDebug—Subdirectory for executable and object files
PLAN—C++ class for PlanManager
PLAN.H
PLAN.CPP
TEST_PLN.CPP
RW—Spaceship 3D simulation using RenderWare. Requires source files in
AGENT, EXPERT, GENETIC, NN, PLAN, and TXT_GAME. For
Microsoft Windows
MAKEFILE—For Watcom 10.0
WIN_GUI.CPP—Main program for simulation
RW_NT —Spaceship 3D simulation using RenderWare. Requires source files
in AGENT, EXPERT, GENETIC, NN, PLAN, and TXT_GAME. For
Microsoft Windows NT.
RW_NT.mak—Microsoft Visual C++ 2.0 makefile
RW_NT.CPP—Main program for simulation
TEST—Contains a C++ test program for the VR Agent Toolkit
TEST.CPP
TXT_GAME—A text-only version of the 3D spaceship simulation
CROGAN.CPP—Implementation of the C++ class Crogan (enemy
spaceships)
CROGAN.DAT—Data file for genetic algorithm chromosome population
CROGAN.H—Header file for the C++ class Crogan (enemy spaceships)
CROGAN.CP2—Experimental code using genetic algorithms and recurrent
neural networks (not part of the simulation)
CROGAN.H2—Experimental code using genetic algorithms and recurrent
neural networks (not part of the simulation)
GAME_VAL.H—Defines all simulation constants
NAV.NET—Trained neural network data file to help in navigation

NAV_AGNT.CPP—C++ class that uses a pretrained neural network and
    object-specific expert system and plan manager rule functions

NAV_AGNT.H

NAV_TRN.CPP—C++ standalone program to train navigational neural
    network (uses source files in ..\ NN)

PLAYER.CPP—C++ class implemetation of Player ship class

PLAYER.H—C++ class interface of Player ship class

PR_SHIP.CPP—C++ class implemetation of Processor ship class

PR_SHIP.H—C++ class interface of Processor ship class

SETUP.CPP—Data initialization for the 3D spaceship simulation

TEST.CPP—Simple test program that creates test objects

TXT_GAME.CPP—Main program and functions for the text version

TXT_GAME.IDE—Borland C++ 4.5 project file

TXT_GAME.WPJ—Watcom C++ 10.0 project file

UTILS—Log file class and classes for VR Agent Toolkit

GEOM_OBJ.H—Header file for C++ class **geometric_object**

GEOM_OBJ.CPP—Implementation file for C++ class **geometric_object**

GAME_OBJ.H—Header file for C++ class **game_object**

GAME_OBJ.CPP—Implementation file for C++ class **game_object**

WORLD.H—Header file for class **World** (container for all
    simulation objects)

WORLD.CPP—Implementation file for class **World** (container for
    all simulation objects)

OUT_LOG.H—Header file for text output logging C++ class

OUT_LOG.CPP—Implementation file for text output logging C++ class

WIN31—Windows 3.1 2D spaceship sample game

TEST_WIN.CPP—Main program and functions for Microsoft Windows
    sample game

TEST_WIN.ICO—Program ICON

TEST_WIN.H—C++ header file

TEST_WIN.WPJ—Watcom C++ 10.0 project file

WIN_BC.IDE—Borland C++ 4.5 project file

The directory SRC\TXT_GAME contains a text-only version
of the 3D spaceship and implementations for the three types of
simulated spaceships: Player, Processor Ship, and Crogan.

The Macintosh version of the sample game is included in the directory SRC\MAC. I include a BinHex (all ASCII file containing a StuffIt version 1.51 file). You should use the Other menu for StuffIt, converting the BinHex file to a binary StuffIt file, which can then be unpacked on your Macintosh. A project file for Symantec C++ version 6.0 and an executable is included in the StuffIt archive. The DOS file VR_SIT.HQX can be written to a DOS floppy disk, and read on your Macintosh using the Apple File Exchange program. Under Macintosh OS 7.5, you can also read the DOS floppy directly. You can also copy the files GUI_MAC.CPP, AGENT.H, AGENT.CPP, EXPERT.H, EXPERT.CPP, GENETIC.H, GENETIC.CPP, NEURAL.H, NEURAL.CPP, PLAN.H, PLAN.CPP, CROGAN.H, CROGAN.CPP, NAV.NET, NAV_AGNT.CPP, PLAYER.H, PLAYER.CPP, PR_SHIP.H, PR_SHIP.CPP, and TXT_GAME.CPP to your Macintosh, and create a project file with your C++ compiler.

The UNIX X Windows version of the sample game is included in the directory SRC\LINUX. You can copy the files TEST_X.CPP, MAKEFILE, AGENT.H, AGENT.CPP, EXPERT.H, EXPERT.CPP, GENETIC.H, GENETIC.CPP, NEURAL.H, NEURAL.CPP, PLAN.H, PLAN.CPP, CROGAN.H, CROGAN.CPP, NAV.NET, NAV_AGNT.CPP, PLAYER.H, PLAYER.CPP, PR_SHIP.H, PR_SHIP.CPP, and TXT_GAME.CPP to your UNIX workstation. Alternatively, there is a UNIX tar file VR_AGENT.TAR in the directory LINUX, which is set up to work with Linux, the Athena Widget set, and the GNU C++ compiler.

In order to build the RenderWare versions of the 3D simulation, you need to purchase the RenderWare developers kit from Criterion software (see the READ.ME file in the directory RENDWARE, and additional information in Chapter 6). The OpenGL example 3D simulation was written under Microsoft Windows NT using Visual C++ 2.0, both of which directly support OpenGL. The example OpenGL simulation should be easily portable to other OpenGL environments.

The SRC directory also contains project files for Borland C++ version 4.5 (extension *.IDE), Watcom C++ version 10.0 (extension *.WPJ), and Visual C++ version 2 for Windows NT (extension *.MAK).

The directory MARK_V contains a demonstration version of the Mark V Systems ObjectMaker program in the two subdirectories: DISK_01 and DISK_02. From Windows, OS/2 Warp, or Microsoft NT, execute the program SETUP.EXE in the subdirectory DISK_01, then execute the program SETUP.EXE in the subdirectory DISK_02. The second SETUP.EXE program will give a warning that you should ignore after it is done installing the demonstration version of ObjectMaker on your hard disk, because the directory DISK_02 only contains rule-sets for the Booch 94 methodology. The full ObjectMaker program is available from Mark V Systems (818-995-7671) with the following methodologies: Booch 94, Jacobson Use Case, MPDM, Rumbaugh, SEI ProNet, STRIM, and Wirfs-Brock. The demonstration program is limited, but you can view the Booch 94 class diagrams that appear in this book, and additional detail diagrams (found in directory DIAGRAMS on the CD-ROM) by specifying the name of a diagram file as a command line argument to the OBJMAKER.EXE program. There is a README.TXT file in the CD-ROM directory MARK_V that gives additional information for running ObjectMaker.

User Assistance and Information

John Wiley & Sons, Inc. is pleased to provide assistance to users of this CD-ROM. Should you have questions regarding the installation of this package, please call our technical support number at 212-850-6194 weekdays between 9 am and 4 pm Eastern Time.

Arrangement of Material in Chapters 2, 3, and 4

There are two software components in the VR Agent Toolkit:

1. A set of C++ AI utility classes for neural networks, genetic algorithms, expert systems, and plan management.
2. A set of C++ base classes for simulating game objects in a game or virtual reality world, a container class **World** to

manage a set of game objects, and a class **Agent** for containing and managing instances of the AI utility classes.

I discuss the requirements, design, and implementation of the AI utility classes in Chapter 2 *before* covering the requirements, design, and implementation of the **game_object** class, the **World** container class, and the **Agent** class in Chapters 3 and 4.

There are forward references in Chapter 2 to the classes **World** and **game_object**. Instances of classes **ExpertSystem** and **PlanManager** are created with references to the **World** object and **game_object** object in which they are contained. For some applications, the reader may want to substitute his or her own (different) implementations of **World** and **game_object** for use with the **ExpertSystem, PlanManager, Neural,** and **genetic** classes developed in Chapter 2.

Arrangement of Material in Chapters 6 and 7

The main themes of this book, the development and use of the C++ VR Agent Toolkit class libraries, are covered in Chapters 1 through 5. Chapters 6 and 7 concentrate on example programs that combine the text-based 3D spaceship simulation in Chapter 5 with the use of the 3D graphics toolkits RenderWare and OpenGL. Chapter 6 will be of interest to readers who either own the RenderWare graphics toolkit, or who may be interested in buying it. Chapter 7 will be of interest to readers who have access to a computer that supports OpenGL 3D graphics. Microsoft has built-in support for OpenGL in both Windows NT 3.5 and Windows 95. OpenGL is available on all Silicon Graphics workstations, and as an optional software product for Sun and HP workstations.

Arrangement of Material in Chapters 8, 9, and 10

The three simple example games in Chapters 8, 9, and 10 are very similar, basically implementing the same game for Microsoft Windows 3.1, the Apple Macintosh, and UNIX X Windows. There is some duplication of material in these chapters so that they can stand independently from each other. For example, if you are a Windows programmer, you probably want to read Chapters 1, 2, 3, 4, 5, and 8. If you are a Macintosh programmer, you probably want to read Chapters 1, 2, 3, 4, 5, and 9. If you are lucky enough to be programming on a UNIX machine running X Windows (including running the public domain Linux system on your PC at home), then you probably want to concentrate on Chapters 1, 2, 3, 4, 5, and 10.

Contacting the Author

You can reach me through electronic mail at:

- mwa@netcom.com (Internet)
- CompuServe 75765,556

I check my Internet e-mail several times daily, but I only check my CompuServe e-mail once a week. Use my Internet address if possible. I am also interested in collaborating with other developers of games and virtual reality experiences.

Introduction

Writing games and virtual reality (VR) simulations uses many programming disciplines. If we view a game as simply a computer program, we are concerned with:

- Real time graphics
- Sound effects
- Data structures
- Simulation model for interacting objects
- Real-time coordination of user inputs with simulation model

If we view the tasks in writing a game as a human computer interaction (HCI), we are concerned with the answers to these questions:

- Does the graphics refresh rate occur frequently enough to engage the game player?
- Do the graphic images look good? Are they pleasing to look at repetitively?
- Do the sound effects add to the sense of realism while playing the game?

- Is the story line for the game engaging? Does the game player have to think, or is it a "twitch" game?

- Do objects in the game act in a reasonable and engaging way?

The purpose of this book is to address the last question: Do objects in the game behave in a reasonable and engaging way? I enjoy experiencing VR worlds that other people create, and I enjoy playing good computer games that combine action ("twitch" games) with interesting problems to solve. I was motivated to write this book because I believe that applying new technologies like genetic algorithms, neural networks, and expert systems to VR simulations and games will result in more engaging and entertaining programs. I have written several shareware games since the days of the Apple II computer (I bought the 71st Apple II computer made), but I do not consider myself to be an expert game programmer. I am an expert in artificial intelligence (AI), object-oriented programming methodology, and C++ software development. My goal in this book is to present AI techniques to game programmers so that they can make this technology their own to use.

My goal in writing this book is to provide a tutorial for the AI techniques that I believe the game and VR simulation programmers should master. After the tutorial material, I design and implement a complete C++ toolkit for integrating these AI technologies into your games.

I start by designing a set of reusable C++ classes for creating intelligent software agents, then write a text-based space war game to test these C++ classes. In later chapters, I add 3D graphics for OpenGL and RenderWare platforms to create a 3D space simulation in which you can move around in the virtual world and watch the intelligent agents at work. I also create a simple interactive 2D game in which a human player can take control of one of the simulated spaceships from a game agent; I implement this 2D demonstration game for Windows, Macintosh, and UNIX X Window environments. For the UNIX X Windows example, I used the free Linux (UNIX clone) operating system, with the Athena Widget Toolkit; Linux, X Windows, and the Athena Toolkit are available for free on the Internet, or can be purchased for a copying charge on CD-ROM (e-mail: info@infomagic.com).

Development Methodology for the Software Contained in this Book

The C++ class libraries provided in this book are the result of an iterative approach to software development. I started by writing a short description of the major software components (such as utility classes for genetic algorithms, expert systems, neural networks, intelligent agent frameworks, and "throw-away" text-based and graphics code for testing the intelligent agent software).

For each software component, I started by naming the component; this name became the C++ class name. I then wrote a short description containing:

- The external behaviors (functionality) of instances of this class.

- Private data structures that each instance would have.

- Shared (static) class data that all instances of a class share.

- The public interface for class behaviors (public member functions).

- The public interface for reading, and possibly modifying, private data structures.

After making a preliminary pass at writing these requirements, I used the Mark V System's ObjectMaker CASE tool (a demo version of this product is included on the CD-ROM included with this book) to draw Booch (Booch 1994) class diagrams. I find these diagrams useful to:

- Serve as a reminder for the public interfaces for all the C++ classes that I use in a system.

- Provide a framework for understanding the relationships between the C++ classes in a system.

- Allow me to quickly iterate on a preliminary design for C++ classes.

When I am satisfied that the C++ class designs as represented in the Booch class diagrams cover the class and system requirements, I write a first-stage implementation of the classes, including short test programs to test the functionality of the classes, and to get experience using the classes.

When using the first-stage C++ class implementations, I (usually) iteratively go back to the requirements and the design, and update both my understanding of the requirements and my initial design ideas. I find that it is worthwhile to spend extra time keeping my requirements specifications, design notes, and Booch class diagrams up-to-date with iterative changes to the software.

CHAPTER 1

Abstract Framework for Specifying VR Worlds

Even though the principle subject of this book is how to use AI techniques to build interesting, entertaining, and engaging software agents for our games, we do need a software foundation for quickly constructing virtual worlds for our AI agents to "live" in. This chapter briefly discusses the game or virtual reality environment, explaining the requirements for real-time virtual experiences.

Requirements

A game program or a VR simulation is a real-time program. Figure 1.1 shows the major components of a VR simulation. There are several good options for the process architecture of a VR simulation or VR-based game, and this figure shows four distinct processes:

- Artificial Intelligence Agent: Well-defined inputs to view the current state of the world. Well-defined outputs for affecting changes in the current state of the world.

1

Sample Process Architecture for a Virtual Reality Simulation or Game

Artificial Intelligence Agents	Virtual World Data
3D Graphics Rendering Engine	Physics models for object interactions and dynamics
IO Control Manager	Network Manager for coordination with linked game simulations
	Interface to IO Manager
	Interface to Graphics Rendering Engine(s)

Figure 1.1   Typical process architecture for a virtual reality simulation.

- Graphics Rendering Engine: This process maintains geometric models for 3D rendering of all objects that can appear in a virtual world. Reads the current positions of world objects and the current viewpoint, and renders an animation frame. This process has read-only privileges to the world model (possible exception: some graphics processors have hardware collision detection; these collision events should be fed back to the world model for efficiency).

- IO Control Manager: This process captures user inputs and controls output devices, like motion platforms.

- World Model: This is a multithreaded process (on operating systems that support this) that maintains the current state of the world.

This process architecture obviously would not fit on top of DOS, for example. Still, even for DOS-based games, it provides a good structure for the software module architecture. Figure 1.2 shows a timing diagram illustrating typical real-time performance requirements. Typically, in real-time simulations for virtual reality, systems impose time restrictions on each system component. This is especially appropriate for standard operations performed by the Graphics Rendering system and the World Model simulation. For the AI Agent process however, there is no real need for such strict real-time performance. I consider it a better design trade-off to allow the AI Agent sufficient time for calculations, even if it makes decisions based on a world view that is slightly out of date.

Timing Diagram

As an example, assume a 20 Hz graphics frame update rate, a 40 Hz physical model update rate, a 5 Hz network update rate, and a 10 Hz input device polling rate:

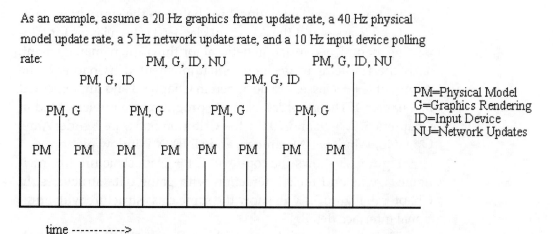

Figure 1.2   Typical timing diagram for a VR system.

Design Decisions

In designing software, especially reusable component libraries, it is important to understand the requirements for the software, and to make decisions as to the relative importance of the system requirements. The following is an ordered list of requirements (most important listed first) that will drive the design decisions for the C++ class libraries developed in this book:

1. Artificial intelligence (AI) components should be loosely coupled with the graphics and simulation components (I anticipate that readers will reuse the AI Intelligent Agent and the Virtual World simulation components, but largely write their own, or buy graphics components).
2. AI components must be extensible to new VR simulation and game environments.
3. Implementation of the graphics and simulation components must be relatively simple for both Windows, UNIX X Window, RenderWare, OpenGL, and Macintosh platforms.

C++ Classes for Intelligent Agents

This section shows the relationships between the simulation database C++ classes and the AI Agent classes. Utility classes for supporting neural networks, genetic algorithms, plan management, and expert systems are designed and implemented in Chapter 2. The AI Agent C++ classes are designed in Chapter 3 and implemented in Chapter 4. The graphics example programs are implemented in Chapters 6, 7, 8, 9, and 10 for the Criterion Software RenderWare, OpenGL, Windows, Macintosh, and UNIX X Window platforms.

Figure 1.3 shows the top-level C++ class structure for intelligent agents and their interaction with game data structures. In Chapter 3, Figure 3.1 will show the same class structure with additional interface detail.

The interested reader should see Booch (1994) for an excellent reference for object-oriented software development methodology. In order to make this book self-contained, I will describe the

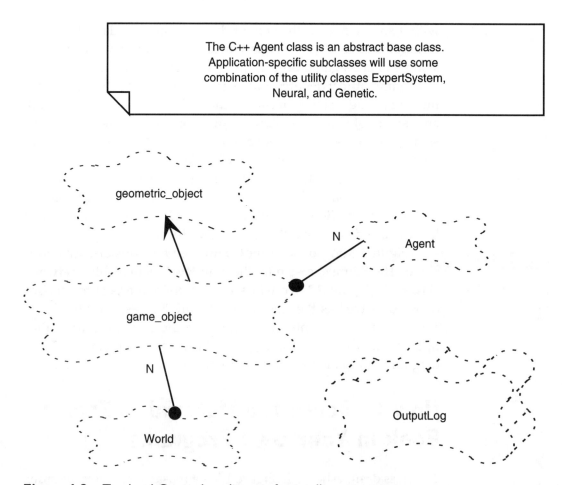

The C++ Agent class is an abstract base class. Application-specific subclasses will use some combination of the utility classes ExpertSystem, Neural, and Genetic.

geometric_object

N   Agent

game_object

N

World

OutputLog

Figure 1.3   Top-level C++ class diagram for intelligent agents.

Booch notation that appears in figures in this book. Figure 1.3 shows five C++ classes: **geometric_object**, **game_object**, **World**, **Agent**, and **OutputLog**. The C++ class **game_object** is derived from class **geometric_object**; this is indicated by the arrow pointing from the derived class (**game_object**) to the base class (**geometric_object**). I only use public C++ inheritance in this book, so all derived C++ classes follow "is a" relationships with their base classes. In this example, "An instance of class **game_object** *is a* type of **geometric_object**." In the Booch notation, containment relationships between C++ classes is denoted by a line drawn between classes, with a solid circle on the side of the "containing" class. In Figure 1.3, an instance of C++ class **World** can contain one or more instances of class **game_object**; the N next to the "Booch cloud" for class **game_object** denotes that instances of class **World** can contain more than one instance of class **game_object**. As seen in Figure 1.3, an instance of C++ class **game_object** can contain one or more instances of class **Agent**, or as per the note in Figure 1.3, one or more instances of classes derived from class **Agent**.

In Figure 1.3, the C++ class symbol for **OutputLog** stands apart from the other classes. Notice that the notation is different for **OutputLog**: the Booch cloud has a shadow, or three-dimensional look. This indicates that the class is a utility class.

Figure 1.3 only denotes the C++ class names inside each Booch cloud. The figure shows only the high-level relationships between classes. In Figure 2.1 we will see the public interface for classes denoted as well as the class name. Figure 3.1 is similar to Figure 1.3, with the public interface denoted in the class diagram. Other figures in this book (such as Figure 5.2) will use Harel state transition diagrams to denote the run-time dynamics of class interactions.

How to Reuse the Material in This Book in Your Own Programs

The class design shown in Figure 1.3 is a reusable resource. In order to reuse the material presented in this book in your own programs, you can use a process similar to the following:

1. Write a short description of your game.
2. Write a set of "use cases" describing different ways of playing your game (such as, start with an on-line tutorial, practice mode, or game mode).
3. Write a short document describing hardware requirements for running the game, supported video resolutions, behavior of game objects, game scoring, and so on.
4. Reuse Figure 1.3, which is specific to software agents and the data objects that they interact with. You will need to add C++ classes for IO control, graphics, and so on.

5. Reuse the C++ classes developed in this book that are appropriate to your game: Artificial Intelligence utility classes developed in Chapter 2; the World data, **geometric_object**, **game_object**, **Agent**, and **OutputLog** classes developed in Chapters 3 and 4.

6. Write your own C++ classes for graphics, IO control, and so forth.

You will find that following this process will yield several benefits:

- It will be easier to explain to other programmers how your game works.

- The object model of development will allow you to reuse not only C++ classes in future games, but you will find that you will also be able to reuse parts of your design in future projects (Booch, 1994).

- It is easier for a team of developers to work on your projects if they all understand the C++ class design, and all agree on the system requirements.

CHAPTER **2**

Multiparadigm Programming

We will use four AI paradigms for constructing intelligent agents: neural networks, genetic algorithms, expert systems, and plan management. Figure 2.1 shows the top-level class diagram for utility C++ classes developed in this chapter. The four utility classes shown in this figure will be used as low-level software components for building software agents, and they will be completely designed and implemented in this chapter. The requirements and design for the remainder of the VR Agent Toolkit will be covered in Chapter 3. The C++ classes designed in Chapter 3 will be implemented in Chapter 4. The remainder of the book, starting at Chapter 5 will provide example programs that use the VR Agent Toolkit.

Neural Networks

Back propagation neural networks are useful for recognizing patterns in data. For game-playing agents, these patterns can be particular sensor values and data values that trigger specific control events. Trained neural networks by themselves simply map an input data pattern to an output data pattern. When a trained back

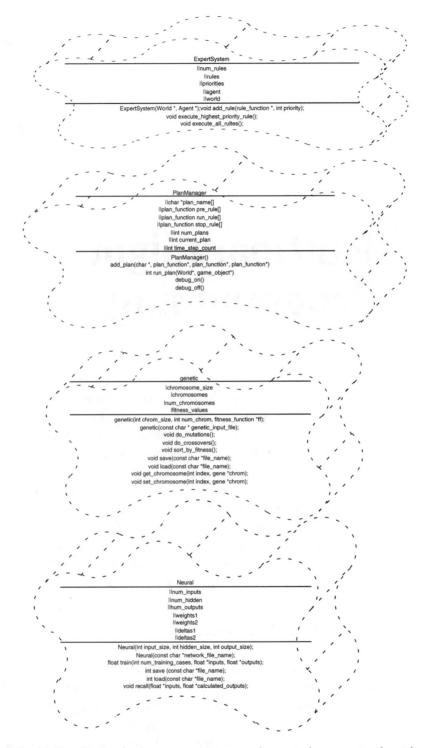

Figure 2.1 Utility C++ classes to support neural networks, genetic algorithms, expert systems, and plan management. This figure serves as a road map for the C++ classes designed and implemented in this chapter.

propagation (or delta rule) neural network is "shown" an input pattern, it matches it with the most similar training input pattern that it has learned, and emits the output data pattern that corresponds to the matched input training pattern. Figure 2.2 shows an example neural network architecture with three input neurons, two "hidden" neurons, and two output neurons.

Each neuron in a network has a numeric value referred to as *activation energy*. Neurons are connected with each other through *connection weights*. A connection weight, or weight, is characterized by a single floating point value. During training, the activation energy of each input neuron is set to a value calculated from a training pattern. The activation energies in the input neurons are allowed to flow through the connection weights (scaled by the numeric connection weight value) to the hidden neurons. Then new activation energies are calculated for the hidden neurons, and these new activation energies are allowed to flow through the connection weights connecting the hidden and output neurons. New activation energies are then calculated for the output neurons, and compared with the desired output values from the training examples. Both sets of weights are numerically adjusted during training to minimize the error between calculated output neuron activation values and the target activation values from the training examples.

For example, in Figure 2.2, if we have a training pattern with three input values, $-0.4 -0.4 +0.4$, and two training output values, $-0.4 +0.4$, then the weights in the network can be modified by using the following procedure (the Sigmoid and SigmoidP functions will be described after this procedure):

1. Copy the training inputs into the input neurons:

```
A_I1 = -0.4
A_I2 = -0.4
A_I3 = +0.4
```

2. Calculate the new hidden neuron activation values:

```
A_H1 = Sigmoid(A_I1 * W_I1_to_H1 + A_I2 * W_I2_to_H1 + A_I3 * W_I3_to_H1)
A_H2 = Sigmoid(A_I1 * W_I1_to_H2 + A_I2 * W_I2_to_H2 + A_I3 * W_I3_to_H2)
```

Architecture for a Neural Network with One Hidden Neuron Layer

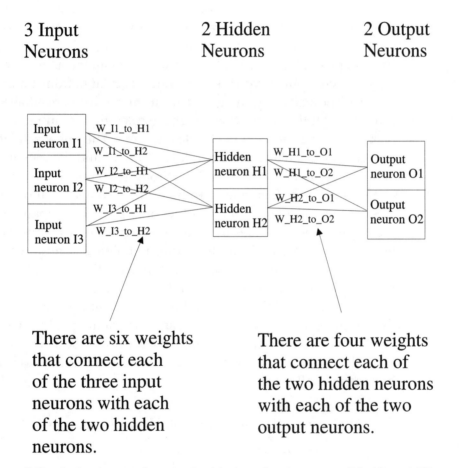

Figure 2.2   A simple neural network with three input neurons (I1, I2, and I3), two hidden neurons (H1 and H2) and two output neurons (O1 and O2). The weights are labeled by the neurons that they connect; for example, W_I2_to_H1 connects input neuron I2 with hidden layer neuron H1. The activation values for neurons can be denoted by, for example, A_H2 for the activation of hidden neuron H2.

3. Calculate the new output neuron values:

```
A_O1 = Sigmoid(A_H1 * W_H1_to_O1 + A_H2 * W_H2_to_O1)
A_O2 = Sigmoid(A_H1 * W_H1_to_O2 + A_H2 * W_H2_to_O2)
```

4. Calculate the error at each output neuron between the calculated values in step 3 and the training output values (-0.4 and $+0.4$):

```
Error_at_O1 = A_O1 - (-0.4)
Error_at_O2 = A_O2 - (+0.4)
```

5. Update the hidden neuron to output neuron weights:

```
Weight_change_H1_to_O1 = Error_at_O1 * Calculated_activation_O1
Weight_change_H2_to_O1 = Error_at_O1 * Calculated_activation_O1
Weight_change_H1_to_O2 = Error_at_O2 * Calculated_activation_O2
Weight_change_H2_to_O2 = Error_at_O2 * Calculated_activation_O2
```

6. Estimate the errors of the hidden layer neurons:

```
Error_at_H1 = SigmoidP(A_I1 * W_I1_to_H1 + A_I2 * W_I2_to_H1 + A_I3 * W_I3_to_H1)
            * (Error_at_O1 * W_H2_to_O1 + Error_at_O2 * W_H2_to_O2)
Error_at_H2 = SigmoidP(A_I1 * W_I1_to_H2 + A_I2 * W_I2_to_H2 + A_I3 * W_I3_to_H2)
            * (Error_at_O1 * W_H2_to_O1 + Error_at_O2 * W_H2_to_O2)
```

7. Update the input neuron to hidden neuron weights:

```
Weight_change_I1_to_H1 = Error_at_H1 * A_H1
Weight_change_I2_to_H1 = Error_at_H1 * A_H1
Weight_change_I3_to_H1 = Error_at_H1 * A_H1
Weight_change_I1_to_H2 = Error_at_H2 * A_H2
Weight_change_I2_to_H2 = Error_at_H2 * A_H2
Weight_change_I2_to_H2 = Error_at_H2 * A_H2
```

In practice, the weight changes are scaled by small values, so the value of each weight changes slowly while the training process loops repetitively over a set of training input/output values.

The hidden neurons allow a network to learn more complex patterns. A network with two hidden layers can learn arbitrarily complex mappings between input and output values. For use in game software, we will use networks with a single hidden layer of neurons as seen in Figure 2.2.

The **Sigmoid** function is a threshold function that limits the absolute value of neuron activation values; we will use a **Sigmoid** function with a minimum value of -0.5 and a maximum value of $+0.5$. The **SigmoidP** function is the derivative of the **Sigmoid** function, and is used to scale weight changes during training. Figure 2.3 shows an example of training a neural network with similar input patterns for the same target output activation values.

We can train neural networks to recognize patterns by showing them many slightly different examples of the same input pattern with the same target output activation energy pattern. During the training process, a network will "learn" to generalize: the common features of similarly classified input patterns are remembered in the connection weight values, while differences are treated as noise and not remembered. For example, in Figure 2.3, if each of the 16 input neurons was set to an activation value based on the fraction

Two Example Input Patterns for a Neural Network with 16 Input Neurons

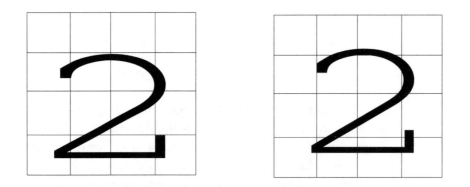

Example of characters mapped on a two-dimensional grid of input neurons

Figure 2.3   Two sample input patterns for a neural network with 16 input neurons.

of the character 2 covering each grid cell in the figure, the numerical values for these two patterns would be very different. However, if both of these patterns were identified as the character 2, then the network would learn the similarities of these patterns, as opposed, for example, to the input patterns from the characters 1 or 3.

In Chapter 5, we will train a neural network to calculate new velocities for a simulated spaceship based on input activation values representing relative positions of nearby objects. We will see that the ability of neural networks to recognize similar, yet different patterns will provide interesting behavior in new situations.

Neural networks combine both chaotic behavior, since they are a nonlinear system, and reasonable, if unexpected behavior since this nonlinearity is controlled by so-called basins of attraction in the memory formed in the connection weight values (as seen in Figure 2.4). If a neural network has N input neurons, then the range of possible input values can be thought of as a hyper-cube in N dimensions. This space is bounded since we typically force the activation energies of neurons to lie in the range -0.5 to $+0.5$. A new set of input values can therefore be thought of as a point inside this N-dimensional hyper-cube. This point will be attracted to the nearest "basin of attraction" inside the N-dimensional hyper-cube. Typically, one basin of attraction is formed for each category of training data (hopefully, the input patterns in Figure 2.3 would both be classified as an output activation energy pattern specifying 2, and would contribute to forming the same basin of attraction).

The behavior of a neural network is chaotic since a very small change in an input pattern can cause the corresponding point in the N-dimensional hyper-cube to be attracted to a different basin of attraction. This behavior of neural networks is very useful for intelligent agents in games and VR simulations since all basins of attraction near the point in the hyper-cube corresponding to an input pattern are likely to represent appropriate actions for that input pattern. For a human observer of a game agent using a neural network for decision-making purposes, it is very difficult to predict what the actions of the agent will be; after the agent has acted, the actions will usually seem reasonable. Figure 2.4 shows a representation of basins of attraction.

Basins of Attraction Formed by Training Data in a Neural Network with Three Input Neurons

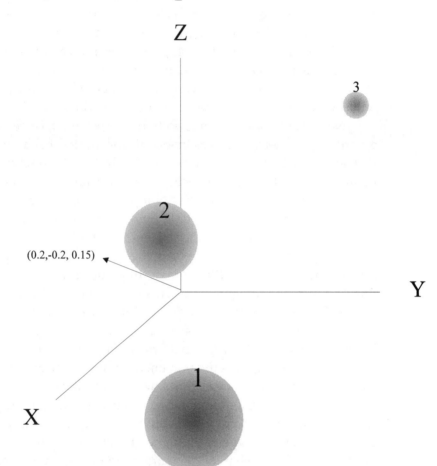

Figure 2.4 The space of possible input values for a neural network with three input neurons is a cube centered at the origin, with sides equal to 0.5. In this figure, three training cases created three basins of attraction inside the unit cube centered at the origin. Here, a new input pattern represented by a vector from the origin (input neuron 1 is set to 0.2, input neuron 2 is set to −0.2, and input neuron 3 is set to 0.15) is shown to be closest to the second basin of attraction, so the output neuron values will be close in value to the target output values for the second training case.

Listing 2.1 shows the C++ class interface for the class **Neural**, as seen in Figure 2.1.

Listing 2.1

```
// File: neural.h
//
// Description: This file contains the C++ class
//              definition for the VR agent neural
//              network utility class.
//
// Copyright 1995, Mark Watson
//

#ifndef NEURAL_H
#define NEURAL_H

#ifdef NT
#define random(x) (rand() % (x))
#endif

class Neural {
 public:
        Neural(int input_size, int hidden_size, int output_size);
        Neural(const char *network_file_name);
        ~Neural();
        float train(int num_training_cases,
                    float *training_inputs,
                    float *training_outputs);
        void save(const char *file_name);
        void load(const char *file_name);
        void recall(float *inputs, float *outputs);
        enum {MAX_INPUTS=16, MAX_HIDDEN=8, MAX_OUTPUTS=8};
 private:
        int num_inputs;
        int num_hidden;
        int num_outputs;
        float w1[MAX_INPUTS][MAX_HIDDEN];
        float w2[MAX_HIDDEN][MAX_OUTPUTS];
};

#endif
```

The library function **random** was not defined in Visual C++ for Microsoft Windows NT, so I use a compile time macro **NT** to define **random**. The first constructor for class **Neural** uses three integer arguments to set the number of input, hidden, and output neurons. The constructor initializes the weights in the network to random values. The second constructor for class **Neural** uses a single-character string argument to specify the file name of a previously trained neural network object. The public member functions **save** and **restore** serve to support data persistence. The public member function recall is used for calculating the output neuron values given a set of input neuron values. Listing 2.2 shows the C++ implementation of the class **Neural**.

Listing 2.2

```
// File: neural.cpp
//
// Description: This file contains the implementation of
//              the C++ class 'Neural'
//
// Copyright 1995, Mark Watson
//

#include <iostream.h>
#include <fstream.h>
#include <stdlib.h>
#include <math.h>

#ifdef NT
#define random(x) (rand() % (x))
#endif

#ifdef WIN31
#define random(x) (rand() % (x))
#endif

#include "neural.h"

Neural::Neural(int input_size, int hidden_size,
               int output_size)
{
```

```
    num_inputs = input_size;
    num_hidden = hidden_size;
    num_outputs = output_size;
    if (num_inputs > MAX_INPUTS) {
#ifdef TEXT_MODE
        cerr << "Input size too large\n";
#endif
        exit(1);
    }

    if (num_hidden > MAX_HIDDEN) {
#ifdef TEXT_MODE
        cerr << "Hidden size too large\n";
#endif
        exit(1);
    }

    if (num_outputs > MAX_OUTPUTS) {
#ifdef TEXT_MODE
        cerr << "Output size too large\n";
#endif
        exit(1);
    }

    // Initialize the w1 and w2 weight arrays:
    for (int i=0; i<MAX_INPUTS; i++)
        for (int j=0; j<MAX_HIDDEN; j++)
            w1[i][j] = ((float)random(1000) - 500.0) * 0.0001;
    for (int k=0; k<MAX_HIDDEN; k++)
        for (int l=0; l<MAX_OUTPUTS; l++)
            w2[k][l] = ((float)random(1000) - 500.0) * 0.0001;
}


// The following constructor reads a network definition
// file (from a previously trained and saved network),
// and constructs a new Neural instance.  The file format
// is of the form <# inputs> <# hidden> <# outputs>
// <list of w1 values> <list of w2 values>.

Neural::Neural(const char *network_file_name)
{
    load(network_file_name);
```

```
}
Neural::~Neural()
{
}


static float Sigmoid(float z)
{
   if (z > 8.0)  z = 8.0;
   if (z <-8.0)  z = -8.0;
   return (1.0 / (1.0 + exp(-z))) - 0.5;
}


static float SigmoidP(float z)
{
   float x = Sigmoid(z) + 0.5f;
   return x * (1.0f - x);
}


// Member function train is called with a set of training
// cases that are used to adjust the network weights to
// reduce the output error averaged over the complete
// training set. The output error over the training set
// is returned as the function value. This function is
// typically called repetitively until this error
// approaches zero.

float Neural::train(int num_training_cases,
                    float *training_inputs,
                    float *training_outputs)
{
   float error = 0.0; // this will be the return value
   int i, j, k;
   float hidden_errors[MAX_HIDDEN];
   float output_errors[MAX_OUTPUTS];
   float input_neurons[MAX_INPUTS];
   float hidden_neurons[MAX_HIDDEN];
   float output_neurons[MAX_OUTPUTS];

   for (int nt=0; nt<num_training_cases; nt++) {
      float * inputs_vals =
         &(training_inputs[nt*num_inputs]);
      float inputs[MAX_INPUTS];
      for (int m=0; m<num_inputs; m++)
```

```
    inputs[m] = inputs_vals[m]
      + (((float)random(1000) - 500.0) * 0.0001);
float *outputs = &(training_outputs[nt*num_outputs]);
// zero out errors:
for (i=0; i<num_hidden; i++)
   hidden_errors[i] = 0.0;
for (i=0; i<num_outputs; i++)
   output_errors[i] = 0.0;
// copy training inputs to the input neurons:
for (i=0; i<num_inputs; i++)
   input_neurons[i] = inputs[i];
// Propagate the activation energy from the
// input neurons, through the w1 weight array to
// the hidden neurons, then from the hidden neurons
// through the w2 weight array to the output neurons:
int from, to;
// from input to hidden neurons:
for (to=0; to<num_hidden; to++) {
   hidden_neurons[to] = 0.0;
   for (from=0; from<num_inputs; from++)
      hidden_neurons[to] +=
         input_neurons[from] * w1[from][to];
}
// from hidden to output neurons:
for (to=0; to<num_outputs; to++)  {
   output_neurons[to] = 0.0;
   for (from=0; from<num_hidden; from++)
      output_neurons[to] +=
         hidden_neurons[from] * w2[from][to];
}
// calculate the error at each output neuron:
for (j=0; j<num_outputs; j++)
   output_errors[j] +=
      (outputs[j] - Sigmoid(output_neurons[j]))
    *SigmoidP(output_neurons[j]);
// calculate the error at each hidden neuron:
for (i=0; i<num_hidden; i++)  {
   hidden_errors[i] = 0.0;
   for (j=0; j<num_outputs; j++)  {
      hidden_errors[i] += output_errors[j] * w2[i][j];
   }
}
```

```
      for (i=0; i<num_hidden; i++) {
         hidden_errors[i] *= SigmoidP(hidden_neurons[i]);
      }
      // update the w2 array that connects the hidden neurons
      // to output neurons:
      for (j=0; j<num_outputs; j++)
         for (i=0; i<num_hidden; i++)
            w2[i][j] += output_errors[j] * hidden_neurons[i];
      // update the w1 array that connects the input
      // neurons to the hidden neurons:
      for (j=0; j<num_hidden; j++)
         for (i=0; i<num_inputs; i++)
            w1[i][j] += hidden_errors[j] * input_neurons[i];
      // sum the error at the output neurons:
      for (i=0; i<num_outputs; i++)
         error += output_errors[i] * output_errors[i];
   }
   return error;
}


void Neural::save(const char *file_name)
{
   filebuf out_file;
   if (out_file.open(file_name, ios::out) == 0) {
#ifdef TEXT_MODE
      cerr << "Could not open output file "
           << file_name << "\n";
#endif
      exit(1);
   }
   ostream out_stream(&out_file);
   out_stream << num_inputs << "\n";
   out_stream << num_hidden << "\n";
   out_stream << num_outputs << "\n";
   int i, j;
   for (i=0; i<num_inputs; i++)
      for (j=0; j<num_hidden; j++)
         out_stream << w1[i][j] << "\n";
   for (i=0; i<num_hidden; i++)
      for (j=0; j<num_outputs; j++)
         out_stream << w2[i][j] << "\n";
}
```

```cpp
void Neural::load(const char *file_name)
{
    filebuf in_file;
    if (in_file.open(file_name, ios::in) == 0) {
#ifdef TEXT_MODE
        cerr << "Could not open input file "
            << file_name << "\n";
#endif
        exit(1);
    }
    istream in_stream(&in_file);
    in_stream >> num_inputs;
    in_stream >> num_hidden;
    in_stream >> num_outputs;
    int i, j;
    for (i=0; i<num_inputs; i++)
        for (j=0; j<num_hidden; j++)
            in_stream >> w1[i][j];
    for (i=0; i<num_hidden; i++)
        for (j=0; j<num_outputs; j++)
            in_stream >> w2[i][j];
}


void Neural::recall(float *inputs, float *outputs)
{
    int i, j;
    float hidden_neurons[MAX_HIDDEN];

    // Propagate the activation energy from the
    // input neurons, through the w1 weight array to
    // the hidden neurons, then from the hidden neurons
    // through the w2 weight array to the output neurons:
    int from, to;
    // from input to hidden neurons:
    for (to=0; to<num_hidden; to++) {
        hidden_neurons[to] = 0.0;
        for (from=0; from<num_inputs; from++)
            hidden_neurons[to] +=
                inputs[from] * w1[from][to];
    }
    // from hidden to output neurons:
    for (to=0; to<num_outputs; to++)  {
```

```
      outputs[to] = 0.0;
      for (from=0; from<num_hidden; from++)
         outputs[to] +=
            hidden_neurons[from] * w2[from][to];
      outputs[to] = Sigmoid(outputs[to]);
  }


}
```

Both constructors for class **Neural** check the requested network size, and compare this size with the class-enumerated constants **MAX_INPUTS, MAX_HIDDEN,** and **MAX_OUTPUTS**. A warning message is printed, and the **exit()** function is called to terminate the program if the requested network is too large. See Watson (1994) for a more complicated network architecture that allocates all storage dynamically and works with one or two hidden layers. For the purposes of this book, it is easier to implement and to understand the implementation of class **Neural** with static allocation of weights based on class-enumerated constants, which can be changed, and file NEURAL.CPP recompiled, if a larger neural network is desired.

The initial values of the connection weights are set to small random values before training in the first class constructor. The second class constructor reads trained connection weights from an ASCII text file. By convention, I use the extension *.NET for the examples later in this book for trained neural network files.

The function **Sigmoid** is often called a *squashing* function. As implemented in file NEURAL.CPP, the maximum value of this function (for large positive values of its input argument) is 0.5, and the minimum value of this function (for large negative values of its input argument) is -0.5. The **Sigmoid** function is used to constrain the output activation energy of any neuron to the range $(-0.5, 0.5)$.

The function **SigmoidP** is the first derivative of the **Sigmoid** function. This function is used internally in the class public member function **train** for adjusting the connection weights during training. The public member function **train** is used to set the values of the network's connection weights to minimize the sum of the error of all of the output neurons over all of the training examples.

The public member function **save** is used after training to write the values of the connection weights to a file. The complementary public member function **load** is used to quickly reload a trained set of weights. All of the example 3D spaceship simulations and the 2D spaceship games implemented later in this book load in a pretrained neural network in file NAV.NET to help navigate a class of simulated spaceships. The public member function **recall** is used to calculate the output neuron values given a set of input neuron values.

The neural network simulator in Listing 2.2 is fairly simple, but it is effective for the purposes of this book. Training time can be reduced by using momentum terms to adjust weights that are grossly incorrect more quickly. To implement training with momentum, you need to remember the weight changes from the previous training cycle, and adjust weights based on the current and the last delta weight values. For a given weight, if the direction of the weight change is in the same direction, the learning rate accelerates.

Listing 2.3 contains a short test program for the C++ class **Neural**. This short program serves as an example for using the following public member functions of class **Neural**:

Neural::Neural(int input_size, int hidden_size, int output_size)

Neural::train(int num_training_examples, float * inputs, float *outputs)

Neural::save(const char *save_file_name)

Neural::load(const char *load_file_name)

Neural::recall(float *inputs, float *outputs)

Listing 2.3

```
// File: nn_test.cpp
//
// Description: This file contains code to test the
//              C++ class 'Neural'.
//
```

```
#include "neural.h"
#include <iostream.h>

void main()
{
  cerr << "Test of the class Neural\n";
  Neural nn(4,4,4);
  float inputs[] = {    // 4 training input sets:
    +0.5, -0.5, -0.5, -0.5,
    -0.5, +0.5, -0.5, -0.5,
    -0.5, -0.5, +0.5, -0.5,
    -0.5, -0.5, -0.5, +0.5
  };
  float outputs[] = {    // 4 training output sets:
    -0.3, +0.3, -0.3, -0.3,  // target 0.3, not 0.5
    -0.3, -0.3, +0.3, -0.3,  // (see text)
    -0.3, -0.3, -0.3, +0.3,
    +0.3, -0.3, -0.3, -0.3
  };
  for (int i=0; i<100; i++) {
    float error = nn.train(4, inputs, outputs);
    cerr << "iteration " << i
        << " training error =" << error << "\n";
  }
  float outs[10];
  for (i=0; i<4; i++) {
    cerr << "\ntesting training pattern " << i << "\n";
    nn.recall(&(inputs[i*4]), outs);
    cerr << outs[0] << ", " << outs[1] << ", "
        << outs[2] << ", " << outs[3] << "\n";
  }
  nn.save("test.net");
  Neural n2("test.net");
  for (i=0; i<4; i++) {
    cerr << "\nStored net: testing training pattern " << i << "\n";
    n2.recall(&(inputs[i*4]), outs);
    cerr << outs[0] << ", " << outs[1] << ", "
        << outs[2] << ", " << outs[3] << "\n";
  }
}
```

Note that the target output neuron activation values are set to −0.3 and +0.3 instead of −0.5 and +0.5. It is very difficult to train a neural network to produce output activation values near the extreme ranges of the **Sigmoid** function. You should build this test program (using source files NEURAL.H, NEURAL.CPP, and NN_TEST.CPP) and run it. The member function **train** returns as its value a measure of how well trained the network is for the current training set; this return value will be large the first few times that member function **train** is called, then decrease toward zero. Larger networks will take longer to train. We will use class **Neural** in Chapter 5 and discuss there its use in the example spaceship simulation. Here are a few general heuristics for effectively using neural networks in your programs:

- *Use an adequate number of training examples.* For small networks, include at least two or three slightly different sets of input neuron activation energy values for each target output activation pattern.

- *Initially select a small subset of the training data.* For large networks that require over 50 training examples, you can usually speed up the training process by selecting a small subset of the training cases for initial training. Once the error from function **train** gets close to zero, retrain the network using all of the training examples.

- *Do not use too many hidden neurons.* A good rule for calculating the number of hidden neurons is to take the log, base 2, of the distinct number of target output patterns, and add one extra hidden neuron. Using a smaller number of hidden neurons forces a neural network to find common patterns in training cases with the same output pattern. If you use too many hidden neurons, the network will be able to simply remember all of the distinct training cases, and will not generalize by ignoring "noise" in the training data.

Genetic Algorithms

Genetic algorithms borrow principles from population biology to efficiently search very large parameter spaces. Genetic algorithms work by applying a fitness function to each chromosome in a population. Unfit chromosomes are replaced by chromosomes produced by crossover and mutation from fit chromosomes. Each chromosome in a genetic population contains a specified number of genes. The data stored in each chromosome is application-dependent. However, experience has shown that usually genes best represent a single bit of information. We will see in Chapter 5 how to code the information for controlling the strategy of a class of a simulated spaceship object in a chromosome, and how to use genetic algorithms to continually modify the strategy of every member of this class of simulated spaceships as the virtual world, or game situation, changes. In this section, we will develop a general understanding of genetic algorithms, develop a C++ class library to make it simple to embed genetic algorithms in C++ programs, and show a very simple test program that uses this C++ utility class.

Listing 2.4 shows the C++ class interface for class **genetic** (as seen in Figure 2.1). An instance of this class contains the following data:

- A population of chromosomes

- A numeric fitness value for each chromosome in the population

The file GENETIC.H in Listing 2.4 contains, in addition to the class definition, a C style *typedef* for a function pointer **fitness_function**. The class **genetic** contains a pointer to a **fitness_function**, which is used to numerically rate the effectiveness of each chromosome in the population for a specified environment. There are two tasks involved in using genetic algorithms in your programs:

1. Determining what data needs to be encoded in a chromosome.
2. Writing a C language fitness function that assigns a numerical fitness rating to a given chromosome.

In principle, you could simply create a large number of random chromosomes, use the fitness function to rank them, and keep the best few chromosomes for your population, but this type of brute force random search is extremely inefficient. Instead, genetic algorithms borrow two ideas from population biology to efficiently search for chromosomes with a high fitness rating:

- Crossover: create a new chromosome by combining two existing chromosomes with high fitness ratings.

- Mutation: occasionally randomly change the value of a gene in a chromosome.

We will look at a simple application of genetic algorithms before implementing the C++ class **genetic**. The educational system in a state has received a federal grant for educational equipment for the 42 junior high schools in the state. The school system expects to receive this money for at least 10 years, and would like to optimize the fraction of money spent on the following nonreusable items:

- Hiring high school students as special tutors

- Renting science movies

- Field trips to science museums

- Field trips to art galleries

- Travel expenses for guest speakers for career guidance

The school system could use a genetic algorithm to optimize the use of these extra funds by following this procedure:

1. Represent each of the five expense items as an integer number represented by 3 bits (this can encode an integer from 0 to 7). A chromosome will contain 15 genes (or bits), representing the relative expenditures in each of the five categories.
2. There will be one chromosome for each school. These 42 chromosomes encode the spending patterns for each junior high school in the state.
3. The fitness function will be the relative yearly test scores of each school. This allows us to roughly judge the relative

value of each chromosome in the genetic population. This fitness score could also be normalized by past performance at each school.

4. Each year, after the yearly test scores are available, the chromosome population is altered by discarding low-rated (unfit) chromosomes, and by using mutation and crossover operations to replace the discarded chromosomes. After the chromosome population is recalculated, the chromosomes in the population are randomly assigned to the schools.

This simple example shows how the genetic crossover and mutation operators can be used to quickly find near optimal setting for a system's control parameters.

Listing 2.4 shows the C++ class definition for the class **genetic**. The C typedef for the prototype of fitness functions is defined before the class definition for **genetic**. The typedef for gene is specified as type *unsigned char*.

Listing 2.4

```
// File: genetic.h
//
// Description: This file contains the C++ class interface
//              for class 'genetic'.
//
// Copyright 1995, Mark Watson
//

#ifndef genetic_h
#define genetic_h

#ifdef NT
#define random(x) (rand() % (x))
#endif

typedef unsigned char gene;

typedef float (*fitness_function)(int chrom_index,
                                  int chrom_size,
                                  unsigned char *chrom);
```

```
class genetic {
 public:
    genetic(int chrom_size, int num_chrom,
            fitness_function ff);
    genetic(const char *genetic_input_file,
            fitness_function ff);
   ~genetic();
    void do_mutations();
    void do_crossovers();
    void sort_by_fitness();
    void save(const char *file_name);
    void load(const char *file_name);
    void set_chromosome(int index, gene *chrom);
    void get_chromosome(int index, gene *chrom);
 protected:
    int chromosome_size;    // # of genes per chromosome
    int num_chromosomes;
    fitness_function fitness_func;
    enum {MAX_CHROMOSOMES=100};
    gene * population[MAX_CHROMOSOMES];
    float fitness_values[MAX_CHROMOSOMES];
    int p_chrom[MAX_CHROMOSOMES];
};


#endif
```

The data in class **genetic** is defined as *protected* instead of *private* so that any classes derived from **genetic** can have direct access to the data defined in the **genetic** class interface.

Listing 2.5 shows the C++ implementation of class **genetic**. Class public member functions **do_crossovers()** and **do_mutations()** are used to create new chromosomes in the population. The class constructor initializes the chromosomes to random gene values. The member function **sort_by_fitness()** uses the fitness function to rank the current chromosome population. Member function **sort_by_fitness()** uses private data to keep a sorted list of chromosome indices in the population (using the array **p_chrom**), rather than physically shuffling chromosomes.

During normal use of this C++ class, we will call these class member functions in this order:

1. **sort_by_fitness**
2. **do_crossovers**
3. **do_mutations**

It is important to sort the chromosomes by fitness before applying the crossover and mutation operations because both crossover and mutation selectively keep fit chromosomes intact, and discard unfit chromosomes. These three functions are not coalesced into a single "training" utility function because sometimes we will not want to use the mutation "operator" on a population. For some cases (such as using genetic algorithms to train neural networks) we might not want to use the crossover operation.

Listing 2.5

```
// File: genetic.cpp
//
// Description: This file contains the C++ class
//              definition for class 'genetic'.
//
// Copyright 1995, Mark Watson
//

#include <iostream.h>
#include <fstream.h>
#include <stdlib.h>
#include <math.h>

#ifdef NT
#define random(x) (rand() % (x))
#endif

#ifdef WIN31
#define random(x) (rand() % (x))
#endif

#include "genetic.h"

genetic::genetic(int chrom_size, int num_chrom,
                 fitness_function ff)
{
```

```
      chromosome_size = chrom_size;
      num_chromosomes = num_chrom;
      if (num_chromosomes > MAX_CHROMOSOMES) {
#ifdef TEXT_MODE
         cerr << "Chromosome size is too large.\n";
#endif
         exit(1);
      }
      fitness_func = ff;
      // Initialize the population:
      for (int i=0; i<num_chromosomes; i++) {
         population[i] = new unsigned char[chromosome_size];
         for (int j=0; j<chromosome_size; j++) {
            if (random(10) < 7)
               population[i][j] = 0;
            else
               population[i][j] = 1;
         }
      }
}


genetic::genetic(const char *genetic_input_file,
                 fitness_function ff)
{
   load(genetic_input_file);
   fitness_func = ff;
}


genetic::~genetic()
{
   for (int i=0; i<num_chromosomes; i++)
      delete population[i];
}


void genetic::do_mutations()
{

   // Copy the best chromosomes:
   for (int m=0; m<2; m++) {
      for (int g=0; g<chromosome_size; g++) {
         population[p_chrom[num_chromosomes -1 -m]][g] =
            population[p_chrom[m]][g];
      }
```

```
    }
    int nskip = 2 + num_chromosomes / 10;
    int threshold = 995 - ((1000 / chromosome_size) / num_chromosomes);
    for (int i=nskip; i<num_chromosomes; i++) { // skip 'nskip'
                                                // best chromosomes
        for (int j=0; j<chromosome_size; j++) {
            if (random(1000) > threshold)
                population[p_chrom[i]][j] =
                        1 - population[p_chrom[i]][j];
        }
    }
}


void genetic::do_crossovers()
{
    // Note: sort_by_fitness() should be called
    //       before this function.
    for (int m=0; m<(num_chromosomes / (num_chromosomes / 2)); m++) {
        // choose one chromosome to change from
        // the "worse" half of the population:
        int c1 = random(num_chromosomes / 2);
        c1 = p_chrom[num_chromosomes - c1 - 1];
        // choose two chromosomes to copy genetic
        // material from fit members of the population
        int s1 = random(num_chromosomes / 4) - 2;
        int s2 = random(num_chromosomes / 4) - 2;
        if (random(10) < 5) {
            s1 /= 2;
            s2 /= 2;
        }
        if (s1 < 0) s1 = 0;  // bias for best chromosome
        if (s2 < 0) s2 = 0;  // bias for best chromosome
        // choose a random allele (gene index)
        // for the crossover operation:
        int cross = 1 + random(chromosome_size - 2);
        for (int i=0; i<cross; i++)
            population[c1][i] = population[s1][i];
        for (i=cross; i<chromosome_size; i++)
            population[c1][i] = population[s2][i];


    }
}
```

```cpp
void genetic::sort_by_fitness()
{
        // Start by calling the fitness function for each
        // chromosome in the population:
        for (int i=0; i<num_chromosomes; i++) {
            fitness_values[i] =
              (*fitness_func)(i, chromosome_size, &(population[i][0]));
        }

        for (i=0; i<num_chromosomes; i++) p_chrom[i] = i;
        // do a "bubble", or exchange sort:
        for (i=0; i<num_chromosomes; i++) {
            for (int j=(num_chromosomes-2); j>=i; j--) {
                if (fitness_values[j] < fitness_values[j+1]) {
                    int k = p_chrom[j];
                    float f = fitness_values[j];
                    p_chrom[j] = p_chrom[j+1];
                    fitness_values[j] = fitness_values[j+1];
                    p_chrom[j+1] = k;
                    fitness_values[j+1] = f;
                }
            }
        }
}


void genetic::save(const char *save_file_name)
{
    filebuf output_file;
    if (output_file.open(save_file_name, ios::out) != 0) {
      // File opened OK:
      ostream out_strm(&output_file);
      out_strm << chromosome_size << "\n";
      out_strm << num_chromosomes << "\n";
      for (int i=0; i<num_chromosomes; i++) {
        for (int j=0; j<chromosome_size; j++) {
            out_strm << (int)population[i][j] << "\n";
        }
      }
    } else {
#ifdef TEXT_MODE
        cerr << "Error opening output chromosome data file\n";
#endif
    }
}
```

```
void genetic::load(const char *file_name)
{
   filebuf input_file;
   if (input_file.open(file_name, ios::in) != 0) {
      // File exists:
      istream in_strm(&input_file);
      in_strm >> chromosome_size;
      in_strm >> num_chromosomes;
      if (num_chromosomes > MAX_CHROMOSOMES) {
#ifdef TEXT_MODE
         cerr << "Chromosome size is too large.\n";
#endif
         exit(1);
      }
      int ii;
      for (int i=0; i<num_chromosomes; i++) {
         for (int j=0; j<chromosome_size; j++) {
            in_strm >> ii;
            population[i][j] = ii;;
         }
      }
   } else {
#ifdef TEXT_MODE
      cerr << "File " << file_name << " does not exist.\n";
      exit(1);
#endif
   }
}


void genetic::set_chromosome(int index, gene *chrom)
{
   if (index < 0)  index = 0;
   if (index > (num_chromosomes - 1)) index = num_chromosomes - 1;
   for (int i=0; i<chromosome_size; i++)
      population[index][i] = chrom[i];
}

void genetic::get_chromosome(int index, gene *chrom)
{
   if (index < 0)  index = 0;
   if (index > (num_chromosomes - 1)) index = num_chromosomes - 1;
   // You must call sort_by_fitness() before
   // calling this function.
```

```
for (int i=0; i<chromosome_size; i++)
    chrom[i] = population[p_chrom[index]][i];
}
```

We use class-enumerated constants defined in the file GENETIC.H (Listing 2.4) to set the maximum size of a chromosome and the maximum population size. The implementation of this C++ class is much easier to understand because we are using fixed-size arrays. See Watson (1994) for an alternative implementation of a genetic algorithm that is suitable for solving problems requiring very large search spaces. The implementation in Listing 2.5 is relatively simple, and is well suited for the small control optimization problems in games, which we will solve with genetic algorithms. Both class constructors check the requested chromosome size and population size to make sure that they are within the fixed limits set by the enumerated constants. When you use class **genetic** in your programs, you can edit the enumerated constants MAX_GENES and MAX_CHROMOSOMES to match your requirements.

Some tuning of parameters in public member functions **do_mutations()** and **do_crossovers()** for mutation rate and crossover selection may be required for some applications. I have attempted to set up functions **do_mutations()** and **do_crossovers()** to handle a wide range of applications without requiring parameter tuning.

Public member function **do_mutations()** calculates, for each gene in each chromosome in the population, a random number between 0 and 999. If this random number is greater than 970, then the gene's value is modified. Public member function **do_crossovers()** uses a simple algorithm to choose which chromosomes to "mate" with a crossover operation to create new chromosomes. I choose chromosomes to mate randomly from the best 25 percent of the population, with the exception that I slightly favor the most fit chromosome in the population. See Goldberg (1987) for an alternative ("roulette wheel") algorithm for choosing chromosomes to mate.

Public member function **sort_by_fitness()** uses an exchange, or *bubble* sort to sort the population of chromosomes by fitness. The C language fitness function is used to assign a numeric fitness value to each member of the population, then the exchange sort is used to sort the array **p_chrom**, which contains chromosomes indices. We sort this array rather than shuffle entire chromosomes during the sorting process to avoid repetitively moving large blocks of data. I used the exchange, or bubble sort because it is simple to understand; however, if you are working with large numbers of chromosomes, it is more efficient to use an alternative sorting algorithm like quick sort or merge sort.

The public member functions **save()** and **restore()** are used to save and restore a chromosome population to a disk file. The public member functions **set_chromosome()** and **get_chromosome()** are used for external access to the individual chromosomes in the population. Member function **set_chromosome()** cannot clobber memory, even with incorrect calling arguments. The caller of member function **get_chromosome()** is responsible for allocating the storage for the returned chromosome value (second calling argument).

Listing 2.6 shows a short test program for class **genetic**. We define a C language fitness function that returns as its value the number of genes (bits) set to 1. This fitness measure has the effect of selecting populations with a large fraction of genes set to 1. While this simple example is not of practical value, it shows how to use the C++ class **genetic**. We will use the C++ class **genetic** in Chapter 5 to dynamically change the control strategy for a class of simulated spaceships.

Listing 2.6

```
// File: test_gen.cpp

#include <iostream.h>

#include "genetic.h"

float fitness_f(int ch_size, unsigned char *chrom)
{
  float ret_val = 0.0;
  for (int i=0; i<ch_size; i++)
    ret_val += chrom[i];
  return ret_val;
}
```

```
const int NUM_GENES = 9;
const int NUM_CHROMOSOMES = 20;

void main()
{
  cerr << "Testing class 'genetic'\n";
  genetic g(NUM_GENES, NUM_CHROMOSOMES, fitness_f);
  for (int iter=0; iter<20; iter++) {
    g.sort_by_fitness();
    g.do_crossovers();
    g.do_mutations();
    gene ch[20];
    cerr << "best chromosomes: ";
    for (int l=0; l<4; l++) {  // 4 best chromosomes
        g.get_chromosome(l, ch);
        for (int j=0; j<NUM_GENES; j++)
          cerr << (int)ch[j];
        cerr << " ";
    }
    cerr << "\n";
  }
}
```

The C language function that you use for a fitness function must return a value of type *float*, and it must take two input arguments of type *int* and unsigned *char**. The interface to the C language fitness function was designed so that an arbitrary fitness function receives all the information that it needs about the data for a chromosome in its argument list; no global data access of the instance of C++ class **genetic** is required. The public member function **sort_by_fitness()** is responsible for calling your C language fitness function correctly.

In the main function in Listing 2.6, the constructor for class **genetic** is called with the two required arguments: number of genes per chromosome and the number of chromosomes in the genetic population. You should build the test program in Listing 2.6 and run it. You will need the files SRC\GENETIC\TEST_GEN.CPP, SRC\GENETIC\GENTIC.CPP, and SRC\GENETIC\GENETIC.H on the CD-ROM to build an executable.

Rule-Based Programming

Rule-based (or expert system) programming allows us to separate domain knowledge from the remainder of a program. In artificial intelligence, so-called expert systems are usually implemented as a set of *if-then* rules. Usually, a separate rule interpreter system interprets the rules at execution time, using the current world data to determine which rules have their if conditions met, and executing the then portion of the rules.

If-then rules typically look like:

If speed $>$ 100 then set speed $=$ 100.

If fuel_level $<$ 0.1 and the distance to base $<$ 100 miles then go to base.

In this example, the rules are too much like English language for most expert system rule interpreters to handle.

For programming intelligent game or virtual reality agents, we want to be able to separate heuristic knowledge in the form of rules from the rest of the system. We especially want to be able to package rules in reusable expert system objects that can be shared by many intelligent agents. For example, an expert system object may contain rules that help to navigate; we want this one object to be able to be shared by perhaps all agents of a specified type, and perhaps by different types of agents that require the heuristic knowledge encoded in an expert system object.

We can now finalize our requirements for a new C++ class, **ExpertSystem**:

1. Separate heuristic knowledge in the form of rules in reusable objects.
2. Simple notation for specifying rules.
3. Debugging tools that allow us to trace the execution of rules.
4. A logical framework that works with **World** and **game_object** classes.

An instance of an **ExpertSystem** will usually be customized (by adding rule functions) to support a single type of game object. However, many instances of a particular type of a game object can share a single instance of an **ExpertSystem** because the **ExpertSystem** class instances contain general knowledge, but contain no specific data pertaining to any particular game object (the rule functions are called with a pointer to the current **World** data object, and to a particular instance of C++ class **game_object**).

C++ class **ExpertSystem** and class **PlanManager**, developed in this chapter, are different from the C++ utility classes **Neural** and **genetic**: **ExpertSystem** and **PlanManager** need knowledge of the classes **World** and **game_object**, which are designed and implemented in Chapters 3 and 4. I still classify **ExpertSystem** and **PlanManager** as general purpose utility classes because they will work with any definition of classes **World** and **game_object**. For example, we will use one design and implementation of class **World** and **game_object** for the spaceship simulation/game (Chapters 3 through 10), and suggest alternative definitions of **World** and **game_object** for other projects in Chapter 11.

Listing 2.7 shows the C++ class interface for **ExpertSystem** (as seen in Figure 2.1). An enumerated constant MAX_RULES sets the maximum number of C language rule functions that can be added to an instance of class **ExpertSystem**. All rule functions must match the prototype in the following C language typedef:

```
typedef int(*rule_function)(World*, game_object*);
```

A rule function is expected to provide the following functionality:

- Test the current state of the game or VR simulation world to see if its preconditions for execution are met; the function should immediately return the value of 0 if its preconditions are not met.

- If its preconditions are met, the rule function is allowed to make any changes to, through the public C++ interfaces of, the **World** or **game_object** instances passed as pointers in the rule functions argument list.

Listing 2.7

```
// File: expert.h
//
// Description: This file contains the interface
//              for the VR agent expert system tools.
//
//              An instance of an ExpertSystem will
//              usually be customized (by adding rule
//              functions) to support a single type of
//              game object.  However, many instances
//              of a particular type of a game object
//              can share a single instance of an
//              ExpertSystem because the ExpertSystem
//              class instances contain general knowledge,
//              but no specific data pertaining to any
//              particular game object (the rule functions
//              are called with a pointer to the current
//              World data object, and to a particular
//              game object).
//
// Copyright 1995, Mark Watson
//

#ifndef expert_h
#define expert_h

#ifdef NT
#define random(x) (rand() % (x))
#endif

#include "world.h"
#include "agent.h"

#include <stdio.h>

typedef int(*rule_function)(World*, game_object*);

class ExpertSystem {
 public:
    ExpertSystem();
    ~ExpertSystem();
    void add_rule(const char * title, rule_function rf, int priority=10);
```

```
    int execute_highest_priority_rule(World *, game_object *);
    void execute_all_rules(World *, game_object *);
    void debug_on() { debug_mode = 1; }
    void debug_off() { debug_mode = 0; }
private:
    enum {MAX_RULES=20};
    int num_rules;
    rule_function rules[MAX_RULES];
    int priorities[MAX_RULES];
    const char * titles[MAX_RULES];
    int debug_mode;
};


#endif
```

The are two class public member functions defined for executing rules: **execute_highest_priority_rule()** and **execute_all_rules()**. Function **execute_highest_priority_rule()** executes rule functions in order of priority until one of them returns a nonzero value, indicating that the rule's preconditions were satisfied, and that the rule executed properly. Member function **execute_all_rules()** calls all rule functions in order of priority.

Member functions **debug_on()** and **debug_off()** can be used to toggle debug output indicating which rules functions are called. Listing 2.8 shows the implementation of the **ExpertSystem** class.

Listing 2.8

```
// File: expert.cpp
//
// Description: This file contains the implementation of
//              the VR agent expert system tools
//
// Copyright 1995, Mark Watson
//

#include <iostream.h>
#include <stdlib.h>
#include "expert.h"
#include "out_log.h"
```

```
ExpertSystem::ExpertSystem()
{
   num_rules = 0;
}


ExpertSystem::~ExpertSystem()
{
}


void ExpertSystem::add_rule(const char *title,
                            rule_function rf,
                            int priority)
{
   int i;
   if (num_rules >= (MAX_RULES - 1)) {
#ifdef TEXT_MODE
      cerr << "Too many rules added to ExpertSystem object.\n";
#endif
      exit(1);
   }
   // Find the index for inserting this rule:
   for (i=0; i<num_rules; i++)
      if (priority > priorities[i])  break;
   // Insert rule at index i:
   for (int j=num_rules; j>i; j--) {
      rules[j] = rules[j-1];
      priorities[j] = priorities[j-1];
      titles[j] = titles[j-1];
   }
   rules[i] = rf;
   priorities[i] = priority;
   titles[i] = title;
   num_rules++;
}


int ExpertSystem::execute_highest_priority_rule(World *w,
                                                game_object *g)
{
   // Starting with the highest priority rules,
   // keep executing rule functions until a rule
   // function returns a non-zero value (indicating
   // that its conditions were met, and it executed
   // correctly):
```

```
    int still_processing = 0;
    int rule_counter = 0;
    while (still_processing == 0 &&
           rule_counter < num_rules)
    {
#ifdef TEXT_MODE
//      if (debug_mode) {
//          cerr << "executing rule '"
//               << titles[rule_counter] << "'\n";
//      }
#endif
        still_processing = (*rules[rule_counter])(w, g);
        rule_counter++;
    }
    return 1 - still_processing;
}


void ExpertSystem::execute_all_rules(World *w, game_object *g)
{
    for (int i=0; i<num_rules; i++) {
#ifdef TEXT_MODE
        if (debug_mode) {
            cerr << "executing rule '"
                 << titles[i] << "'\n";
        }
#endif

        (*rules[i])(w, g);

    }
}
```

The class constructor for **ExpertSystem** simply sets the current rule count to 0. There is nothing for the class destructor to do since there is no dynamically allocated storage.

Class member function **add_rule** adds a new rule function to an internal list of rules, in order of decreasing priority. The rule name is only used for debug output.

Figure 2.5 shows the interaction of an instance of class **ExpertSystem** with the (currently) abstract classes **World** and

Interactions between an Instance of Class ExpertSystem and Instances of Classes World and game_object

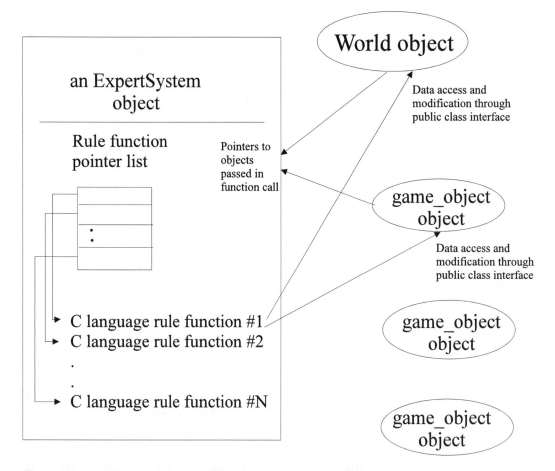

Figure 2.5 When the public member functions **execute_highest_priority_rule()** and **execute_all_rules()** are called, they require pointers to an instance of class **World** and an instance of class **game_object**. These pointers are passed through to the C language rule functions, which can both access and modify these data objects through their public class interface, referenced through these pointers.

game_object, which will be designed and implemented in Chapters 3 and 4 for the spaceship simulation example programs in Chapters 5 through 10. Listing 2.9 shows a short test program demonstrating how an instance of the class **ExpertSystem** is created, and how to add rules to the instance.

Listing 2.9

```cpp
// File: test_exp.cpp

#include <iostream.h>
#include "world.h"
#include "game_obj.h"
#include "expert.h"


int test_function1(World *w, game_object *g)
{
    cerr << "Entered test function 1\n";
    return 1;
}

int test_function2(World *w, game_object *g)
{
    cerr << "Entered test function 2\n";
    return 1;
}

void main()
{
    World world;
    game_object g1(&world);
    ExpertSystem es;
    es.add_rule("rule 1", test_function1, 20);
    es.add_rule("rule 2", test_function2, 40);
    es.debug_on();
    es.execute_highest_priority_rule(&world, &g1);
    es.execute_all_rules(&world, &g1);
}
```

Plan Manager

As defined in this book, a Plan Manager is similar to an Expert System. A Plan Manager uses three types of plan functions:

1. Identifies when the current game situation matches the pre-conditions for a plan template.
2. Plans execution function that is executed each time step that a plan is active.
3. Terminates condition function that tests for conditions indicating plan termination.

A plan template is a set for each of these plan functions. The C++ class for **PlanManager** is similar to **ExpertSystem** with the following differences: an instance of class **ExpertSystem** is stateless between game simulation cycles. That is, an expert system object does not remember its actions from the previous time its functions **execute_highest_priority_rule()** or **execute_all_rules()** were called. In contrast, an instance of the C++ class **PlanManager** maintains state, or memory, between game simulation cycles.

I considered creating an abstract base class for both **ExpertSystem** and **PlanManager** (they would be subclasses of the same abstract base class), but I decided not to do this for two reasons:

1. C++ classes **ExpertSystem** and **PlanManager** use rule functions that are different both in argument lists and execution strategy.
2. The implementations of both classes are only a few dozen lines of code.

One of the big payoffs to using derived classes is the reduction in the number of lines of code required for similar functionality. A drawback of using derived classes is a slight increase in complexity; it is more difficult for the programmer using the classes to read and modify the code. Usually, reduction of the required number of lines of code to implement a system is a deciding factor to use inheritance.

In developing class libraries, it is common to first implement *flat* class hierarchies; that is, to use inheritance sparingly. Often experience with an initial system implementation will suggest ways to find common data and behavior in similar classes, suggesting the use of an abstract base class in the next system implementation. Listing 2.10 shows the C++ interface to class **PlanManager** seen in Figure 2.1.

Listing 2.10

```
// File: plan.h
//
// Description: This file contains the interface
//              for the VR agent expert system tools.
//
//              An instance of a PlanManager will
//              usually be customized (by adding rule
//              functions) to support a single type of
//              game object.  However, many instances
//              of a particular type of a game object
//              can share a single instance of a
//              PlanManager because the PlanManager
//              class instances contain general knowledge,
//              but no specific data pertaining to any
//              particular game object (the rule functions
//              are called with a pointer to the current
//              World data object, and to a particular
//              game object).
//
// Copyright 1995, Mark Watson
//

#ifndef plan_h
#define plan_h

#ifdef NT
#define random(x) (rand() % (x))
#endif

#include "world.h"
#include "agent.h"
```

```
#include <stdio.h>

typedef int(*plan_function)(World*, game_object*, int);

class PlanManager {
 public:
    PlanManager();
   ~PlanManager();
    void add_plan(const char *plan_title = "no_name_plan",
                  plan_function pre_condition_rule = NULL,
                  plan_function plan_execution = NULL,
                  plan_function termination_condition = NULL);
    int run_plan(World *w, game_object *g);
    void debug_on() { debug_mode = 1; }
    void debug_off() { debug_mode = 0; }
 private:
    enum {MAX_PLANS=4};
    const char * plan_name[MAX_PLANS];
    plan_function pre_rule[MAX_PLANS];
    plan_function run_rule[MAX_PLANS];
    plan_function stop_rule[MAX_PLANS];
    int num_plans;
    int debug_mode;
    enum {NO_RUN_STATE = 0, RUN_STATE = 1};
    int run_state;
    int current_plan;
    int time_step_count;
    enum {MAX_RUN_CYCLES = 10};
};

#endif
```

You can see the similarity of class **PlanManager** with class **ExpertSystem**. The following questions will help you decide between the use of the **PlanManager** or the **ExpertSystem** class:

- Do you want software agents to take specific, immediate actions when certain conditions in the agent's environment are satisfied? If this is true, then use the **ExpertSystem** class.

- Do you want your software agents to execute a series of tasks when certain conditions in the agent's environment are satisfied? If this is true, then use the **PlanManager** class.

Listing 2.11 shows the implementation of class **PlanManager** seen in Figure 2.1.

Listing 2.11

```
// File: plan.cpp
//
// Description: This file contains the prototype code
//              for the VR agent plan manager tools
//
// Copyright 1995, Mark Watson
//

#include <iostream.h>
#include <stdlib.h>
#include "plan.h"
#include "out_log.h"

PlanManager::PlanManager()
{
   run_state = NO_RUN_STATE;
   num_plans = 0;
}


PlanManager::~PlanManager()
{
}


void PlanManager::add_plan(const char *plan_title,
                           plan_function pre_condition_rule,
                           plan_function plan_execution,
                           plan_function termination_condition)
{
   if (termination_condition == NULL) {
#ifdef TEXT_MODE
      cerr << "Error: PlanManager::add_plan needs 4 arguments\n";
#endif
      exit(1);
   }
   plan_name[num_plans] = plan_title;
   pre_rule[num_plans]  = pre_condition_rule;
   run_rule[num_plans]  = plan_execution;
```

```
    stop_rule[num_plans] = termination_condition;
    num_plans++;
}

int PlanManager::run_plan(World *w, game_object *g)
{
    if (run_state == NO_RUN_STATE) {
        for (int n=0; n<num_plans; n++) {
            // use the pre-condition rule function to see if
            // this plan object is appropriate to schedule:
            if ((*pre_rule[n])(w, g, 0)) {
                run_state = RUN_STATE;
                current_plan = n;
                time_step_count = 0;
                return 1;
            }
        }
    }

    if (run_state == RUN_STATE) {
        // start by executing the run function for this time step:
        time_step_count++;
        (*run_rule[current_plan])(w, g, time_step_count);
        // check to see if this plan is no longer appropriate to run:
        if ((*stop_rule[current_plan])(w, g, time_step_count)) {
            run_state = NO_RUN_STATE;
            return 0;
        }
        if (time_step_count > MAX_RUN_CYCLES)  {
            run_state = NO_RUN_STATE;
            return 0;
        }
        return 1;
    }
    return 0;

}
```

The public class member function **run_plan()** passes three arguments to the plan functions:

1. A pointer to an instance of C++ class **World**.
2. A pointer to an instance of C++ class **game_object**.
3. A count of the number of time steps in the game or virtual reality simulation that the plan has been in effect.

The third argument is especially useful. The count of simulation time steps since the start of the plan execution can be used in the plan termination function to determine when the plan has been running long enough to terminate. It is often better to delete a running plan after a few time steps, and then reinitiate the plan if it is still appropriate for the current game situation. Listing 2.12 shows a short test program for C++ class **PlanManager**.

Listing 2.12

```cpp
// File: test_pln.cpp

#include <iostream.h>
#include "world.h"
#include "game_obj.h"
#include "plan.h"


int pre_function(World *w, game_object *g, int dummy)
{
    cerr << "Entered test pre condition function 1\n";
    return 1;
}

int run_function(World *w, game_object *g, int time_step)
{
    cerr << "Entered test run function 2\n";
    return 0;
}

int stop_function(World *w, game_object *g, int time_step)
{
```

```
    cerr << "Entered test for stop function 2\n";
    if (time_step < 5) return 0;
    else                return 1;
}
void main()
{
    World world;
    game_object g1(&world);
    PlanManager pm;
    pm.add_plan("test plan", pre_function, run_function, stop_function);
    pm.debug_on();
    for (int i=0; i<10; i++) {
        pm.run_plan(&world, &g1);
    }
}
```

Three plan template functions (defining a single plan) are defined in this listing: **pre_function()**, **run_function()**, and **stop_function()**. In this example, the plan precondition function **pre_function()** always returns a nonzero value, indicating to an instance of the **PlanManager** class that this plan is always appropriate for the current game situation. Usually, a plan precondition function will check the state of the game world and return zero if the plan is not appropriate, and a nonzero value if the plan is appropriate to use in the current game situation. The instance of class **PlanManager** that contains this plan template will execute the C function **run_function()** in Listing 2.12 every time cycle until the termination test function **stop_function()** in Listing 2.12 returns a nonzero value, indicating that the plan is no longer appropriate and should be terminated.

The main function in Listing 2.12 simply creates instances of classes **World**, **game_object**, and **PlanManager**. The member function **PlanManager::add_plan()** is used to create a new plan template and add it to the instance of the **PlanManager** class. The member function **PlanManager::run_plan()** checks to see if any plan is currently running; if no plan is running, then each plan template is checked by calling the plan's precondition test function to see if that plan is appropriate to execute.

Summary of Utility Classes for the Intelligent Agent Toolkit

Neural networks are useful for pattern recognition tasks when there may be either considerable random noise in the pattern that you are trying to recognize, or when the pattern is incomplete. In order to effectively use the C++ **Neural** class, we need to be able to encode some environmental features as input neuron activation values, and specify how we interpret the output neuron activation values. We also need to create a set of training cases that will cover the types of input patterns that the neural network will need to process as part of a software agent.

Genetic algorithms are very effective tools for searching large data spaces. In order to effectively use the C++ class **genetic**, we need to identify a set of control parameters that we use to control a software agent. Ideally, an application of a software agent using genetic algorithms will require many agents that are identical, except for the values of a set of control parameters. As we will see in Chapter 5, the C++ class **genetic** can be effectively used to quickly adapt the control parameters of a set of similar agents in response to a changing environment. We will also see that an added benefit for games and VR simulations is that the use of C++ class **genetic** provides a population of fit, yet often different members of the same population. This is useful in game play since a human opponent must be able to deal with a variety of efficient adversaries whose collective strategy evolves continually in response to changes in the game situation.

Expert systems have proven to be one of the few successful artificial intelligence techniques for real-world applications. A decade ago, I wrote and marketed LISP-based expert system tools for hardware LISP machines and the Apple Macintosh. The C++ class **ExpertSystem** developed in this chapter is rather simple compared to commercial expert system tools, especially those written in the language LISP (see Watson, 1991). I tailored the design of class **ExpertSystem** specifically for games and real-time simulations. It is useful to be able to organize heuristic rules as sets of C language functions. Some commercial expert system tools provide support for advanced features that the class **ExpertSystem** does not support, such as:

- Nonmonatomic reasoning: being able to retract logical inferences

- Built-in support for uncertainty in rules

- Efficient preparsing of semantic networks to factor out common conditional tests

Still, the functionality of the **ExpertSystem** class seems appropriate for the main requirement of this book: to present easy-to-use tools that help programmers add interesting behavior to the objects in their games and VR simulations.

Plan management is a current research topic in artificial intelligence. One practical application of planning is robot vehicles navigating rough terrains. I have tailored the concept of using schema, or templates, to represent possible plans to a game programming environment. Here, our plan templates are based on the simple set of three plan functions:

- Precondition rule function

- Execution function

- Termination rule function

The C++ class **PlanManager** provides a convenient, well-structured notation for specifying canned execution scenarios that should be executed during several game time steps in response to a specified game situation.

Introduction to the VR Agent Toolkit

Chapter 2 contained the requirements, design, and implementation of the AI utility classes **Neural, genetic, ExpertSystem,** and **PlanManager.** In this chapter, we will cover the requirements and design of the VR Agent Toolkit. The AI utility classes provide the underlying functionality of the VR Agent Toolkit, while the **World, game_object,** and **Agent** C++ classes provide a structural framework and high-level control behavior.

Requirements for the VR Agent Toolkit

How does an AI agent work? How do we construct it? What are its limitations? These are the appropriate questions to ask. Most people are skeptical about artificial intelligence, and with good cause! The field of AI has been plagued by premature claims of expected short-term results. Sadly, building general purpose AI software system has proved well beyond our current abilities.

The successful AI applications have always been in narrow problem domains like diagnostic expert systems, speech recognition, and data analysis in limited application domains. Fortunately, our current applications (games and VR simulations) have several things in common with problem domains for successful AI problems solvers, including:

- Limited domain and finite number of objects.

- Available physics models for predicting and computationally "understanding" the interaction of objects.

- Limited system inputs.

- Limited system outputs.

The important limitation of AI systems is that the problem domain be small. VR simulations and games provide such a small, relatively simple environment (as compared to the real world, where AI software often seems to fail). There are two kinds of interactions that our AI agents will be able to handle, with very different techniques used for implementation (which are shown indented in the following list):

- Interaction with the physical world. Steering and moving objects. Collision avoidance.

    Genetic programming dynamically changes control strategies in response to changing game situations.

    Neural networks are used for control functions, trained with carefully prepared training data.

    Expert system rule functions encapsulate heuristic rules that are triggered by a set of preconditions in the current game world, and whose execution occurs completely at one instant in simulated time.

    Plan manager rule function sets are similar to Expert system rule functions, except that when a plan set is activated by conditions in the current game world, execution of the plan rule function set occurs multiple times during the game simulation until a terminating condition is satisfied.

- Interaction with other agents (computer and human). Very domain (game) specific.

    Rule-based programming is very specific to a well-codified set of possible interaction types.

    Procedural programming is very specific to a particular game or VR simulation.

    Plan-based programming is very specific to a particular game or VR simulation.

There is another interesting aspect to the implementation (including software tools for preparing training data and scenarios) of world interaction capability: the AI agent's interaction with the game or VR simulation world can evolve over time by using these same techniques for agent training, but training with data from current game situations. Game scenarios in which a human opponent "wins" (whatever that means in the current application) are most appropriate for "on-the-fly" retraining. Is this simple to implement? No! However, adaptable computer opponents will greatly increase our enjoyment of future games and VR simulations.

Making the interactions with other agents change in response to opponent behavior does not have a straightforward solution. The Agent software toolkit that we are going to develop will support multiple rule sets and procedures that can be selected based on agent failures against a given opponent; we will use a genetic algorithm in the example programs to alter strategy according to the current game situation. There is no self-adaptive learning here since we will be selecting preprogrammed strategies (and combinations of strategies), but the effect for the human opponent will be realistic.

The AI C++ utility classes developed in Chapter 2 provide low-level tools for creating intelligent software agents. The VR Agent Toolkit must also provide a higher level framework for both organizing game objects into manageable collections, and for organizing and controlling the various AI components.

C++ Class Design for the VR Agent Toolkit

The VR Agent Toolkit class library will contain C++ classes for both game, or virtual reality simulation objects, and for building intelligent agents. Figure 3.1 shows the class **World** and the type of object that it can contain: instances of C++ class **game_object**. Class **geometric_object** provides data for the position and shape of a three-dimensional object. The C++ class **game_object** is derived from class **geometric_object** (public inheritance), adding support for using instances of application-specific subclasses of the C++ class **Agent** to provide "intelligent" behavior.

   An instance of class **game_object** can contain agent objects, which can examine and change the internal state of game objects (through public member functions of classes **geometric_object** and **game_object**). It makes sense to make class **game_object** a subclass of **geometric_object** for these reasons:

- It removes duplicate code for manipulating three-dimensional, viewable objects.

- Instances of both classes are useful for writing game programs and VR simulations.

- An instance of a **game_object** correctly follows an is-a type relationship on which to base class **geometric_object**.

   As seen in Figure 3.1, the C++ class **World** is a container class for instances of **game_object**, which is derived from class **geometric_object**. The requirements for the class **geometric_object** are that it:

- Contains data for specifying the location and size of an object in 3D space.

- Provides built-in support for simple geometrical shapes such as spheres and cubes.

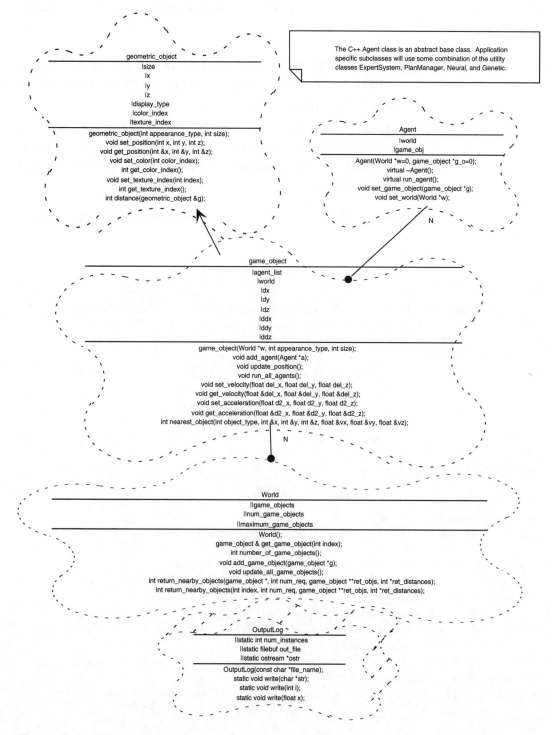

The C++ Agent class is an abstract base class. Application specific subclasses will use some combination of the utility classes ExpertSystem, PlanManager, Neural, and Genetic.

geometric_object
|size
|x
|y
|z
|display_type
|color_index
|texture_index

geometric_object(int appearance_type, int size);
void set_position(int x, int y, int z);
void get_position(int &x, int &y, int &z);
void set_color(int color_index);
int get_color_index();
void set_texture_index(int index);
int get_texture_index();
int distance(geometric_object &g);

Agent
|world
|game_obj

Agent(World *w=0, game_object *g_o=0);
virtual ~Agent();
virtual run_agent();
void set_game_object(game_object *g);
void set_world(World *w);

N

game_object
|agent_list
|world
|dx
|dy
|dz
|ddx
|ddy
|ddz

game_object(World *w, int appearance_type, int size);
void add_agent(Agent *a);
void update_position();
void run_all_agents();
void set_velocity(float del_x, float del_y, float del_z);
void get_velocity(float &del_x, float &del_y, float &del_z);
void set_acceleration(float d2_x, float d2_y, float d2_z);
void get_acceleration(float &d2_x, float &d2_y, float &d2_z);
int nearest_object(int object_type, int &x, int &y, int &z, float &vx, float &vy, float &vz);

N

World
||game_objects
||num_game_objects
||maximum_game_objects

World();
game_object & get_game_object(int index);
int number_of_game_objects();
void add_game_object(game_object *g);
void update_all_game_objects();
int return_nearby_objects(game_object *, int num_req, game_object **ret_objs, int *ret_distances);
int return_nearby_objects(int index, int num_req, game_object **ret_objs, int *ret_distances);

OutputLog
||static int num_instances
||static filebuf out_file
||static ostream *ostr

OutputLog(const char *file_name);
static void write(char *str);
static void write(int i);
static void write(float x);

Figure 3.1 Top-level class diagram for game world data objects and intelligent agents.

- Acts as a base class for creating new types of 3D objects which could contain data for specifying rotation, and visual properties, if required.

- Provides behavior for instances of this class and derived classes for common operations like specifying object position and calculating the distance between objects of this class and derived classes.

Listing 3.1 shows the C++ class interface for **geometric_object**.

Listing 3.1

```
// File: geom_obj.h
//
// Description: This file contains the class definitions
//              for a base class of geometric objects.
//
// 3/25/95 modification: use float instead of int for internal
//                       representation for position so that
//                       position updates less than 1.0 are
//                       not lost.  Keep the set_position
//                       and get_position interface set to
//                       int values.
//
// Copyright 1995, Mark Watson
//

#ifndef geom_obj_h
#define geom_obj_h

class geometric_object {
 public:
    enum {CUBE=1, SPHERE=2};
    enum {RED=1, BLUE=2, GREEN=3, BLACK=4, GRAY=5};
    geometric_object(int appearance_type = SPHERE,
                     int size=10);
    virtual ~geometric_object() {  } ;
    void set_position(int x1, int y1, int z1) {
        x = x1;
        y = y1;
        z = z1;
    };
```

```
    void get_position(int &x1, int &y1, int &z1) {
        x1 = x;
        y1 = y;
        z1 = z;
    };
    void set_color(int color1) { color = color1; }
    int get_color() { return color; }
    void set_texture_index(int texture1) { texture = texture1; }
    int get_texture_index() { return texture; }
    float distance(geometric_object &g);

protected:
    int size;
    float x;
    float y;
    float z;
    int o_type;
    int color;
    int texture;
};

#endif
```

The direct support for representing spheres and cubes suffices for the example spaceship simulation in three dimensions and the example two-dimensional spaceship game developed in this book. Since I support several different graphics environments (including Macintosh, Windows, Windows NT, OpenGL, and UNIX X Window) in the examples in this book, I found it more convenient to design class **geometric_object** to contain data specifying its shape type, but not behavior for drawing itself. In order to keep the class design fairly abstract (that is, it is not tied to any given graphics environment), the behavior for drawing instances of class **geometric_object** is written in the client applications that use the class. Another reason for not including drawing behavior in the class is in order to support both an all-text simulation for effectively writing and debugging software agents, and graphics simulations for viewing agent behavior.

Notice that the destructor for this class is virtual. Since the data contained in the class instances is created and destroyed automatically by the compiler, there is no requirement to ensure that the base class destructor is called, so in principle, the base class destructor does not have to be virtual. (Destructors in base classes must be virtual when you need the base class destructor and the derived class destructor called when you destroy an instance of the class.) The C++ compiler generates code to allocate and free instance data that is not created with calls to the C++ operator *new*. However, it is likely that classes derived from **geometric_object** will in turn be base classes to other derived classes. If you make any destructor in a class hierarchy virtual, you should make all base class destructors virtual.

In addition to instances of C++ class **geometric_object**, which have three-dimensional visual characteristics and a position in space, I wanted a class of objects that could move and interact with their environment using the AI utility classes developed in Chapter 2. Class **game_object** is derived, using public inheritance, from class **geometric_object**, adding data for:

- Velocity.

- Acceleration.

- A reference to an instance of the container class **World** that contains this object.

- A list of instances of C++ class **Agent**.

Class **game_object** adds behavior for:

- Setting the reference of the **World** container object.

- Returning the number of software agents used by this object.

- Returning a reference to a particular software agent used by this object.

- Adding a new software agent.

- Updating the position of an object based on its old position, velocity, and acceleration.

- Executing all software agents used by this object.

- Setting and reading the values for velocity and acceleration.

Listing 3.2 shows the C++ class interface for **game_object**.

Listing 3.2

```
// File: game_obj.h
//
// Description: This file contains the C++ class interface
//              for the 'game_object', which is derived
//              from class geometric_object.
//              An instance of game_object is either a
//              sphere or cube object which contains
//              one or more agent objects to control
//              its behavior.
//
// Copyright 1995, Mark Watson
//

#ifndef GAME_OBJ
#define GAME_OBJ

#include "geom_obj.h"
class World;
class Agent;

class game_object : public geometric_object {
 public:
    game_object(World *w=0,
                const char * my_name = "no_name",
                int appearance_type=geometric_object::SPHERE,
                int size=10);
    virtual ~game_object();
    void set_world(World *w) { world = w; }
    void set_type(int my_type) { object_type = my_type; }
    int get_type() { return object_type; }
    int number_of_agents() { return num_agents; }
    Agent & get_agent(int index) { return *agent_list[index]; }
    enum {MAX_AGENTS=5};

    void add_agent(Agent &a);
```

```
    // Utility functions to be used by derived classes:
    void update_position();
    void run_all_agents();

    int nearest_object(int object_type, int &x, int &y, int &z,
                       float &vx, float &vy, float &vz);

    // Data access functions:
    void set_velocity(float del_x, float del_y, float del_z);
    void get_velocity(float &del_x, float &del_y, float &del_z);
    void set_acceleration(float d2_x, float d2_y, float d2_z);
    void get_acceleration(float &d2_x, float &d2_y, float &d2_z);
    const char * get_name() { return name; }

// Note: the following storage is protected instead of private
//       because this class will be subclassed for a specific
//       game to add special data and behavior specific to
//       that game.
protected:
    const char * name;
    Agent *agent_list[MAX_AGENTS];
    int num_agents;
    int object_type;
    World *world;
    // A geometric object contains data for position. We need
    // to add velocity and acceleration:
    float dx; // first derivative of position in x direction
    float dy; // first derivative of position in y direction
    float dz; // first derivative of position in z direction
    float ddx; // second derivative of position in x direction
    float ddy; // second derivative of position in y direction
    float ddz; // second derivative of position in z direction
};

#endif
```

We will only use instances of class **game_object** in the example programs in this book, but class **geometric_object** has good potential for reuse in other applications. It is good design practice to build shallow hierarchies of C++ classes. Class hierarchies should not be too deep; in fact, it is usually a bad idea to have more than two or three levels in a class hierarchy. For example, this code fragment represents a reasonable depth of public inheritance:

```
class geometric_object { ...};
class game_object : public geometric_object { ... };
class networked_game_object : public game_object {... };
```

Here, I added a new class **networked_game_object** which inherits the data and behavior of class **game_object**, adding support for running on a local network of computers. For a shallow class structure, it is easy for the class designer, the class implementor, and the users of the class to remember the relationship between the derived classes. When you extend class libraries written by other people, and design and implement your own, please remember to use object-oriented design and implementation to reduce complexity and to encourage reuse of software assets.

Just as it is a mistake to use too deep an inheritance hierarchy, it is also a mistake to not use inheritance at all. Inheritance is very useful for reducing the size of libraries, and has the added benefit that code for specific functionality only appears in one place; therefore, modifications only have to be made in one place. For example, the first stage implementation of the VR Agent Toolkit was used for writing the text-based three-dimensional spaceship simulation program in Chapter 5. Ship positions were stored as integers. This worked fine for a text-based simulation with a relatively large simulated time step. However, with the 3D graphics versions of the spaceship simulations in Chapters 6 and 7 (for RenderWare and OpenGL), I used a small time step, where velocities and acceleration values were reduced; and using integer values for positions then produced unwanted truncation errors. Because the position data is maintained in the base class **geometric_object**, modifying the position data type to a floating point values is simple: fix the base class, and the behavior of all derived classes is also fixed. The public interface for reading the position still uses integers, and no code in the rest of the VR Agent Toolkit or example programs is broken by the modification.

The C++ collection class **World**, which we saw referenced in the **ExpertSystem** and **PlanManager** classes in Chapter 2, requires data elements for:

- A list of instances of C++ class **game_object** contained in this object.

- A count of the number of instances of C++ class **game_object** contained in this object.

Instances of class **World** are required to have the following behavior:

- Return a reference to a specified **game_object** instance stored in this collection.

- Return the number of **game_object** instances stored in this collection.

- Add a **game_object** instance to this collection.

- Update all game objects in this collection by calling the **game_object** member functions **update_position** and **run_all _agents**.

Listing 3.3 shows the C++ class interface for **World**.

Listing 3.3

```
// File: world.h
//
// Description: The C++ class 'World' is a container class
//              for game_objects.  Each game object contains
//              zero or more Agent objects.
//
// Copyright 1995, Mark Watson
//

#ifndef world_h
#define world_h

#include "geom_obj.h"
#include "game_obj.h"
#include "agent.h"

class World {
 public:
```

```
    World();
    virtual ~World();
    enum {MAX_GAME_OBJECTS=40};
    game_object & get_game_object(int index)
    { return *game_objects[index]; }
    int get_game_object_index(game_object *g);
    int number_of_game_objects()
    { return num_game_objects; }
    void add_game_object(game_object &g);

    // The following member function iterates over all
    // contained game objects, calling update_position
    // and run_all_agents for each game_object.
    void update_all_game_objects();

    // The following member functions returns a list of
    // nearby game_objects, and the distances to
    // these objects.  Note that the caller needs
    // to allocate space for the returned lists, but
    // should NOT delete the game_objects pointed to
    // by the elements in the returned list! The function
    // returns the actual number of objects returned.
    int return_nearby_objects(game_object *g,
                              int number_requested,
                              game_object **objs,
                              int *distances);
    int return_nearby_objects(int game_object_index,
                              int number_requested,
                              game_object **objs,
                              int *distances);
private:
    game_object *game_objects[MAX_GAME_OBJECTS];
    int num_game_objects;
};

#endif
```

The C++ class **World** is a container class and its primary
purpose is to contain and control instances of another class,
game_object. It is my design style to include organizational behavior in container classes. For class **World**, I include two public
member functions for returning a list of all game objects contained

in the **World** object that are close to a specified contained instance of class **game_object**. This returned list is sorted by distance to the specified **game_object** instance. I believe that behavior specific to a particular **game_object** instance should be implemented as member functions of the class **game_object**, while behavior dealing with relationships between instances of the class **game_object** are best implemented as member functions of the container class.

A good design alternative is to implement behavior dealing with relationships between instances of the class **game_object** in the base class to class **game_object**, which is **geometric_object**. Regardless of which design strategy you use, it is important to be consistent. I always prefer to place organizational behavior and utility functions dealing with more than one contained object in the definition of the container class **World**.

The C++ class **Agent** is a base class that provides the following data to derived classes:

- A pointer to the instance of class **World** that this software agent acts in.

- A pointer to the **game_object** that uses this software agent.

The **Agent** class provides the following behavior to derived classes:

- A virtual function **run_agent**, which needs to be defined in the derived class.

- Functions to set the value of the contained **World** and **game_object** data pointers.

The **Agent** class is an abstract base class, and therefore, you cannot create instances of class **Agent**; you must derive subclasses from it. Listing 3.4 shows the C++ class interface for **Agent**.

Listing 3.4

```
// File: agent.h
//
```

```
#ifndef agent_h
#define agent_h

#ifdef NT
#define random(x) (rand() % (x))
#endif

#include "world.h"
#include "game_obj.h"

class Agent {
 public:
    Agent(World *w, game_object *g);
    virtual ~Agent();
    virtual void run_agent() = 0;
    void set_game_object(game_object *g)
    {
       game_obj = g;
    }
    void set_world(World *w)
    {
       world = w;
    }
// Note: The following storage is protected, instead of private,
// since Agent classes derived from this base class need to
// be able to efficiently access 'world' and 'game_obj'.  A good
// alternative would be to have a public member function return
// a reference to these encapsulated data items.
 protected:
    World *world;
    game_object *game_obj;
};

#endif
```

In the example spaceship simulation program developed in Chapter 5, we will create a derived class from **Agent**, class **NavigationAgent**. Instances of class **NavigationAgent** will be used by both Player and Processor ships.

In order to generate *debug printout* from our software agents, I wanted to create a C++ class that would:

- Provide a method for writing text and numbers to a log file.

- Provide a mechanism for turning off debug output without editing the VR Agent Toolkit source code.

One good way to provide this functionality is to derive a new stream class from the C++ library class **ostream**. I chose an alternative approach that uses static class member functions to write character strings to a file that is opened when an instance of the class is created (the class constructor expects a file name). If no class instances exist, then the member write functions do nothing. The class destructor closes the log file. In the example programs in this book, I simply construct an instance of the class **OutputLog** in the main function to enable debug output to a log file. Commenting out this statement turns off all debug printout in both the example program and in the VR Agent Toolkit. Listing 3.5 shows the C++ class interface for **OutputLog**.

Listing 3.5

```
// File: out_log.h
//
// Description: This is a utility class that provides
//              static member functions to write out
//              strings, integers, and floats to a
//              log file.  One instance of this class
//              must exist (the constructor opens a
//              file, and the destructor closes it).
//
// Copyright 1995, Mark Watson
//

#ifndef OUT_LOG
#define OUT_LOG

#include <iostream.h>
#include <fstream.h>

class OutputLog {
 public:
```

```
    OutputLog(const char *file_name = "log.dat");
   ~OutputLog();
    static void write(char * str);
    static void write(const char * str);
    static void write(int i);
    static void write(long i);
    static void write(float x);
    static void write(double x);
 private:
    static int num_instances;   // must == 1 to write output
    static filebuf out_file;
    static ostream *ostr;
};

#endif
```

Implementation of the VR Agent Toolkit in C++

In Chapter 3, we discussed the requirements, and designed and specified the C++ interfaces for the following C++ classes:

- **geometric_object**
- **game_object**
- **World**
- **Agent**
- **OutputLog**

In this chapter, we will write the C++ implementations for these classes. Then, in Chapter 5, we will extend these classes using public inheritance to write a space game, complete with several types of software agents.

For graphics-related C++ classes like **geometric_object** and **game_object**, it would be a reasonable design decision to include member functions for drawing the object; as discussed in Chap-

75

ter 3, I decided not to include class behavior for drawing members of these C++ classes because my planned use, or requirement, for these classes covered applications that were text-based, and support graphics in Microsoft Windows, Windows NT, Apple Macintosh, UNIX X Window, OpenGL, and RenderWare programming environments. It was this requirement that triggered the design decision not to include self-drawing behavior in these classes. This is another example of why it so important to view the software process as encompassing requirements analysis, design, and implementation. Software that is supported with up-to-date requirements specifications and design documentation is a valuable, potentially reusable, resource.

The C++ class **World** acts as a container class for instances of class **game_object**. As we saw in Chapter 3, in addition to providing the standard behavior of a container class (that is, support for accessing the contained objects), class **World** also has a public member function for calling all software agents used by all contained instances of class **game_object**. Also discussed was that the C++ class **Agent** is an abstract base class that is used as a control framework for the Artificial Intelligence utility classes **Neural, genetic, ExpertSystem,** and **PlanManager**. Because class **Agent** is an abstract base class, you cannot create instances from this class directly; you must derive your own classes from C++ class **Agent**.

The C++ class **OutputLog** is a simple utility class for adding diagnostic output to your programs. This output can be easily turned off, if desired.

Listing 4.1 shows the contents of the file SRC\TEST\TEST.CPP on the CD-ROM. This simple program does nothing, but it serves as a short example of creating instances of the VR Agent Toolkit C++ classes. I include the test program prior to the implementation of the remaining VR Agent Toolkit C++ classes in order to illustrate their use; we have already seen the C++ class interface for these classes in Chapter 3, and the implementation of these classes will be easier to understand after a short example of their use. Listing 4.3 is similar to Listing 4.1, except that instances of the classes **game_object, Agent,** and **World** are created with the C++ *new* operator. In the implementation of these C++ classes, I want the behavior: When an instance of class **World** is deleted, I want to ensure that all objects contained in the **World** class instance are also deleted, including objects that are inside other included objects.

Listing 4.1

```
// File: test.cpp
//
// Description: This file contains a text mode test
//              program for testing the C++ classes:
//
//                  game_object
//                  Agent
//                  World
//                  OutputLog
//
// Copyright 1995, Mark Watson

#include "world.h"
#include "game_obj.h"
#include "agent.h"

#include "out_log.h"

#include <stdio.h>

class myAgent : public Agent {
 public:
    myAgent(World *w = NULL, game_object *g = NULL);
    ~myAgent();
    void run_agent();
};

myAgent::myAgent(World *w, game_object *g) : Agent(w,g)
{
   OutputLog::write("Entering constructor for myAgent class\n");
   // You would create instances of NeuralNet, genetic,
   // ExpertSystem, and PlanManager here
}

myAgent::~myAgent()
{
   OutputLog::write("Entering destructor for myAgent class\n");
```

```
    // delete any objects created in the constructor here
}

void myAgent::run_agent()
{
    OutputLog::write("Entering myAgent::run_agent\n");
}

void main()
{
    OutputLog log("test.log");
    OutputLog::write("Testing VR Agent C++ Classes.\n\n");

    World world;
    game_object g1(&world);
    OutputLog::write("Create an instance of class myAgent 'a1':\n");
    myAgent a1(&world, &g1);
    OutputLog::write("Add myAgent instance 'a1' to game_object 'g1':\n");
    g1.add_agent(a1);
    OutputLog::write("Add game_object 'g1' to the world:\n");
    world.add_game_object(g1);
    world.update_all_game_objects();
    OutputLog::write("Done with test. Compiler will call destructors:\n");
}
```

The instances of **World, game_object**, and **myAgent** are created statically in the main function: The compiler calls the constructors and destructors for you. Listing 4.2 shows the output from running this test program.

Listing 4.2

```
Testing VR Agent C++ Classes.

Entering constructor for class World
Entering game_object constructor
Create an instance of class myAgent 'a1':
Entering constructor for Agent class
Entering constructor for myAgent class
Add myAgent instance 'a1' to game_object 'g1':
Add game_object 'g1' to the world:
Entering myAgent::run_agent
```

```
Done with test. Compiler will call destructors:
Entering destructor for myAgent class
Entering destructor for Agent class
Entering game_object destructor
Entering destructor for Agent class
Entering destructor for class World
Entering game_object destructor
Entering destructor for Agent class
```

In this listing there seem to be several extra calls to the destructor for the derived C++ class **myAgent**. What is going on here? In Chapter 3, we correctly defined the destructor for the base class **Agent** to be a virtual member function, so you may be asking yourself why you only see calls to the base class destructor. There is a good reason for this. As you will see shortly, the destructor for class **game_object** deletes all of the agents that it uses. Even if multiple instances of class **game_object** share the same agent, this works because the C++ *delete* operator does nothing if it is used on an object that has already been deleted. We will see later that the destructor for class **World** deletes all of the instances of class **game_object** that it contains.

The first time that the destructor for the instance of **myAgent a1** is called in Listing 4.2, we see, as expected, first the derived class destructor is called, then the base class destructor is called. Once this object is deleted, and its destructor is called during the "cleanup" operation of the destructors for classes **World** and **game_object**, only the base class destructor is called, which does nothing with the already deleted object; the derived class destructor does not need to be called again.

In normal use, we will be creating instances of class **game_object** and derived classes of **Agent** using the C++ *new* operator. The behavior of the destructors for classes **World** and **game_object** to delete any objects that they contain is useful to avoid memory leaks in programs using the VR Agent Toolkit C++ classes.

Listing 4.3 shows a test program that is identical to the one shown in Listing 4.1 except that instances of **game_object** and **myAgent** are created using the C++ *new* operator.

Listing 4.3

```
// File: test2.cpp
//
// Description: This file contains a text mode test
//              program for testing the C++ classes:
//
//                     game_object
//                     Agent
//                     World
//                     OutputLog
//
// Note: This example is identical to file test.cpp
//       except that instances of class myAgent and game_object
//       are created with the 'new' operator, with no
//       corresponding 'delete' calls. We let the destructors
//       for classes World and game_object delete all objects
//       that they contain.
//
// Copyright 1995, Mark Watson

#include "world.h"
#include "game_obj.h"
#include "agent.h"

#include "out_log.h"

#include <stdio.h>

class myAgent : public Agent {
 public:
    myAgent(World *w = NULL, game_object *g = NULL);
    ~myAgent();
    void run_agent();
};

myAgent::myAgent(World *w, game_object *g) : Agent(w,g)
{
    OutputLog::write("Entering constructor for myAgent class\n");
    // You would create instances of NeuralNet, genetic,
    // ExpertSystem, and PlanManager here
}
```

```
myAgent::~myAgent()
{
   OutputLog::write("Entering destructor for myAgent class\n");
   // delete any objects created in the constructor here
}

void myAgent::run_agent()
{
   OutputLog::write("Entering myAgent::run_agent\n");
}

void main()
{
   OutputLog log("test.log");
   OutputLog::write("Testing VR Agent C++ Classes.\n\n");

   World * world = new World();
   game_object * g1 = new game_object(world);
   OutputLog::write("Create an instance of class myAgent 'a1':\n");
   myAgent * a1 = new myAgent(world, g1);
   OutputLog::write("Add myAgent instance 'a1' to game_object 'g1':\n");
   g1->add_agent(*a1);
   OutputLog::write("Add game_object 'g1' to the world:\n");
   world->add_game_object(*g1);
   world->update_all_game_objects();

   delete world;  // This should also delete all contained objects
}
```

In the example program in this listing, the destructor for class **World** deletes all instances of class **game_object** that it contains. During this process, the destructor for class **game_object** deletes all the instances of classes derived from class **Agent**. Listing 4.4 shows the output created by the static class member function **OutputLog::write** in the program in Listing 4.3.

Listing 4.4

```
Testing VR Agent C++ Classes.

Entering constructor for class World
Entering game_object constructor
```

```
Create an instance of class myAgent 'a1':
Entering constructor for Agent class
Entering constructor for myAgent class
Add myAgent instance 'a1' to game_object 'g1':
Add game_object 'g1' to the world:
Entering myAgent::run_agent
Entering destructor for class World
Entering game_object destructor
Entering destructor for myAgent class
Entering destructor for Agent class
```

Implementation of C++ Class geometric_object

The constructor for class **geometric_object** has two arguments: an appearance type and a size. If not specified, the appearance type defaults to the constant **geometric_object::SPHERE**, and the size defaults to the value 10. As seen in the class definition found in file GEOM_OBJ.H listed in Chapter 3, there are also member functions for setting and reading position, color, and texture values from instances of class **geometric_object**.

The class member function **distance** calculates the distance between any instance of class **geometric_object** (or a derived class) and another instance of this class (or a derived class). Listing 4.5 shows the implementation of class **geometric_object**.

Listing 4.5

```
// File: geom_obj.cpp
//
// Description: This file contains the class implementation
//              for a base class of geometric objects.
//
// Copyright 1995, Mark Watson
//
```

```
#include "geom_obj.h"
#include "out_log.h"
#include <math.h>
geometric_object::geometric_object(int appearance_type,
                                   int size1)
{
    x = 0;
    y = 0;
    z = 0;
    size = size1;
    o_type = appearance_type;
    int color = RED;
    int texture = -1; // no texture assigned
}


// Utility to detect the distance to another
// geometric_object.  A distance < 0 implies a collision.

float geometric_object::distance(geometric_object &g)
{
    float del_x, del_y, del_z;
    del_x = x - g.x;
    del_y = y - g.y;
    del_z = z - g.z;

    float dist =
        sqrt((double)(del_x*del_x + del_y*del_y + del_z*del_z));
    if (dist > 5000.0)  dist = 5000.0;

    return dist;
}
```

Implementation of C++ Class game_object

In Chapter 3, we presented the requirements and C++ class interface for the class **geometric_object**, and we implemented this class in the preceding section. In Chapter 3 we also specified the C++

class interface for the derived class **game_object**, which we will implement in this section.

Figure 4.1 shows the relationship between the base class **geometric_object** and the derived class **game_object**. Class **geometric_object** contains data and behavior specific to supporting an object moving in a three-dimensional space. Class **game_object** adds data and behavior for containing software agents built from the AI utility classes developed in Chapter 2. Listing 4.6 shows the implementation of class **game_object**.

Listing 4.6

```cpp
// File: game_obj.cpp
//
// Description: This file contains the C++ class interface
//              for the 'game_object', which is derived
//              from class geometric_object.
//              An instance of game_object is either a
//              sphere or cube object which contains
//              one or more agent objects to control
//              its behavior.
//
// Copyright 1995, Mark Watson
//

#include "geom_obj.h"
#include "game_obj.h"
#ifdef TEXT_MODE
#include <iostream.h>
#endif
#include <stdlib.h>
#include "out_log.h"
#include "agent.h"
#include "game_val.h"

const float MAX_VEL_COMPONENT = MAX_VELOCITY;
const float MAX_ACC_COMPONENT = 4.0 * SMALL_ACCELERATION;

game_object::game_object(World *w,
                         const char * my_name,
                         int appearance_type,
                         int size)
```

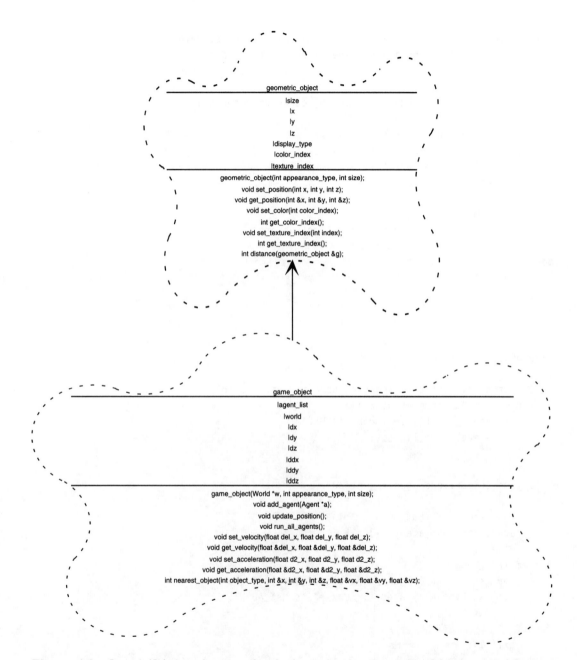

Figure 4.1 Booch '94 class diagrams for the base class **geometric_object** and the derived class **game_object**.

```cpp
    : name(my_name),                              // set const data
      geometric_object(appearance_type, size) // call base
                                               // class constructor
{
    OutputLog::write("Entering game_object constructor\n");
    dx = 0;   dy = 0;   dz = 0;
    ddx= 0;   ddy= 0;   ddz= 0;
    for (int i=0; i<MAX_AGENTS; i++)
      agent_list[i] = (Agent *)NULL;
    num_agents = 0;
    if (w == (World *)NULL) {
#ifdef TEXT_MODE
        cerr << "Error in game_object contructor."
             << " Null World *.\n";
#endif
        exit(1);
    }
    world = w;
}


game_object::~game_object()
{
    OutputLog::write("Entering game_object destructor\n");
    for (int i=0; i<num_agents; i++)
      if (agent_list[i] != (Agent *)NULL)
        delete agent_list[i];
}


void game_object::add_agent(Agent &a)
{
    if (num_agents < (MAX_AGENTS - 1)) {
      agent_list[num_agents++] = &a;
    } else {
#ifdef TEXT_MODE
        cerr << "Error in game_object::add_agent: "
             << "too many agents.  Max =" << MAX_AGENTS
             << "\n";
#endif
        exit(1);
    }
}


void game_object::update_position()
```

```cpp
{
    // Update velocity:
    dx += ddx;
    dy += ddy;
    dz += ddz;

    // Update position:
    x += dx;
    y += dy;
    z += dz;
}

void game_object::run_all_agents()
{
    for (int i=0; i<num_agents; i++) {
        agent_list[i]->run_agent();
    }
}

void game_object::set_velocity(float vx, float vy, float vz)
{
    if (vx < -MAX_VEL_COMPONENT)  vx = -MAX_VEL_COMPONENT;
    if (vx >  MAX_VEL_COMPONENT)  vx =  MAX_VEL_COMPONENT;
    if (vy < -MAX_VEL_COMPONENT)  vy = -MAX_VEL_COMPONENT;
    if (vy >  MAX_VEL_COMPONENT)  vy =  MAX_VEL_COMPONENT;
    if (vz < -MAX_VEL_COMPONENT)  vz = -MAX_VEL_COMPONENT;
    if (vz >  MAX_VEL_COMPONENT)  vz =  MAX_VEL_COMPONENT;

    dx = vx;
    dy = vy;
    dz = vz;
}

void game_object::get_velocity(float &vx, float &vy, float &vz)
{
    vx = dx;
    vy = dy;
    vz = dz;
}
```

```
void game_object::set_acceleration(float ax, float ay, float az)
{
    if (ax < -MAX_ACC_COMPONENT)  ax = -MAX_ACC_COMPONENT;
    if (ax >  MAX_ACC_COMPONENT)  ax =  MAX_ACC_COMPONENT;
    if (ay < -MAX_ACC_COMPONENT)  ay = -MAX_ACC_COMPONENT;
    if (ay >  MAX_ACC_COMPONENT)  ay =  MAX_ACC_COMPONENT;
    if (az < -MAX_ACC_COMPONENT)  az = -MAX_ACC_COMPONENT;
    if (az >  MAX_ACC_COMPONENT)  az =  MAX_ACC_COMPONENT;

    ddx = ax;
    ddy = ay;
    ddz = az;
}

void game_object::get_acceleration(float &ax, float &ay, float &az)
{
    ax = ddx;
    ay = ddy;
    az = ddz;
}


int game_object::nearest_object(int object_type, int &x, int &y, int &z,
                                float &vx, float &vy, float &vz)
{
    game_object *objs[20];
    int distances[20];
    int num = world->return_nearby_objects(this,
                                            20,
                                            objs,
                                            distances);
    for (int i=0; i<num; i++) {
        if (objs[i]->get_type() == object_type) {
            objs[i]->get_position(x, y, z);
            int x0, y0, z0;
            get_position(x0, y0, z0);
            vx = x - x0;
            vy = y - y0;
            vz = z - z0;
            float dist = distance(*objs[i]);
            vx /= dist;
            vy /= dist;
            vz /= dist;
```

```
        return 1;  // success
    }
  }
  return 0;  // failure to find an object of the correct type
}
```

The constructor **game_object::game_object()** initializes the data for a class instance by setting the **const char * name** pointer using initialization and calling the base class **geometric_object** constructor. The velocity and acceleration components are initialized to 0. The constructor requires a non-NULL first argument, which is a pointer to the **World** container object that will contain the **game_object** instance that is being constructed. This pointer to a **World** container object is defaulted to NULL in the class header seen in Chapter 3, and the constructor checks to see if the pointer is equal to NULL, in which case an error message is displayed, and the **exit()** function is called to terminate the program. This test is important, as is the default NULL value for the pointer in the class header. The C++ compiler would normally write a constructor requiring no arguments; therefore, if a game object was incorrectly constructed like this:

```
game_object *ship = new game_object();
```

then the constructor supplied by the C++ compiler would be called instead of the constructor in Listing 4.6. With the default values specified, this incorrect game object construction would be equivalent to:

```
game_object *ship =
  new game_object(NULL, "no_name", geometric_object::SPHERE, 10);
```

The constructor in Listing 4.6 will detect the NULL **World** pointer, and prevent incorrect program behavior.

The destructor **game_object::~game_object()** calls the destructor for all members of classes derived from the abstract base class **Agent**. The member function **game_object::add_agent(Agent &a)** adds a reference from an instance of any class derived from the abstract base class **Agent**, to a **game_object** instance. In order to simplify the class implementation, I allocate a small array to hold references to software agents; this could be changed to a linked list, or a dynamically sized array if required by an application that had a huge variation in the expected number of software agents used in **game_object** instances.

The member function **game_object::update_position** simply updates the velocity based on the current acceleration, then the position based on the updated velocity. Note that the acceleration are not in units of 1 / seconds squared, but rather in units of 1 / (simulation time step) squared. This function is called indirectly for each instance of class **game_object** contained in an instance of class **World** when the member function **World::update_all_game_objects()** is called, usually once per simulation time step.

The member function **game_object::run_all_agents()** executes each software agent used by this game object. This function is called indirectly for each instance of class **game_object** contained in an instance of class **World** when the member function **World::update_all_game_objects()** is called, usually once per simulation time step.

The utility member function **game_object::nearest_object(int object_type, int &x, int &y, int &z, float &vx, float &vy, float &vz)** is used to locate the nearest game object of a specified type (the object type is an inherited data member from class **geometric_object**). I added this function to the public interface of this class after the first implementation of the spaceship simulation developed in Chapter 5. This function uses the utility function **World::return_nearby_objects()**; if required, this function could be reimplemented slightly more efficiently by not calling **World::return_nearby_objects()**, and searching directly just for objects of the required type.

Implementation of C++ Class World

We specified the requirements and designed the class interface for the C++ class **World** in Chapter 3. Recall that class **World** acts as a generic container class for instances of class **game_object**, with added behavior for executing all software agents and updating positions of each contained instance of class **game_object**. C++

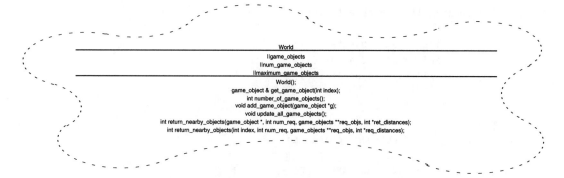

Figure 4.2   Booch '94 class diagram for C++ class **World**.

class **World** provides utility member functions for returning a list of specified size of contained game objects that are closest to any game object in the game world. Figure 4.2 shows the class diagram for **World**. Listing 4.7 shows the implementation of class **World**.

Listing 4.7

```
// File: world.cpp
//

#include "world.h"
#include "out_log.h"
#include <stdlib.h>
#include <iostream.h>

World::World()
{
   OutputLog::write("Entering constructor for class World\n");
   num_game_objects = 0;
}

World::~World()
{
   OutputLog::write("Entering destructor for class World\n");
   for (int i=0; i<num_game_objects; i++)
     if (game_objects[i] != (game_object *)NULL)
        delete game_objects[i];
}
```

```
void World::update_all_game_objects()
{
    for (int i=0; i<num_game_objects; i++) {
        game_objects[i]->run_all_agents();
        game_objects[i]->update_position();
    }
}


void World::add_game_object(game_object &g)
{
    if (num_game_objects < (MAX_GAME_OBJECTS - 1)) {
        game_objects[num_game_objects++] = &g;
    }
    // Make sure that all contained objects have pointers
    // back to this world:
    g.set_world(this);
    for (int i=0; i<g.number_of_agents(); i++) {
        (g.get_agent(i)).set_world(this);
    }
}


int World::get_game_object_index(game_object *g)
{
    for (int i=0; i<num_game_objects; i++)
        if (g == game_objects[i])   return i;
    // Error: object not found.  I choose to make this
    // a fatal error, since this condition should never
    // occur.
#ifdef TEXT_MODE
    cerr << "Fatal error in world.cpp:World::get_game_object_index.\n"
         << "Illegal game object pointer.\n";
#endif
    exit(1);
    return 0;  // never reach this statement.
}


// The following member function returns a list of
// nearby game_objects, and the distances to
// these objects.  Note that the caller needs
// to allocate space for the returned lists, but
// should NOT delete the game_objects pointed to
// by the elements in the returned list! The function
// returns the actual number of objects returned.
```

```
int World::return_nearby_objects(game_object *g,
                                 int number_requested,
                                 game_object **objs,
                                 int *distances)
{
   int g_distances[MAX_GAME_OBJECTS];
   int g_indices[MAX_GAME_OBJECTS];
   int i, j;
   for (i=0; i<num_game_objects; i++) {
      g_indices[i] = i;
      g_distances[i] = g->distance(*game_objects[i]);
   }
   if (number_requested > (num_game_objects - 1))
       number_requested = num_game_objects - 1;
   // Bubble sort the distances:
   for (i=0; i<num_game_objects; i++) {
      for (j=(num_game_objects-2); j>=i; j--) {
         if (g_distances[j] > g_distances[j+1]) {
            int k = g_indices[j];
            int f = g_distances[j];
            g_indices[j] = g_indices[j+1];
            g_distances[j] = g_distances[j+1];
            g_indices[j+1] = k;
            g_distances[j+1] = f;
         }
      }
   }
   for (i=0; i<number_requested; i++) {
      objs[i] = game_objects[g_indices[i + 1]];
      distances[i] = g_distances[i+1];
   }
   return number_requested;
}


// The following member function returns a list of
// nearby game_objects, and the distances to
// these objects.  Note that the caller needs
// to allocate space for the returned lists, but
// should NOT delete the game_objects pointed to
// by the elements in the returned list! The function
// returns the actual number of objects returned.
```

```
int World::return_nearby_objects(int game_object_index,
                                 int number_requested,
                                 game_object **objs,
                                 int *distances)
{
    game_object *g = game_objects[game_object_index];
    return return_nearby_objects(g, number_requested, objs, distances);
}
```

The implementation of C++ class **World** is fairly simple. It is fairly common to spend much more time thinking about the requirements and class interface for a new class than actually writing the code to implement it. This is especially true when several classes work together in a framework, like the C++ classes **World, game_object**, and **Agent**; the interactions of members of a class framework are much more complex than the classes themselves.

The class constructor **World::World()** simply initializes the count of contained **game_object** instances to 0. The destructor **World::~World()** calls the destructor for each contained instance of class **game_object**; the destructor for class **game_object** calls the destructor of every contained software agent object.

The member function **World::update_all_game_objects()** executes all software agents for each game object in the game world, and then calls the member function **game_object::update_position()** to move the object. This function is typically called once every game of virtual reality simulation time step.

The member function **World::add_game_object(game_object &g)** adds a reference to a game object to an instance of class **World**. In order to simplify the class implementation, I statically allocate a small array to hold references to game objects; this could be changed to a linked list, or a dynamically sized array if required by an application that had a huge variation in the expected number of game objects used in a game world.

Member function **World::return_nearby_objects()** is overloaded: the first argument can either be a pointer to an instance of class **game_object**, or an integer index into the array of **game_object** pointers contained in the **world** object.

Implementation of C++ Class Agent

As already stated, the C++ class **Agent** is an abstract base class. In C++, we define a class to be an abstract base class (or pure virtual) by declaring at least one virtual function, and setting the initial value of the function to 0. (This is a strange syntax, but it works!) Application programs cannot create instances directly from an abstract base class; they must define a derived class of the abstract base class, and then create instances of the derived class.

As we will see in the example programs in Chapters 5 through 10, the instances of derived classes of **Agent** behave as focal points for controlling the execution of neural networks, genetic algorithms, expert systems, and plan managers. Figure 4.3 shows the class diagram for **Agent**. Listing 4.8 shows the implementation of class **Agent**.

Listing 4.8

```
// File: agent.cpp
//

#include <iostream.h>
#include <stdlib.h>

#include "game_obj.h"
#include "world.h"
#include "agent.h"
#include "out_log.h"


Agent::Agent(World *w, game_object *g)
{
   OutputLog::write("Entering constructor for Agent class\n");
   if (w == (World *)NULL || g == (game_object *)NULL) {
#ifdef TEXT_MODE
      cerr << "Error: Agent constructor must be called "
           << "with a World* and Agent *\n";
#endif
      exit(1);
```

```
   }
   game_obj = g;
   world = w;
}

Agent::~Agent()
{
   OutputLog::write("Entering destructor for Agent class\n");
}

void Agent::run_agent()
{
   OutputLog::write("Entered virtual base Agent::run_agent\n");
   // Dummy test code:
   game_obj->set_acceleration(1.0, 0.0, 0.0);
   int x, y, z;
   game_obj->get_position(x, y, z);
   if (x > 50)
       game_obj->set_acceleration(1.0, 0.0, 0.0);
}
```

The constructor **Agent::Agent(World *w, game_object *g)** should be called in the constructor of classes derived from **Agent**. For example, in Chapter 5 we will derive a class whose constructor calls **Agent::Agent**.

```
NavigationAgent::NavigationAgent(World *w, game_object *g)
   : Agent(w,g)
{
   ...
}
```

C++ class **Agent** is an abstract base class. The member function **run_agent()** needs to be redefined in derived classes. The example code in **Agent::run_agent()** is an example of accessing the instance of class **game_object**, which is using the agent. Note that the example code in **Agent::run_agent()** can never be executed; this public member function is pure virtual, and must be overridden in derived classes.

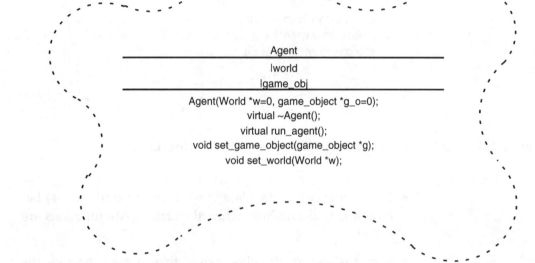

The C++ Agent class is an abstract base class. Application-specific subclasses will use some combination of the utility classes ExpertSystem, PlanManager, Neural, and Genetic.

Agent
lworld
lgame_obj
Agent(World *w=0, game_object *g_o=0);
virtual ~Agent();
virtual run_agent();
void set_game_object(game_object *g);
void set_world(World *w);

Figure 4.3   Booch '94 class diagram for C++ class **Agent**.

Implementation of C++ Class OutputLog

We specified the requirements and designed the class interface for C++ class **OutputLog** in Chapter 3. This class is unusual because:

- Its behavior is static (class) behavior, not associated with any instance of the class.

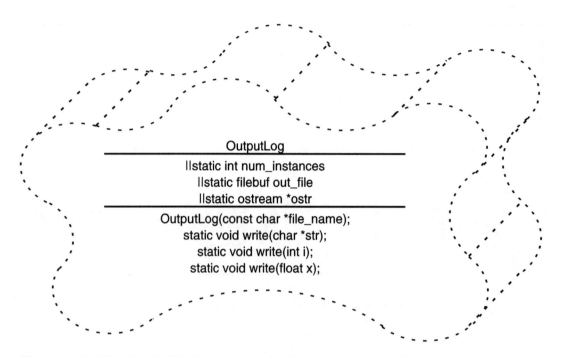

Figure 4.4   The Booch '94 class diagram for C++ class **OutputLog**.

- If no instances of the class exist, then the static (class) behavior is to do nothing when the static write functions are called.

- If an instance of the class exists, then output through the static (class) write functions is enabled.

Figure 4.4 shows the class diagram for class **OutputLog**. Listing 4.9 shows the implementation of class **OutputLog**.

Listing 4.9

```
// File: out_log.cpp
//
// Description: This is a utility class that provides
//              static member functions to write out
//              strings, integers, and floats to a
```

```
//              log file.  One instance of this class
//              must exist (the constructor opens a
//              file, and the destructor closes it).
//
// Copyright 1995, Mark Watson
//

#include <iostream.h>
#include <fstream.h>
#include <stdlib.h>

#include "out_log.h"

OutputLog::OutputLog(const char * file_name)
{
    if (OutputLog::num_instances == 0) {
        OutputLog::num_instances = 1;
        if (OutputLog::out_file.open(file_name, ios::out) == 0) {
#ifdef TEXT_MODE
            cerr << "Could not open log file "
                << file_name << "\n";
#endif
            exit(1);
        }
        OutputLog::ostr = new ostream(&out_file);
    }
}


OutputLog::~OutputLog()
{
    if (OutputLog::num_instances == 1) {
        OutputLog::out_file.close();
        OutputLog::num_instances = 0;
    }
}


void OutputLog::write(char * str)
{
    if (OutputLog::num_instances == 1) {
        *(OutputLog::ostr) << str;
    }
}
```

```
void OutputLog::write(const char * str)
{
    if (OutputLog::num_instances == 1) {
        *(OutputLog::ostr) << str;
    }
}

void OutputLog::write(int i)
{
    if (OutputLog::num_instances == 1) {
        *(OutputLog::ostr) << i;
    }
}

void OutputLog::write(long i)
{
    if (OutputLog::num_instances == 1) {
        *(OutputLog::ostr) << i;
    }
}

void OutputLog::write(float x)
{
    if (OutputLog::num_instances == 1) {
        *(OutputLog::ostr) << x;
    }
}

void OutputLog::write(double x)
{
    if (OutputLog::num_instances == 1) {
        *(OutputLog::ostr) << x;
    }
}
int OutputLog::num_instances = 0;
filebuf OutputLog::out_file;
ostream * OutputLog::ostr;
```

The last three lines in this listing are required to allocate storage for static (class) variables. Note that every instance of a class shares the same single copy of static (class) variables. Static variables defined inside a class can be global variables if defined in the *public* section of the class definition, or accessible to just instances of the class if they are defined in the *private* section of the class definition, or available to both instances of the class and instances of derived classes if defined in the *protected* section of the class definition.

Text-Based Spaceship Simulation: Trade Commodities and Avoid Enemy Ships

As stated, the purpose of this book is to provide reusable analysis, design, and C++ class libraries that you can freely use for developing your own virtual reality simulations and games. This material was covered in Chapters 1 through 4. The remainder of this book provides examples of using the VR Agent Toolkit, which will, I hope, give you good ideas for creating your own games.

In this chapter, we will design and implement software agents for controlling three types of simulated spaceships. The same simulation scenario is used for the text-based simulation in this chapter, the RenderWare-based 3D simulation in Chapter 6, the OpenGL-based 3D simulation in Chapter 7, the Microsoft Windows-based 2D game in Chapter 8, the Apple Macintosh-based 2D game in

Chapter 9, and the UNIX X Windows-based 2D game in Chapter 10. All of the software for controlling the three ship types is developed in this chapter, and reused in later chapters.

Game Description and Program Overview

The spaceship simulation uses three types of ships: the Player ship, the Processor ship, and the Crogan ship. The Processor ships accept Magnozate ore that the Player ship has collected from asteroids, and it barters with the player for energy conversion costs. This bartering is instigated by the Player ship offering an energy conversion rate, which a Processor ship will either accept or ignore. Processor ships will not trade if they already contain too much Magnozate ore. The Crogan ships are like mosquitoes. There are many of them, and they slowly steal energy from nearby Player or Processor ships. Crogan ships use genetic algorithms to continually evolve their game strategy to become better opponents. The Player ship "stays alive" in this game by mining for Magnozate, bartering for energy conversion with any of the Processor ships, and avoiding Crogans. The Player ship has an intelligent agent that can help the human player maneuver the ship and barter. In the 2D game version of the simulation (Chapters 8, 9, and 10), the intelligent agent on the Player ship can be turned on and off, allowing manual control of the ship. Figure 5.1 shows the simulated world, which consists of four asteroids, one Player ship, several Processor ships, and many Crogan ships. Figure 5.2 shows a Harel state transition diagram (Booch, 1994) of the text-based spaceship simulation program developed in this chapter.

As seen in Figure 5.2, when the program starts, a data setup function is called which creates an instance of C++ class **World**, a set of contained instances of class **game_object**, and the instances of classes derived from C++ class **Agent** to control the instances of class **game_object**. Since there is no real time behavior in the text-based simulation, the program simply calls two update functions each time step: **World::update_all_game_objects()**

Objects in the example game world

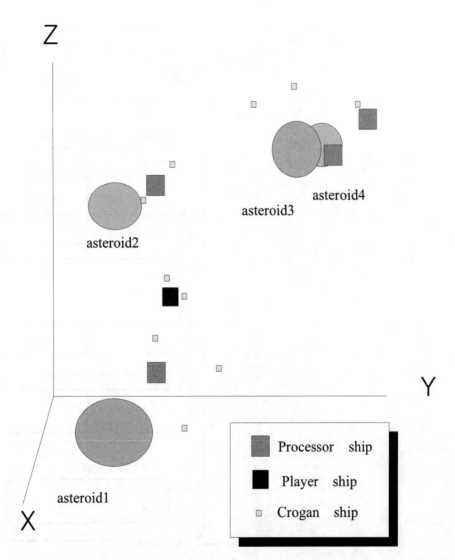

Figure 5.1 Three-dimensional game world. The four asteroids are located between the origin ($x = y = z = 0$) and the bounding box created by the point ($x = y = z = 800$).

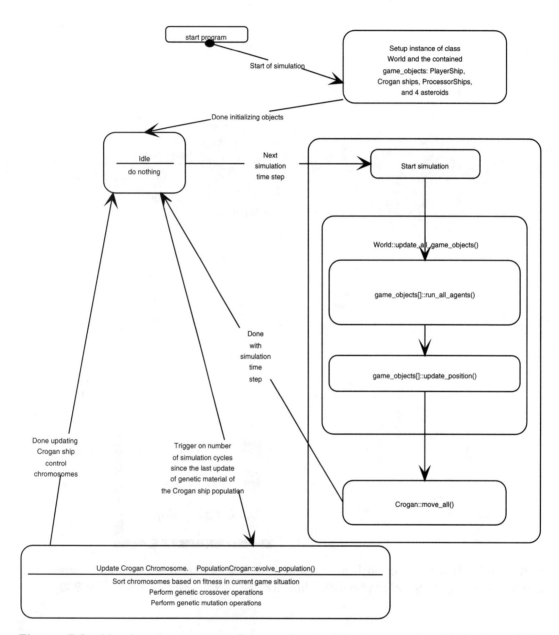

Figure 5.2 Harel state transition diagram showing the event-ordered behavior of the text-based 3D spaceship simulation program.

and **Crogan::move_all()**. The member function **World::update_all_ game_objects()** simply calls the functions **game_object::run_all_ agents()** and **game_object::update_position()** for each instance of class **game_object** contained in the **World** data object.

The Crogan ships are handled differently. The C++ class **Crogan** is derived, using public inheritance, from the C++ class **genetic** developed in Chapter 2. Class **Crogan** uses static class data to maintain control parameters for each Crogan ship; these control parameters are encoded in chromosomes, and evolved using a genetic algorithm. The chromosomes controlling the behavior of the Crogan ships are modified periodically by the text-based simulation, enabling the Crogan ships to optimize their strategy for the current game situation.

Using Neural Networks for Player Ship and Processor Ship Navigation

Figure 5.1 showed the three-dimensional coordinate system of our game world. The navigational behavior of Processor and Player ships is similar, so we will train a neural network object to provide navigational cues. In upcoming sections we will create expert system executives for Processor and Player ships that use this neural network object.

We will use a neural network object (instance of C++ class **Neural**) to control velocity and acceleration in a single direction based on sensor readings in that direction. Use of the same neural network object, with different inputs and control outputs for each of the X, Y, Z, −X, −Y, and −Z directions in space, will provide full navigational control for a ship based on the local positions of asteroids and other ships. Treating the directions in space separately sometimes results in "funky" behavior, but it is much easier to create training data for one direction. We could use only three neural network objects, but our representation is easier if we don't have to deal with negative distances in any direction.

As we saw in Chapter 2, neural networks accept inputs as floating point numbers in the range −0.5 to 0.5, and set their output neuron's activation energy to values in the same range. We need a representation of the space surrounding a ship that can be easily converted to the input values for a trained navigational neural network. We also need a representation for the ship controls that allows mapping output neuron values to the ship control representation.

We want the ship to react, in increasing order of priority, to the following objects in its immediate vicinity:

- Nearby asteroids

- Enemy Crogan ships

- Processor/Player ship when in a "need to trade" mode

In other words, if a Processor or Player ship has nothing better to do, it should slowly maneuver close to an asteroid to mine Magnozate ore. If there are Crogan ships around, the Processor and Player ships should move away from the Crogans, when convenient to do so. When Processor ships have excess R4 fuel (converted Magnozate ore), they want to trade it away to a Player ship (the more energy in the form of R4 that a Processor ship has, the faster it can lose energy to Crogan ships). When the Player ship is running low on R4 fuel, it needs to get to an asteroid, mine Magnozate ore, and find a Processor ship to trade for R4; the human player "loses" the game when the Player ship's energy level (amount of R4) goes to 0.

For the Processor ships, a trading partner must be the Player ship. For the Player ship, a trading partner can be any Processor ship. So, each Player and Processor ship will use six neural network objects for navigation to separately handle the X, Y, Z, $-X$, $-Y$, and $-Z$ directions in space. Each of these six navigational neural networks has the following inputs:

1. If distance to an asteroid in this direction is between 0 and 10 distance units, set this input to ON, otherwise to OFF.
2. If distance to an asteroid in this direction is between 11 and 100 distance units, set this input to ON, otherwise to OFF.
3. If distance to an asteroid in this direction is between 101 and 200 distance units, set this input to ON, otherwise to OFF.

4. If distance to a Crogan ship in this direction is less than 50 units, set this input to ON, otherwise to OFF.

5. If distance to a Crogan ship is between 51 and 100 distance units, set this input to ON, otherwise to OFF.

6. If in "need to trade" mode, and a trading partner is between 0 and 10 units in this direction, set this input to ON, otherwise to OFF.

7. If in "need to trade" mode, and a trading partner is between 11 and 80 distance units, set this input to ON, otherwise to OFF.

8. If in "need to trade" mode, and a trading partner is between 81 and 200 distance units, set this input to ON, otherwise to OFF.

This input representation, modeled after a binary decision tree, would work, but it does not take full advantage of the nonlinear decision surfaces that the use of neural networks for control can provide. Instead of setting input neuron values to ON or OFF (about 0.5 or −0.5 for our neural networks), we can add two additional neuron values:

9. Amount of R4 fuel: a value of OFF for no R4, scaled linearly to ON for full fuel tanks.

10. Amount of Magnozate ore: a value of OFF for no Magnozate ore, scaled linearly to ON for a full load.

Now, if we have appropriate training data for the neural network, the ship navigation will vary smoothly according to several input factors.

The navigation expert system that uses six navigational neural networks will have to take some care in choosing which neural network control signals (outputs of the neural networks) to actually use. For each of the six directions, we have the following control outputs:

1. Stop ship, set velocity to 0.
2. Accelerate.
3. Decelerate.

The control output for an "all stop" condition is easy: if the output neuron is over a threshold value, we set the velocity for that direction (and the negative of that direction) to 0. Handling acceleration and deceleration is harder, because back-propagation networks do not reliably scale their outputs; that is, treating an output value of, for example, 0.45 as faster acceleration than 0.41 is risky.

Listing 5.1 shows a short C++ training program for creating a neural network weight set for navigation in one direction.

Listing 5.1

```cpp
// File: nav_trn.cpp
//
// Description: This file contains code to train a neural
//              neural network to help navigate a ship.
//

#include "neural.h"
#include <iostream.h>
#include <math.h>

#include "game_val.h"

const int NUM_EXAMPLES = 30;
const int INPUT_SIZE = 12;
const int OUTPUT_SIZE = 3;

static float inputs[NUM_EXAMPLES][INPUT_SIZE];
static float outputs[NUM_EXAMPLES][OUTPUT_SIZE];
static int num_examples;

static void init_data()
{
    int i, j;
    for (i=0; i<NUM_EXAMPLES; i++) {
        for (j=0; j<OUTPUT_SIZE; j++)  outputs[i][j] = OFF;
        for (j=0; j<INPUT_SIZE; j++)   inputs[i][j] = OFF;
    }
    int ic = 0;  // training set counter

    inputs[ic][CLOSE] = ON;
    outputs[ic][STOP] = ON;
```

```
ic++;
inputs[ic][CLOSE] = ON;
inputs[ic][FULL_ORE] = ON;
outputs[ic][DECELERATE] = ON;  // change velocity away from asteroid
ic++;
inputs[ic][NEAR] = ON;
inputs[ic][FULL_ORE] = ON;
ic++;
outputs[ic][DECELERATE] = 0.6 * ON;  // change velocity
                                     // away from asteroid
ic++;
inputs[ic][NEAR] = ON;
outputs[ic][ACCELERATE] = 0.6 * ON;
ic++;
inputs[ic][FAR] = ON;
outputs[ic][ACCELERATE] = ON;
ic++;
inputs[ic][NEED_TO_TRADE_PARTNER_CLOSE] = ON;
outputs[ic][STOP] = ON;
ic++;
inputs[ic][NEED_TO_TRADE_PARTNER_NEAR] = ON;
outputs[ic][ACCELERATE] = 0.6 * ON;
ic++;
inputs[ic][NEED_TO_TRADE_PARTNER_FAR] = ON;
outputs[ic][ACCELERATE] = ON;
ic++;
inputs[ic][DO_NOT_NEED_R4_PARTNER_CLOSE] = ON;
outputs[ic][DECELERATE] = ON;
ic++;
inputs[ic][DO_NOT_NEED_R4_PARTNER_NEAR] = ON;
outputs[ic][DECELERATE] = 0.6 * ON;
ic++;
inputs[ic][CROGAN_CLOSE] = ON;
outputs[ic][DECELERATE] = ON;
ic++;
inputs[ic][CROGAN_NEAR] = ON;
outputs[ic][DECELERATE] = 0.6 *ON;
ic++;

inputs[ic][CLOSE] = ON;
inputs[ic][NEED_TO_TRADE_PARTNER_NEAR] = ON;
outputs[ic][ACCELERATE] = 0.6 * ON;
ic++;
```

```
    inputs[ic][NEAR] = ON;
    inputs[ic][NEED_TO_TRADE_PARTNER_NEAR] = ON;
    outputs[ic][ACCELERATE] = 0.6 * ON;
    ic++;

    inputs[ic][CLOSE] = ON;
    inputs[ic][NEED_TO_TRADE_PARTNER_FAR] = ON;
    outputs[ic][ACCELERATE] = ON;
    ic++;

    inputs[ic][NEAR] = ON;
    inputs[ic][NEED_TO_TRADE_PARTNER_FAR] = ON;
    outputs[ic][ACCELERATE] = ON;
    ic++;

    num_examples = ic;
}


void main()
{
    cerr << "Using C++ class 'Neural' to train for navigation\n";
init_data();
// See note in text for why we choose 6 hidden neurons:
Neural * nn = new Neural(INPUT_SIZE,6,OUTPUT_SIZE);
    int i, j, c=0, d=0;
    float ins[400], outs[100];
    cerr << "Number or training examples=" << num_examples << "\n";
    for (i=0; i<num_examples; i++) {
        for (j=0; j<INPUT_SIZE; j++) ins[c++] = inputs[i][j];
        for (j=0; j<OUTPUT_SIZE; j++) outs[d++] = outputs[i][j];
    }
for (i=0; i<600; i++) {
float error = nn->train(num_examples, ins, outs);
if ((i % 30) == 0)
        cerr << "iteration " << i
    << " training error =" << error << "\n";
}

#if 0
for (i=0; i<num_examples; i++) {
    cerr << "\ntesting training pattern " << i << "\n";
nn->recall(&(ins[i*num_examples]), outs);
cerr << outs[0] << ", " << outs[1] << ", "
```

```
    << outs[2] << "\n";
}
#endif
nn->save("nav.net");

    delete nn;
}
```

There are only four hidden neurons in the network that we trained for navigation in one direction. If we consider that, roughly speaking, each hidden neuron can have an ON or OFF value, then 16 (2 raised to the fourth power) different input training examples can be encoded in the hidden neural activation values.

The training cases that we have to deal with fortunately are limited for controlling motion in one direction. It would be better to train a navigation neural network to work directly in three dimensions (we will require some code to decide which navigational hint from six separate neural network navigation objects to use), but the amount of training data required would be enormous. We can roughly estimate that the number of training examples necessary to cover navigation in three dimensions would be:

```
num_3D_training_cases =
    num_1D_training_cases *
    num_1D_training_cases *
    num_1D_training_cases *
    num_ship_types
```

We needed about 12 cases for the one-dimensional (1D) case, and we have three ship types, so we would need at least 5,000 fairly unique training cases that would span the required behavior for navigating in three dimensions. Training a 3D navigation neural network would take a while, but would not be inherently difficult; the difficulty would be in creating the huge set of required training cases.

The neural network model for three-dimensional navigation would require two hidden layers of neurons, not just the one layer that we use here. See Watson (1991 and 1994) for a discussion of more complex neural networks. Working with two hidden neuron layer networks is not inherently more difficult than the networks

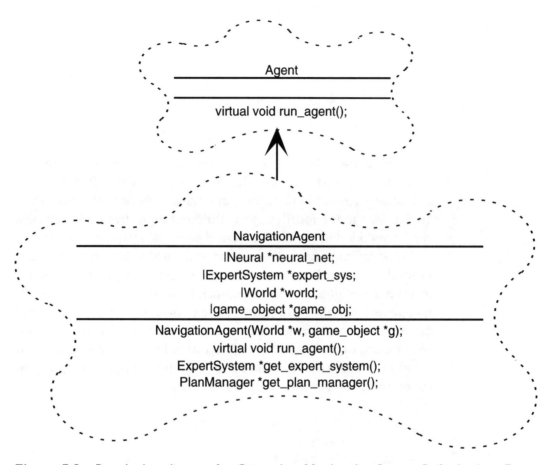

Figure 5.3   Booch class diagram for C++ class **NavigationAgent**. Refer back to Figure 4.3 for the complete interface for the base class **Agent**.

that we use here, except that training time is substantially longer. Figure 5.3 shows a Booch '94 class diagram for the C++ class **NavigationAgent**. Listing 5.2 of file NAV_AGNT.H shows the C++ class interface for **NavigationAgent**.

Listing 5.2

```
// File: nav_agnt.h
//
// Description: This file contains the interface for the
//              C++ class 'NavigationAgent'.  It is written
```

```
//              specifically to navigate a ship in the book's
//              example space war game.
//
// Copyright 1995, Mark Watson.  This software may be used
// in compiled form without restriction.  All source code
// rights retained.
//

#ifndef nav_agent_h
#define nav_agent_h

#include "world.h"
#include "neural.h"
#include "expert.h"
#include "plan.h"

#include "game_val.h"

class NavigationAgent : public Agent {
 public:
    NavigationAgent(World *w, game_object *g);
   ~NavigationAgent();
    virtual void run_agent();
    ExpertSystem * get_expert_system() { return expert_sys; }
    PlanManager * get_plan_manager() { return plan_manager; }
 protected:
    Neural *neural_net;
    ExpertSystem *expert_sys;
    PlanManager *plan_manager;
    World *world;
    game_object * game_obj;
 };

#endif
```

The class data for **NavigationAgent** is *protected*. I anticipated that I would want to make subclasses of **NavigationAgent** in the future in one of my own game projects, and would want access to the class data in derived classes. For the purposes of this book, this class data could be declared *private*. The member function **NavigationAgent::run_agent()** is called indirectly when an instance of class **World** calls the member function **World::update_all_game_objects()**.

This causes each game object to call the member function **game_object::run_all_agents()**, which causes the virtual function **Agent::run_agent()** to be called for each software agent attached to each game object. Listing 5.3 of file NAV_AGNT.CPP shows the C++ implementation of class **NavigationAgent**.

Listing 5.3

```
// File: nav_agnt.cpp
//
// Description: This file contains the interface for the
//              C++ class 'NavigationAgent'.  It is written
//              specifically to navigate a ship in the book's
//              example space war game.
//
// Copyright 1995, Mark Watson.  This software may be used
// in compiled form without restriction.  All source code
// rights retained.
//

#include <iostream.h>
#include <stdlib.h>

#include "world.h"
#include "pr_ship.h"
#include "player.h"
#include "expert.h"
#include "genetic.h"
#include "nav_agnt.h"

#include "out_log.h"

#include <stdio.h>

NavigationAgent::NavigationAgent(World *w, game_object *g)
  : Agent(w,g)
{
    neural_net = new Neural("nav.net");
    // Note: an instance of the class ExpertSystem is not created
    // knowing about particular World and game_object instances;
    // the member functions for executing rule functions are passed
    // pointers to a particular World object and an Agent object.
```

```
    // This is done so a single ExpertSystem instance can be used
    // for many game_object/Agent pairs.
    expert_sys = new ExpertSystem();
    plan_manager = new PlanManager();
    world = w;
    game_obj = g;
}

NavigationAgent::~NavigationAgent()
{
    delete neural_net;
    delete expert_sys;
    delete plan_manager;
}

void NavigationAgent::run_agent()
{   int i, j;
    float vx, vy, vz, ax, ay, az;

    if (game_obj->get_type() == PLAYER) {
        PlayerShip *ps = (PlayerShip *)game_obj;
        if (ps->get_automatic_flag() == 0) {
            // This is a player ship, and it is in manual
            // mode (i.e., the player has turned off the
            // AI capabilities of his or her ship).  We assume that
            // the ship's acceleration is set externally, so
            // here we want to just update the velocity and
            // position.  We still execute the expert system
            // rules for the ship (although some of these rules
            // might look at the state of this ship, notice that
            // it is in manual fly mode, and does nothing).

            float vx, vy, vz, ax, ay, az;
            game_obj->get_velocity(vx, vy, vz);
            game_obj->get_acceleration(ax, ay, az);
            vx += ax;
            vy += ay;
            vz += az;
            game_obj->set_velocity(vx, vy, vz);
            game_obj->update_position();

            // Run all the rules in the expert system object:
```

```
      if (plan_manager->run_plan(world, game_obj) == 0)
        expert_sys->execute_all_rules(world, game_obj);
      return;
    }
  }


  // We will start by finding the 4 closest objects to the
  // game object containing this agent:
  int distances[4];
  game_object *objs[4];
  int num_close_objects =
    world->return_nearby_objects(game_obj,
                                 4,
                                 objs,
                                 distances);
  int x, y, z, x0, y0, z0;  // this ship, other ship coordinates
  float vx0, vy0, vz0;
#ifdef DEBUG
  game_obj->get_position(x0, y0, z0);
  OutputLog::write("\nPosition of ");
  OutputLog::write(game_obj->get_name());
  OutputLog::write(": x: ");
  OutputLog::write(x0);
  OutputLog::write(", y: ");
  OutputLog::write(y0);
  OutputLog::write(", z: ");
  OutputLog::write(z0);
  OutputLog::write(" vel: ");
  game_obj->get_velocity(vx0, vy0, vz0);
  OutputLog::write(vx0);
  OutputLog::write(" ");
  OutputLog::write(vy0);
  OutputLog::write(" ");
  OutputLog::write(vz0);
  OutputLog::write("\n");
  OutputLog::write("\nClosest objects:\n");
  for (i=0; i<num_close_objects; i++) {
    objs[i]->get_position(x, y, z);
    OutputLog::write(i);
    OutputLog::write(" : ");
    OutputLog::write(objs[i]->get_name());
    OutputLog::write(", x: ");
```

```
        OutputLog::write(x);
        OutputLog::write(", y: ");
        OutputLog::write(y);
        OutputLog::write(", z: ");
        OutputLog::write(z);
        OutputLog::write(", distance = ");
        OutputLog::write(distances[i]);
        OutputLog::write("\n");
    }
#endif
    // Set acceleration values based on application of the
    // neural network 1D navigation object in each of
    // 6 directions (see text for explanation of why we
    // only deal with positive directions here, requiring
    // 6 calculations instead of 3) for +x, +y, +z, -x, -y, -z:

    // inputs for 6 application of the neural network for
    // directions: +x, +y, +z, -x, -y, -z:

    float inputs[6][Neural::MAX_INPUTS];
    for (i=0; i<6; i++)
        for (j=0; j<Neural::MAX_INPUTS; j++)
            inputs[i][j] = OFF;

    // Look at the closest objects (at (x0,y0,z0)):
    objs[0]->get_position(x0, y0, z0);  // closest object
    game_obj->get_position(x, y, z);  // this object
    game_obj->get_velocity(vx, vy, vz);
    game_obj->get_acceleration(ax, ay, az);
    int del_x, del_y, del_z;

    int closest_type = objs[0]->get_type();

    if (game_obj->get_type() == PROCESSOR &&
        closest_type == PROCESSOR) {
      objs[1]->get_position(x0, y0, z0);  // 2nd closest object
      closest_type = objs[1]->get_type();
    }

    if (game_obj->get_type() == PROCESSOR &&
        closest_type == PROCESSOR) {
      objs[2]->get_position(x0, y0, z0);  // 2nd closest object
```

```
      closest_type = objs[2]->get_type();
}


int need_to_trade = 0;

// Check for a full load of Magnozate:
if (game_obj->get_type() == PLAYER) {
   if (((PlayerShip *)game_obj)->get_Magnozate() <
       PlayerShip::MAX_MAGNOZATE / 2) {
       need_to_trade = 1;
   }
}
// Check for a full load of Magnozate:
if (game_obj->get_type() == PROCESSOR) {
   if (((ProcessorShip *)game_obj)->get_Magnozate() <
       ProcessorShip::MAX_MAGNOZATE) {
       need_to_trade = 1;
   }
}


if (game_obj->get_type() == PROCESSOR) {
    if (((ProcessorShip *)game_obj)->get_R4() >
        ProcessorShip::MAX_R4 - 10) {
      for (i=0; i<6; i++)
        inputs[i][FULL_R4] = ON;
    }
    if (((ProcessorShip *)game_obj)->get_Magnozate() >
        ProcessorShip::MAX_MAGNOZATE - 10) {
      for (i=0; i<6; i++)
        inputs[i][FULL_ORE] = ON;
    }
}


if (game_obj->get_type() == PLAYER) {
    if (((PlayerShip *)game_obj)->get_R4() >
        PlayerShip::MAX_R4 - 10) {
      for (i=0; i<6; i++)
        inputs[i][FULL_R4] = ON;
    }
    if (((PlayerShip *)game_obj)->get_Magnozate() >
        PlayerShip::MAX_MAGNOZATE - 10) {
      for (i=0; i<6; i++)
        inputs[i][FULL_ORE] = ON;
```

```
        }
    }

    if (need_to_trade &&
        game_obj->get_type() != closest_type &&
        closest_type != ASTEROID)
    {
        del_x = x0 - x;
        if (del_x > 0)
        {
          if (del_x < 11)
          {
             inputs[0][NEED_TO_TRADE_PARTNER_CLOSE] = ON;
                   // index 0 == +X direction
          } else  if (del_x < 101) {
               inputs[0][NEED_TO_TRADE_PARTNER_NEAR] = ON;
          } else if (del_x < 300) {
                 inputs[0][NEED_TO_TRADE_PARTNER_FAR] = ON;
          }
        } else  {
          if (del_x > -11)
          {
             inputs[3][NEED_TO_TRADE_PARTNER_CLOSE] = ON;
                   // index 3 == -X direction
          } else  if (del_x > -101) {
                 inputs[3][NEED_TO_TRADE_PARTNER_NEAR] = ON;
          } else if (del_x > -300) {
                 inputs[3][NEED_TO_TRADE_PARTNER_FAR] = ON;
          }
        }

        del_y = y0 - y;
        if (del_y > 0)
        {
          if (del_y < 11)
          {
             inputs[1][NEED_TO_TRADE_PARTNER_CLOSE] = ON;
                   // index 1 == +Y direction
          } else  if (del_y < 101) {
                 inputs[1][NEED_TO_TRADE_PARTNER_NEAR] = ON;
          } else if (del_y < 300) {
                 inputs[1][NEED_TO_TRADE_PARTNER_FAR] = ON;
```

```
        }
    } else {
      if (del_y > -11)
      {
          inputs[4][NEED_TO_TRADE_PARTNER_CLOSE] = ON;
                // index 4 == -Y direction
      } else  if (del_y > -101) {
              inputs[4][NEED_TO_TRADE_PARTNER_NEAR] = ON;
      } else if (del_y > -300) {
                inputs[4][NEED_TO_TRADE_PARTNER_FAR] = ON;
      }
    }


    del_z = z0 - z;
    if (del_z > 0)
    {
      if (del_z < 11)
      {
          inputs[2][NEED_TO_TRADE_PARTNER_CLOSE] = ON;
                // index 2 == +Z direction
      } else  if (del_z < 101) {
              inputs[2][NEED_TO_TRADE_PARTNER_NEAR] = ON;
      } else if (del_z < 300) {
                inputs[2][NEED_TO_TRADE_PARTNER_FAR] = ON;
      }
    } else {
      if (del_z > -11)
      {
          inputs[5][NEED_TO_TRADE_PARTNER_CLOSE] = ON;
                // index 5 == -Z direction
      } else  if (del_z > -101) {
              inputs[5][NEED_TO_TRADE_PARTNER_NEAR] = ON;
      } else if (del_z > -300) {
                inputs[5][NEED_TO_TRADE_PARTNER_FAR] = ON;
      }
    }
}


if (closest_type == ASTEROID)
{
    del_x = x0 - x;
    if (del_x > 0)
```

```
{
  if (del_x < 11)
  {
    inputs[0][CLOSE] = ON;
          // index 0 == +X direction
  } else  if (del_x < 101) {
        inputs[0][NEAR] = ON;
  } else if (del_x < 300) {
          inputs[0][FAR] = ON;
  }
} else {
  if (del_x > -11)
  {
    inputs[3][CLOSE] = ON;
          // index 3 == -X direction
  } else  if (del_x > -101) {
        inputs[3][NEAR] = ON;
  } else if (del_x > -300) {
          inputs[3][FAR] = ON;
  }
}

del_y = y0 - y;
if (del_y > 0)
{
  if (del_y < 11)
  {
    inputs[1][CLOSE] = ON; // index 1 == +Y direction
  } else  if (del_y < 101) {
        inputs[1][NEAR] = ON;
  } else if (del_y < 300) {
          inputs[1][FAR] = ON;
  }
} else {
  if (del_y > -11)
  {
    inputs[4][CLOSE] = ON;
          // index 4 == -Y direction
  } else  if (del_y > -101) {
        inputs[4][NEAR] = ON;
  } else if (del_y > -300) {
          inputs[4][FAR] = ON;
```

```
    }
  }

  del_z = z0 - z;
  if (del_z > 0)
  {
    if (del_z < 11)
    {
       inputs[2][CLOSE] = ON;
             // index 2 == +Z direction
    } else  if (del_z < 101) {
         inputs[2][NEAR] = ON;
    } else if (del_z < 300) {
             inputs[2][FAR] = ON;
    }
  } else  {
    if (del_z > -11)
    {
       inputs[5][CLOSE] = ON;
             // index 5 == -Z direction
    } else  if (del_z > -101) {
         inputs[5][NEAR] = ON;
    } else if (del_z > -300) {
             inputs[5][FAR] = ON;
    }
  }
}


if (closest_type == CROGAN)
{
    del_x = x0 - x;
    if (del_x > 0)
    {
      if (del_x < 11)
      {
         inputs[0][CROGAN_CLOSE] = ON;
               // index 0 == +X direction
      } else  if (del_x < 101) {
           inputs[0][CROGAN_NEAR] = ON;
      }
    } else  {
      if (del_x > -11)
```

```
      {
        inputs[3][CROGAN_CLOSE] = ON;
                // index 3 == -X direction
      } else  if (del_x > -101) {
            inputs[3][CROGAN_NEAR] = ON;
      }
    }

del_y = y0 - y;
if (del_y > 0)
{
  if (del_y < 11)
  {
    inputs[1][CROGAN_CLOSE] = ON;
            // index 1 == +Y direction
  } else  if (del_y < 101) {
        inputs[1][CROGAN_NEAR] = ON;
  }
} else  {
  if (del_y > -11)
  {
    inputs[4][CROGAN_CLOSE] = ON;
            // index 4 == -Y direction
  } else  if (del_y > -101) {
        inputs[4][CROGAN_NEAR] = ON;
  }
}

del_z = z0 - z;
if (del_z > 0)
{
  if (del_z < 11)
  {
    inputs[2][CROGAN_CLOSE] = ON;
            // index 2 == +Z direction
  } else  if (del_z < 101) {
        inputs[2][CROGAN_NEAR] = ON;
  }
} else  {
  if (del_z > -11)
  {
    inputs[5][CROGAN_CLOSE] = ON;
            // index 5 == -Z direction
```

```
        }  else  if (del_z > -101) {
            inputs[5][CROGAN_NEAR] = ON;
        }
    }
}

float outs0[Neural::MAX_OUTPUTS];
float outs1[Neural::MAX_OUTPUTS];
float outs2[Neural::MAX_OUTPUTS];
float outs3[Neural::MAX_OUTPUTS];
float outs4[Neural::MAX_OUTPUTS];
float outs5[Neural::MAX_OUTPUTS];
// Use neural network navigation object for acceleration in +X:
neural_net->recall(inputs[0], outs0);
// Use neural network navigation object for acceleration in +Y:
neural_net->recall(inputs[1], outs1);
// Use neural network navigation object for acceleration in +Z:
neural_net->recall(inputs[2], outs2);
// Use neural network navigation object for acceleration in -X:
neural_net->recall(inputs[3], outs3);
// Use neural network navigation object for acceleration in -Y:
neural_net->recall(inputs[4], outs4);
// Use neural network navigation object for acceleration in -Z:
neural_net->recall(inputs[5], outs5);

// Test starting with lowest priority actions (start with
// accelerate, decelerate, then test for full stop condition):

// X direction:
if (outs0[1] > NEURAL_NETWORK_THRESHOLD)
    ax += SMALL_ACCELERATION + outs0[1];
if (outs0[2] > NEURAL_NETWORK_THRESHOLD)
    ax -= SMALL_ACCELERATION - outs0[2];
if (outs3[1] > NEURAL_NETWORK_THRESHOLD)
    ax -= SMALL_ACCELERATION - outs3[1];
if (outs3[2] > NEURAL_NETWORK_THRESHOLD)
    ax += SMALL_ACCELERATION + outs3[2];
if (outs0[0] > NEURAL_NETWORK_THRESHOLD) {       // +X
    // Full stop in this direction:
    vx = 0.0;
    ax = 0.0;
} else {
```

```
     if (outs3[0] > NEURAL_NETWORK_THRESHOLD) {   // -X
        // Full stop in this direction:
        vx = 0.0;
        ax = 0.0;
     }
  }

  // Y direction:
  if (outs1[1] > NEURAL_NETWORK_THRESHOLD)
     ay += SMALL_ACCELERATION + outs1[1];
  if (outs1[2] > NEURAL_NETWORK_THRESHOLD)
     ay -= SMALL_ACCELERATION - outs1[2];
  if (outs4[1] > NEURAL_NETWORK_THRESHOLD)
     ay -= SMALL_ACCELERATION - outs4[1];
  if (outs4[2] > NEURAL_NETWORK_THRESHOLD)
     ay += SMALL_ACCELERATION + outs4[2];
  if (outs1[0] > NEURAL_NETWORK_THRESHOLD) {      // +Y
     // Full stop in this direction:
     vy = 0.0;
     ay = 0.0;
  } else {
     if (outs4[0] > NEURAL_NETWORK_THRESHOLD) {   // -Y
        // Full stop in this direction:
        vy = 0.0;
        ay = 0.0;
     }
  }

  // Z direction:
  if (outs2[1] > NEURAL_NETWORK_THRESHOLD)
     az += SMALL_ACCELERATION + outs2[1];
  if (outs2[2] > NEURAL_NETWORK_THRESHOLD)
     az -= SMALL_ACCELERATION - outs2[2];
  if (outs5[1] > NEURAL_NETWORK_THRESHOLD)
     az -= SMALL_ACCELERATION - outs5[1];
  if (outs5[2] > NEURAL_NETWORK_THRESHOLD)
     az += SMALL_ACCELERATION + outs5[2];
  if (outs2[0] > NEURAL_NETWORK_THRESHOLD) {      // +Z
     // Full stop in this direction:
     vz = 0.0;
     az = 0.0;
  } else {
     if (outs5[0] > NEURAL_NETWORK_THRESHOLD) {   // -Z
```

```
        // Full stop in this direction:
        vz = 0.0;
        az = 0.0;
    }
}


// Reset velocity and acceleration vectors based on advice
// from the neural network navigator (after clamping max
// velocity and acceleration):

vx += ax;
vy += ay;
vz += vz;

float max_accel = 3.0 * SMALL_ACCELERATION;
float max_vel = 3.0 * SMALL_VELOCITY;

if (vx < -max_vel) vx = -max_vel;
if (vx >  max_vel) vx =  max_vel;
if (vy < -max_vel) vy = -max_vel;
if (vy >  max_vel) vy =  max_vel;
if (vz < -max_vel) vz = -max_vel;
if (vz >  max_vel) vz =  max_vel;

if (ax < -max_accel) ax = -max_accel;
if (ax >  max_accel) ax =  max_accel;
if (ay < -max_accel) ay = -max_accel;
if (ay >  max_accel) ay =  max_accel;
if (az < -max_accel) az = -max_accel;
if (az >  max_accel) az =  max_accel;

// Check the fuel level:
if (game_obj->get_type() == PLAYER) {
    PlayerShip *ps = (PlayerShip *)game_obj;
    if (ps->get_R4() < 1) {
        vx = vy = vz = ax = ay = az = 0;
    }
}

if (game_obj->get_type() == PROCESSOR) {
    ProcessorShip *ps = (ProcessorShip *)game_obj;
    if (ps->get_R4() < 1) {
```

```
            vx = vy = vz = ax = ay = az = 0;
        }
    }

#ifdef DO_NOT_MOVE_PROCESSOR_SHIPS
    vx = vy = vz = ax = ay = az = 0;
#endif

    // If no plan is running, update the position from neural
    // network, and execute expert system:

    if (plan_manager->run_plan(world, game_obj) == 0) {
        game_obj->set_velocity(vx, vy, vz);
        game_obj->set_acceleration(ax, ay, az);
        game_obj->update_position();
        expert_sys->execute_highest_priority_rule(world, game_obj);
    }

}
```

Class **NavigationAgent** will be used in later sections for implementing the software agents for both Player and Processor ship types. The constructor **NavigationAgent::NavigationAgent(world *w, game_object *g)** calls the base class constructor **Agent::Agent (world *w, game_object *g)** to initialize base class data. The base class constructor **Agent::Agent(world *w, game_object *g)** checks that both the **World** pointer and **game_object** pointer are non-null. The instance variable **neural_net** is initialized to a new instance of class **Neural**, which reads an existing (pretrained) neural network file NAV.NET. The instance variable **expert_sys** is initialized to a new empty expert system object. The instance variable **plan_manager** is initialized to a new empty plan manager object. The destructor **NavigationAgent::~NavigationAgent()** simply destroys the expert system and plan manager objects created in the class constructor.

The interesting behavior in this class is supplied by the member function **NavigationAgent::run_agent()**. This member function is called indirectly when an instance of class **World** calls the member function **World::update_all_game_objects()**, which causes each game object to run all of its software agents. This C++ class was implemented to support both Player and Processor ships. This member function is hard coded for these two types of ships; the first part of the function is specific to Player ships in manual run mode.

I do not require all C++ classes to be reusable. Classes like **NavigationAgent** are "at the top of the food chain"; that is, they consume or use generic, reusable classes like those supplied in the VR Agent Toolkit to solve application-specific problems. On the other hand, C++ class designs and implementation evolve with reuse. When I use class **NavigationAgent** in a planned project, I will probably rework the class design to make it a base class; this is fair play, because in software design and development, we are trying to develop software in the most economical way possible. As software developers, we should put real effort into designing software classes, but realize that, often, ideas for enhancements occur more readily as we reuse the classes in a series of development projects.

Member function **NavigationAgent::run_agent()**, after checking for a Player ship in manual run mode (that is, the software agent is turned off; this option will only be used in the example 2D games in Chapters 8, 9, and 10), calculates the position of the four objects closest to the ship using this instance of a **NavigationAgent**. Input values for the control neural network are set up based on the relative positions of these nearby objects.

After applying changes to the ships velocity and acceleration based on advice of the neural network, the code at the end of member function **NavigationAgent::run_agent()** checks to see if the plan manager object is currently executing a plan. If no plan is running, and no new plan can be instantiated from the current game situation, then the highest priority rule is executed. As a matter of fact, the member function **ExpertSystem::execute_highest_priority_rule()** usually will run more than one rule function because a rule function that returns a zero value will cause **ExpertSystem::execute_highest_priority_rule()** function to execute the next highest priority rule; this execution sequence continues until either a rule function returns a nonzero value, or the list of rule function pointers is exhausted.

Suggested Project

I chose to look only for the four nearest objects because this produces an interesting behavior: when many Crogan ships cluster around a Processor or Player ship, that ship loses "sight" of other nearby objects as far as the neural network is concerned. In both this text-based simulation and especially in one of the 2D example games in Chapters 8, 9, or 10, try experimenting with increasing the number nearby objects by changing the constants in this code:

```
// We will start by finding the 4 closest objects to the
// game object containing this agent:
int distances[4];
game_object *objs[4];
int num_close_objects =
  world->return_nearby_objects(game_obj,
                               4,
                               objs,
                               distances);
```

You may want to make this an input parameter for the game or simulation. You may also want to ignore all but the nearest Crogan ship when setting up the input for the neural network.

Using an Expert System Executive for Controlling Processor Ships

A Processor ship uses an instance of the class **NavigationAgent** to control the movement and behavior of each class instance. The constructor for the class **ProcessorShip** adds expert system rule functions to the instance of class **ExpertSystem** used by class **NavigationAgent**. The constructor for class **ProcessorShip** does not use an instance of the class **PlanManager**.

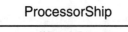

ProcessorShip

||float R4;

||int Magnozate;

||NavigationAgent *nav_agent;

ProcessorShip(World *w, char *name, int shape, int size);

void set_R4(float new_value);

float get_R4();

void set_Magnozate(int new_value);

int get_Magnozate();

int want_to_trade(float trade_ratio, int amount);

Figure 5.4   Booch class diagram for C++ class **ProcessorShip**.

Figure 5.4 shows a Booch class diagram for **ProcessorShip**. Listing 5.4 of file PR_SHIP.H shows the C++ class interface for the class **ProcessorShip**.

Listing 5.4

```
// File: pr_ship.h
//
// Description: This file contains the C++ class interface
//              definition for class 'ProcessorShip', which
//              is a subclass of 'game_object', and which
//              encapsulates the behavior and data for computer-
//              controlled processor ships.
//
```

```
// Copyright 1995, Mark Watson.  This software can be used
// in compiled form without restriction.
//

#ifndef pr_ship_h
#define pr_ship_h

#include "game_obj.h"
#include "agent.h"
#include "nav_agnt.h"


class ProcessorShip : public game_object {
 public:
    ProcessorShip(World *w=0,
                  const char * my_name = "no_name",
                  int appearance_type=geometric_object::SPHERE,
                  int size=10);
    ~ProcessorShip();
    enum {MAX_R4=440, MAX_MAGNOZATE=280};
    void set_R4(int new_val) { R4 = new_val; }
    float get_R4() { return R4; }
    void set_Magnozate(int new_val) { Magnozate = new_val; }
    float get_Magnozate() { return Magnozate; }
    int want_to_trade(float trade_ratio, int amount);
 private:
    float R4;
    float Magnozate;
    NavigationAgent *nav_agnt;
};



#endif
```

In the first stage implementation of the class **ProcessorShip**, I used integer values for the amount of R4 fuel and Magnozate ore on a Processor ship. This worked fine when I was debugging the text version of the space simulation, but when I added a graphic user interface, the graphical version of the simulation ran hundreds of simulation cycles per minute, so I reduced the rate of fuel use. In order to avoid truncation errors, I wanted to change the class definition to use floating point values for both the quantity of R4 fuel and Magnozate ore on hand. Because all access to the amount of R4 and Magnozate (outside of class member functions) is through public access functions (including **ProcessorShip::get_R4()**, **ProcessorShip::set_R4()**, **ProcessorShip::get_Magnozate()**, **Proces-**

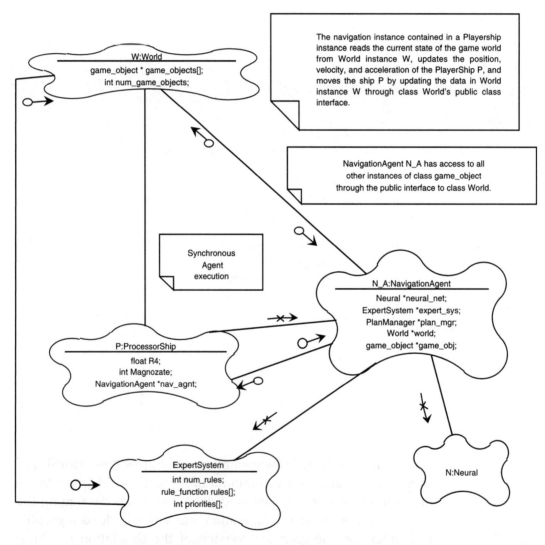

Figure 5.5   Booch object diagram showing the interactions on instances of classes **World**, **ProcessorShip**, **NavigationAgent**, **Neural**, and **ExpertSystem**.

sorShip::set_Magnozate()), I could make this change locally to the **ProcessorShip** class definition without "breaking" anything in the rest of the spaceship simulation. Figure 5.5 shows a Booch '94 object diagram that depicts the interaction between instances of classes **World, ProcessorShip, NavigationAgent, Neural,** and **ExpertSystem**. Listing 5.5 of file PR_SHIP.CPP shows the implementation of C++ class **ProcessorShip**.

Listing 5.5

```
// File: pr_ship.cpp
//
// Description: This file contains the C++ class implementation
//              for the C++ class 'ProcessorShip', which
//              is a subclass of 'game_object', and which
//              encapsulates the behavior and data for computer-
//              controlled processor ships.
//
// Copyright 1995, Mark Watson.  This software can be used
// in compiled form without restriction.
//

#include <iostream.h>
#include <math.h>
#include <stdlib.h>

#include "world.h"
#include "pr_ship.h"
#include "nav_agnt.h"
#include "expert.h"
#include "genetic.h"

#include "out_log.h"

#include <stdio.h>

// Rule functions for the navigation expert system:

static int rule_for_fuel_use(World *w, game_object *g)
{
    OutputLog::write("Entered test function for pr_ship fuel use\n");
    ProcessorShip *ps = (ProcessorShip *)g;
```

```
    float vx, vy, vz;
    g->get_velocity(vx, vy, vz);
    float fuel_use = fabs(vx) + fabs(vy) + fabs(vz);
    fuel_use *= 0.002;
    int R4 = ps->get_R4() - fuel_use;
    if (ps->get_Magnozate() > 0) {
        ps->set_Magnozate(ps->get_Magnozate() - 0.5);
        R4 += 0.5;
    }
    if (R4 < 0) R4 = 0;
    ps->set_R4(R4);
    OutputLog::write("    new R4 level=");
    OutputLog::write(R4);
    OutputLog::write("\n");
    if (R4 < 0) {
        ps->set_velocity(0, 0, 0);
        ps->set_acceleration(0, 0, 0);
    }
    // Return zero, to the next rule in the priority
    // chain is checkd:
    return 0;
}

static int rule_for_motion_correction(World *w, game_object *g)
{
    OutputLog::write("Entered rule function for motion correction for ");
    OutputLog::write(g->get_name());
    OutputLog::write("\n");
    ProcessorShip *ps = (ProcessorShip *)g;

    // if velocity is zero, set velocity to a very small value:
    float vx, vy, vz, ax, ay, az;

    g->get_velocity(vx, vy, vz);

    // check to see if the ship is far from the center of the asteroid
    // field; if it is, then send it back:

    int x, y, z;
    g->get_position(x, y, z);
    long del_x = (x - X_CENTER);
    long del_y = (y - Y_CENTER);
    long del_z = (z - Z_CENTER);
```

```cpp
        vx = 0.0;
        vy = 0.0;
        vz = 0.0;
        if (del_x*del_x + del_y*del_y + del_z*del_z  > 9000L) {
            if (del_x > del_y && del_x > del_z) {
                if (del_x > 0)  vx = -4 * SMALL_VELOCITY;
                else            vx =  4 * SMALL_VELOCITY;
            } else  if (del_y > del_x && del_y > del_z) {
                if (del_y > 0)  vy = -4 * SMALL_VELOCITY;
                else            vy =  4 * SMALL_VELOCITY;
            } else {
                if (del_z > 0)  vz = -4 * SMALL_VELOCITY;
                else            vz =  4 * SMALL_VELOCITY;
            }
            g->set_velocity(vx, vy, vz);
            OutputLog::write("   setting course back to asteroid field\n");
            return 1;
        }

        float vel = fabs(vx) + fabs(vy) + fabs(vz);
        if (vel < 1.0) {
            OutputLog::write("  Stopped ship (");
            OutputLog::write(vx);
            OutputLog::write(" ");
            OutputLog::write(vy);
            OutputLog::write(" ");
            OutputLog::write(vz);
            OutputLog::write("): setting small random velocity\n");
            vx += random(5) - 2.0;
            vy += random(5) - 2.0;
            vz += random(5) - 2.0;
            g->set_velocity(vx, vy, vz);
            return 1;
        }

        return 0;
}


static int rule_for_avoiding_Crogans(World *w, game_object *g)
{
    OutputLog::write("Entered rule function for avoiding Crogans\n");
    float vx, vy, vz;
```

```
    g->get_velocity(vx, vy, vz);
    if ((fabs(vx) + fabs(vy) + fabs(vz)) > 8) {
        OutputLog::write(" .. processor ship velocity already sufficient
to avoid Crogan\n");
        return 0;
    }
    ProcessorShip *ps = (ProcessorShip *)g;

    // We will start by finding the 3 closest objects to the
    // game object containing this agent:
    int distances[3];
    game_object *objs[3];
    int num_close_objects =
      w->return_nearby_objects(g,
                               3,
                               objs,
                               distances);
    for (int i=0; i<num_close_objects; i++) {
        if (objs[i]->get_type() == CROGAN) {
            int dist = g->distance(*objs[i]);
            if (dist < 20) {
                OutputLog::write("  ..too close to a Crogan\n");
                vx += random(9) - 4;
                vy += random(9) - 4;
                vz += random(9) - 4;
                g->set_velocity(vx, vy, vz);
                g->update_position();
                float R4 = ps->get_R4() - 1;
                if (R4 < 0) R4 = 0;
                ps->set_R4(R4);
                return 1;
            }
        }
    }

    return 0;
}


ProcessorShip::ProcessorShip(World *w,
                             const char * my_name,
                             int appearance_type,
                             int size)
    : game_object(w, my_name, appearance_type, size)
```

```
{
   nav_agnt = new NavigationAgent(w, this);
   add_agent(*nav_agnt);
   R4 = MAX_R4 / 2 +  2 * random(MAX_R4 / 2);
   Magnozate = random(MAX_MAGNOZATE / 4);

   // Create rule set for the Processor Ship expert system:
   ExpertSystem *es = nav_agnt->get_expert_system();
   // Strategy for using ExpertSystem object rules:
   // We always want the fuel use rule to run, so we give
   // this rule a high priority, but have the rule function
   // return a zero value, so the next rule in the priority
   // chain is checked.
   es->add_rule("rule for fuel use", rule_for_fuel_use, 200);
   es->add_rule("rule for motion correction",
             rule_for_motion_correction, 100);
   es->add_rule("rule for avoiding Crogan ships",
             rule_for_avoiding_Crogans, 30);
}

ProcessorShip::~ProcessorShip()
{
   delete nav_agnt;
}

int ProcessorShip::want_to_trade(float trade_ratio, int amount)
{
   // Check on Magnozate level:
   if (Magnozate < (MAX_MAGNOZATE / 4)) {
      OutputLog::write(" ** trade accepted by empty processor ship\n");
      Magnozate += amount;
      return 1;
   } else if (Magnozate < MAX_MAGNOZATE) {
      if (trade_ratio > (float)Magnozate / (float)MAX_MAGNOZATE) {
         OutputLog::write(" ** trade accepted by processor ship\n");
         Magnozate += amount;
         return 1;
      } else {
         OutputLog::write(" ** trade NOT accepted by processor ship\n");
         return 0;
      }
   } else {
```

```
    OutputLog::write(" ** trade NOT accepted by FULL processor ship\n");
    return 0;
  }
}
```

The class constructor for the C++ class **ProcessorShip** is given at the end of Listing 5.5; the expert system rule functions are defined first in Listing 5.5, and referenced in the constructor.

The expert system rule function **rule_for_fuel_use(World *w, game_object *g)** reduces the amount of R4 fuel each time step. This rule function uses a trick: the amount of R4 fuel is reduced, but the rule function returns 0, so the expert system object will execute the next lower priority rule.

The expert system rule function **rule_for_motion_correction (World *w, game_object *g)** checks for two environmental conditions:

- If the ship is far from the center of the asteroid field, then change the velocity to move back toward the center of the asteroid field.

- If the ship's velocity is very small, set it to a small random value.

The expert system rule function **rule_for_avoiding_Crogans (World *w, game_object *g)** checks to see if the ship is very close to a Crogan ship; and if it is, it moves in the opposite direction.

The constructor **ProcessorShip::ProcessorShip(World *w, const char * my_name, int appearance_type, int size)** has one mandatory argument, a pointer to an instance of class **World**, and three optional arguments. The constructor calls the base class constructor **game_object::game_object()** to initialize base class data. The constructor then creates a navigational agent and adds it to the processor ship's software agent list:

```
nav_agnt = new NavigationAgent(w, this);
add_agent(*nav_agnt);
```

The constructor next initializes class data for the amount of R4 fuel and Magnozate. Then it gets a pointer to the expert system object created in the constructor for the navigation agent, and adds the three rule functions to the expert system object contained in the navigation agent object:

```
ExpertSystem *es = nav_agnt->get_expert_system();
es->add_rule("rule for fuel use", rule_for_fuel_use, 200);
es->add_rule("rule for motion correction",
            rule_for_motion_correction, 100);
es->add_rule("rule for avoiding Crogan ships",
            rule_for_avoiding_Crogans, 30);
```

The class destructor **ProcessorShip::~ProcessorShip()** simply deletes the navigation agent used by the Processor ship object being destroyed. The member function **ProcessorShip::want_to_trade (float trade_ratio, int amount)** returns a zero or nonzero value in response to a request to trade conversion of Magnozate or from a Player ship.

Using an Expert System Executive for Computer Assistant on Player Ship

A Player ship uses an instance of the class **NavigationAgent** to control the movement and behavior of each class instance. The constructor for the class **PlayerShip** adds expert system rule functions to the instance of class **ExpertSystem** used by class **Navigation Agent**, and plan rule functions used by an instance of the class **PlanManager**. Figure 5.6 shows a Booch class diagram for **PlayerShip**. Listing 5.6 of file PLAYER.H shows the class interface for C++ class **PlayerShip**.

Listing 5.6

```
// File: player.h
//
// Description: This file contains the C++ class interface
//              definition for class 'PlayerShip', which
//              is a subclass of 'game_object', and which
//              encapsulates the behavior and data for computer-
//              controlled player ships. Usually, during play,
//              the human player can either use his or her on-board
```

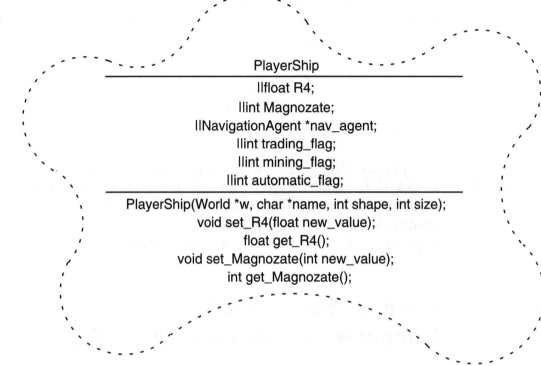

Figure 5.6   Booch class diagram showing C++ class **PlayerShip**.

```
//              "AI" to run the ship, or override any actions.
//
// Copyright 1995, Mark Watson.  This software can be used
// in compiled form without restriction.
//

#ifndef player_h
#define player_h

#include "game_obj.h"
#include "agent.h"
#include "nav_agnt.h"


class PlayerShip : public game_object {
 public:
```

```
    PlayerShip(World *w=0,
              const char * my_name = "no_name",
              int appearance_type=geometric_object::SPHERE,
              int size=10);
  ~PlayerShip();
   enum {MAX_R4=640, MAX_MAGNOZATE=310};
   void set_R4(float new_val) { R4 = new_val; }
   float get_R4() { return R4; }
   void set_Magnozate(int new_val) { Magnozate = new_val; }
   int get_Magnozate() { return Magnozate; }
   int get_trading_flag() { return trading_flag; }
   void set_trading_flag(int val) { trading_flag = val; }
   int get_mining_flag() { return mining_flag; }
   void set_mining_flag(int val) { mining_flag = val; }
   int get_automatic_flag() { return automatic_flag; }
   void set_automatic_flag(int val) { automatic_flag = val; }
private:
   float R4;
   int Magnozate;
   NavigationAgent *nav_agnt;
   int trading_flag;
   int mining_flag;
   int automatic_flag;
};
#endif
```

Figure 5.7 shows a Booch (Booch, 1994) object interaction diagram. It illustrates the control and data flow interactions between instances of the classes **World, PlayerShip, Navigation-Agent, PlanManager, ExpertSystem,** and **Neural**. Listing 5.7 of file PLAYER.CPP shows the implementation of C++ class **PlayerShip**.

Listing 5.7

```
// File: player.cpp
//
// Description: This file contains the C++ class implementation
//              for the C++ class 'PlayerShip', which
//              is a subclass of 'game_object', and which
//              encapsulates the behavior and data for AI computer
//              control of the player's ship. The human player
//              can override the on-board "AI".
```

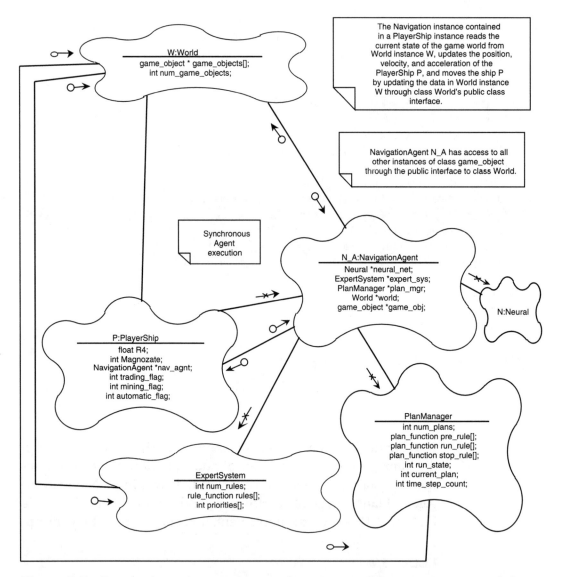

Figure 5.7 Booch object diagram showing the interactions between instances of classes **World, PlayerShip, NavigationAgent, PlanManager, ExpertSystem,** and **Neural.**

```cpp
//
// Copyright 1995, Mark Watson.  This software can be used
// in compiled form without restriction.
//

#include <iostream.h>
#include <math.h>
#include <stdlib.h>

#include "world.h"
#include "player.h"
#include "pr_ship.h"
#include "nav_agnt.h"
#include "expert.h"
#include "plan.h"
#include "genetic.h"

#include "out_log.h"

#include <stdio.h>

//
//          Rule functions for the navigation expert system:
//
static int rule_for_fuel_use(World *w, game_object *g)
{
   OutputLog::write("Entered test function for fuel use in player ship\n");
   PlayerShip *ps = (PlayerShip *)g;
   float vx, vy, vz;
   g->get_velocity(vx, vy, vz);
   float fuel_use = fabs(vx) + fabs(vy) + fabs(vz);
   fuel_use *= 0.015;
   float R4 = ps->get_R4() - fuel_use;
   if (R4 < 0.0) R4 = 0.0;
   ps->set_R4(R4);
   OutputLog::write("    new R4 level=");
   OutputLog::write(R4);
   OutputLog::write("\n");
   // return 0 so that the next rule in the priority chain is checked:
   return 0;
}
```

```cpp
static int rule_for_moving_to_asteroid_field(World *w, game_object *g)
{

    OutputLog::write("Entered rule function for moving back to asteroid field\n");
    PlayerShip *ps = (PlayerShip *)g;

    if (ps->get_automatic_flag() == 0) {
        OutputLog::write(".. in manual fly mode\n");
        return 0;
    }
    float vx, vy, vz;
    g->get_velocity(vx, vy, vz);

    // check to see if the ship is far from the center of the asteroid
    // field; if it is, then send it back:

    int x, y, z;
    g->get_position(x, y, z);
    long del_x = (x - X_CENTER);
    long del_y = (y - Y_CENTER);
    long del_z = (z - Z_CENTER);

    vx = 0.0;
    vy = 0.0;
    vz = 0.0;
    if (del_x*del_x + del_y*del_y + del_z*del_z  > 150000L) {
        if (del_x > del_y && del_x > del_z) {
            if (del_x > 0)  vx = -4 * SMALL_VELOCITY;
            else            vx =  4 * SMALL_VELOCITY;
        } else  if (del_y > del_x && del_y > del_z) {
            if (del_y > 0)  vy = -4 * SMALL_VELOCITY;
            else            vy =  4 * SMALL_VELOCITY;
        } else {
            if (del_z > 0)  vz = -4 * SMALL_VELOCITY;
            else            vz =  4 * SMALL_VELOCITY;
        }
        g->set_velocity(vx, vy, vz);
        g->update_position();
        OutputLog::write("   setting course back to asteroid field\n");
        return 1;
    }
    return 0;
}
```

```
static int rule_for_mining_asteroid(World *w, game_object *g)
{
   OutputLog::write("Entered rule function for mining asteroid\n");
   PlayerShip *ps = (PlayerShip *)g;

   ps->set_mining_flag(0);
   if (ps->get_Magnozate() > (PlayerShip::MAX_MAGNOZATE - 20))
      return 0;
   // We will start by finding the 22 closest objects to the
   // game object containing this agent:
   int distances[22];
   game_object *objs[22];
   int num_close_objects = w->return_nearby_objects(g,22,objs,distances);
   for (int i=0; i<num_close_objects; i++) {
      if (objs[i]->get_type() == ASTEROID) {
         int dist = g->distance(*objs[i]);
         if (dist < 7) {
            OutputLog::write("  ..mining asteroid\n");
            ps->set_Magnozate(PlayerShip::MAX_MAGNOZATE);
            ps->set_mining_flag(1);
            return 1;
         }
      }
   }
   return 0;
}

static int rule_for_avoiding_Crogans(World *w, game_object *g)
{
   OutputLog::write("Entered rule function for avoiding Crogans\n");
   PlayerShip *ps = (PlayerShip *)g;


   // We will start by finding the 5 closest objects to the
   // game object containing this agent:
   int distances[5];
   game_object *objs[5];
   int num_close_objects = w->return_nearby_objects(g,5,objs,distances);
   for (int i=0; i<num_close_objects; i++) {
      if (objs[i]->get_type() == CROGAN) {
         int dist = g->distance(*objs[i]);
         if (dist < 12) {
            if (ps->get_automatic_flag() == 1) {
```

```
                OutputLog::write("  ..too close to a Crogan\n");
                float vx, vy, vz;
                ps->get_velocity(vx, vy, vz);
                vx += random(3) - 1;
                vy += random(3) - 1;
                vz += random(3) - 1;
                ps->set_velocity(vx, vy, vz);
            }
            float R4 = ps->get_R4() - 1;
            if (R4 < 0) R4 = 0;
            ps->set_R4(R4);
            return 1;
        }
      }
   }
   return 0;
}


static int rule_for_trading(World *w, game_object *g)
{
   OutputLog::write("Entered rule function for trading\n");
   PlayerShip *ps = (PlayerShip *)g;

   ps->set_trading_flag(0);

   // We will start by finding the 8 closest objects to the
   // game object containing this agent:
   int distances[8];
   game_object *objs[8];
   int num_close_objects = w->return_nearby_objects(g,8,objs,distances);

   for (int i=0; i<num_close_objects; i++) {
      if (objs[i]->get_type() == PROCESSOR) {
         ProcessorShip *proc_ship = (ProcessorShip *)objs[i];
         int dist = g->distance(*objs[i]);
         if (dist < 7) {
            OutputLog::write("  ..starting trade negotiation with ");
            OutputLog::write(objs[i]->get_name());
            OutputLog::write("\n");
            // call member function on processor ship object to see
            // if the processor ship object wants to trade:
            int mgzt = ps->get_Magnozate();
            if (mgzt > 5)  {
```

```
            if (((ProcessorShip *)objs[i])->want_to_trade(0.7, mgzt))
            {
               OutputLog::write("  .. trade accepted\n");
               ps->set_R4(ps->get_R4() + mgzt * 0.7 );
               ps->set_Magnozate(0);
               ps->set_trading_flag(1);
               proc_ship->set_Magnozate(proc_ship->get_Magnozate() + mgzt);
            } else {
               OutputLog::write("  .. trade not accepted\n");
               ps->set_trading_flag(-1);
            }
         }
         return 1;
      }
   }
   }
   return 0;
}


//
//          Rule functions for the plan manager object:
//

static float p1_vx, p1_vy, p1_vz;

static int test_low_Magnozate(World *w, game_object *g, int cycle_count)
{
   OutputLog::write("## entered plan pre test rule\n");
   PlayerShip *ps = (PlayerShip *)g;
   if (ps->get_automatic_flag() == 0) {
      OutputLog::write(".. pre test rule: in manual fly mode\n");
      return 0;
   }
   if (ps->get_Magnozate() < 10 && ps->get_R4() > 0) {
      OutputLog::write(".. pre test rule: low supply of Magnozate\n");
      int x, y, z;
      int ok = ps->nearest_object(ASTEROID, x, y, z,
                                  p1_vx, p1_vy, p1_vz);
      if (ok) {
         ps->set_velocity(p1_vx, p1_vy, p1_vz);
         ps->set_acceleration(0.0, 0.0, 0.0);
         return 1;
      }
   }
```

```
      return 0;
}

static int go_to_asteroid(World *w, game_object *g, int cycle_count)
{
    PlayerShip *ps = (PlayerShip *)g;
    if (ps->get_automatic_flag() == 0) {
        OutputLog::write(".. in manual fly mode\n");
        return 0;
    }

    ps->set_velocity(p1_vx, p1_vy, p1_vz);
    ps->set_acceleration(0.0, 0.0, 0.0);
    ps->update_position();

    rule_for_fuel_use(w, g);
    return 1;
}

static int end_go_to_asteroid(World *w, game_object *g, int cycle_count)
{
    PlayerShip *ps = (PlayerShip *)g;
    if (ps->get_automatic_flag() == 0) {
        OutputLog::write(".. in manual fly mode\n");
        return 0;
    }
    if (cycle_count < 10)  return 0;  // keep going with the plan
    return 1;  // stop plan execution
}

static int test_trade_Magnozate(World *w, game_object *g, int cycle_count)
{
    OutputLog::write("## entered plan pre test rule for finding pr_ship\n");
    PlayerShip *ps = (PlayerShip *)g;
    if (ps->get_automatic_flag() == 0) {
        OutputLog::write(".. pre test rule: in manual fly mode\n");
        return 0;
    }
    if (ps->get_Magnozate() > 50 && ps->get_R4() > 0)  {
        OutputLog::write(".. pre test rule: large supply of Magnozate to trade\n");
        int x, y, z;
        int ok = ps->nearest_object(PROCESSOR, x, y, z,
                                    p1_vx, p1_vy, p1_vz);
```

```
      if (ok) {
         ps->set_velocity(p1_vx, p1_vy, p1_vz);
         ps->set_acceleration(0.0, 0.0, 0.0);
         return 1;
      }
   }
   return 0;
}

static int go_to_pr_ship(World *w, game_object *g, int cycle_count)
{
   PlayerShip *ps = (PlayerShip *)g;
   if (ps->get_automatic_flag() == 0) {
      return 0;
   }

   ps->set_velocity(p1_vx, p1_vy, p1_vz);
   ps->set_acceleration(0.0, 0.0, 0.0);
   ps->update_position();

   rule_for_fuel_use(w, g);
   return 1;
}

static int end_go_to_pr_ship(World *w, game_object *g, int cycle_count)
{
   PlayerShip *ps = (PlayerShip *)g;
   if (ps->get_automatic_flag() == 0) {
      OutputLog::write(".. in manual fly mode\n");
      return 0;
   }
   if (cycle_count < 10)  return 0;  // keep going with the plan
   return 1;  // stop plan execution
}

PlayerShip::PlayerShip(World *w, const char * my_name, int appearance_type, int size)
   : game_object(w, my_name, appearance_type, size)
{
   nav_agnt = new NavigationAgent(w, this);
   add_agent(*nav_agnt);
   R4 = MAX_R4;
   Magnozate = 0;
   trading_flag = 0;
```

```
  mining_flag = 0;
  automatic_flag = 1;
  // Create rule set for the Processor Ship expert system:
  ExpertSystem *es = nav_agnt->get_expert_system();
  es->add_rule("rule for fuel use", rule_for_fuel_use, 200);
  es->add_rule("rule for returning to field",
               rule_for_moving_to_asteroid_field, 100);
  es->add_rule("rule for mining asteroid",
               rule_for_mining_asteroid, 90);
  es->add_rule("rule for avoiding Crogans",
               rule_for_avoiding_Crogans, 10);
  es->add_rule("rule for trading", rule_for_trading, 92);

  // Create PlanManager objects for this PlayerShip:
  PlanManager *pm = nav_agnt->get_plan_manager();
  pm->add_plan("get Magnozate", test_low_Magnozate,
               go_to_asteroid,  end_go_to_asteroid);
  pm->add_plan("trade Magnozate", test_trade_Magnozate,
               go_to_pr_ship, end_go_to_pr_ship);
}


PlayerShip::~PlayerShip()
{
  delete nav_agnt;
}
```

The class constructor for the C++ class **PlayerShip** is given at the end of Listing 5.7; the expert system rule functions are defined first, the rules plan templates for the plan manager. The rule functions are added to the expert system contained in the navigation agent object, and plan template functions are added to the plan manager object contained in the navigation object in the Player ship being created.

The expert system rule function **rule_for_fuel_use(World *w, game_object *g)** reduces the amount of R4 fuel each time step. This rule function uses a trick: the amount of R4 fuel is reduced, but the rule function returns 0, so the expert system object will execute the next lower priority rule.

The expert system rule function **rule_for_moving_to_asteroid _field(World *w, game_object *g)** checks to see if a ship is far from the center of the asteroid field; if it is, it then changes the velocity to move back toward the center of the asteroid field. The expert system rule function **rule_for_mining_asteroid(World *w, game_object *g)** looks for nearby asteroids at which to mine for Magnozate ore. The rule function **rule_for_avoiding_Crogans(World *w, game_object *g)** looks for nearby Crogans, and sets the ship's velocity to move away from any Crogan ships. The expert system rule function **rule_for_mining_asteroid(World *w, game_object *g)** looks for nearby Processor ships to attempt to trade with.

The plan for moving to an asteroid uses three plan functions:

- **test_low_Magnozate()**: This precondition test function checks for low Magnozate supply and, if necessary, sets up a plan to move the ship close to an asteroid.

- **go_to_asteroid()**: This plan execution function moves the ship toward the target asteroid.

- **end_go_to_asteroid()**: This plan termination test function checks to see if the ship is near an asteroid, or if the plan has executed too long.

The plan for finding a Magnozate trade partner uses the following three plan template functions:

- **test_trade_Magnozate()**: This precondition test function checks to see if the Player ship has enough Magnozate to trade; if so, a goal is set to move toward the nearest Processor ship.

- **go_to_pr_ship()**: This plan execution function moves the ship toward the target Processor ship.

- **end_go_to_pr_ship()**: this plan termination test function determines whether the Player ship is close enough to the target Processor ship, or if the plan has executed for too long.

The constructor **ProcessorShip::ProcessorShip(World *w, const char * my_name, int appearance_type, int size)** has one mandatory argument, a pointer to an instance of class **World**, and three optional arguments. The constructor calls the base class constructor **game_object::game_object()** to initialize base class data.

The constructor then creates a navigational agent and adds it to the Processor ship's software agent list:

```
nav_agnt = new NavigationAgent(w, this);
add_agent(*nav_agnt);
```

The constructor then initializes class data for the amount of R4 fuel and Magnozate. The constructor next gets a pointer to the expert system object created in the constructor for the navigation agent, and adds the three rule functions to the expert system object contained in the navigation agent object:

```
ExpertSystem *es = nav_agnt->get_expert_system();
es->add_rule("rule for fuel use", rule_for_fuel_use, 200);
es->add_rule("rule for returning to field",
            rule_for_moving_to_asteroid_field, 100);
es->add_rule("rule for mining asteroid",
            rule_for_mining_asteroid, 90);
es->add_rule("rule for avoiding Crogans",
            rule_for_avoiding_Crogans, 10);
es->add_rule("rule for trading", rule_for_trading, 92);
```

The two plan template functions are then added to the plan manager object:

```
PlanManager *pm = nav_agnt->get_plan_manager();
pm->add_plan("get Magnozate", test_low_Magnozate,
            go_to_asteroid,  end_go_to_asteroid);
pm->add_plan("trade Magnozate", test_trade_Magnozate,
            go_to_pr_ship, end_go_to_pr_ship);
```

The class destructor **PlayerShip::~PlayerShip()** simply deletes the navigation agent used by the Player ship object being destroyed.

Using Genetic Algorithms to Dynamically Change Crogan Ship Strategy

Crogan ships use several distinct playing strategies. Each Crogan ship action is determined by a combination of three state variables that determine:

1. Should a Crogan ship move in a straight line, or zigzag to reach a destination?
2. Should a Crogan ship favor slowly drawing energy from asteroids, or hunt Processor and Player ships?
3. Should a Crogan ship move at a moderately slow speed, or move quickly (using energy at a faster rate)?

How should these variables be set for optimum strategy? Different settings of these parameters will be optimal for different game situations. Ideally, we want the Crogan ships to adapt in real time as a game progresses. Genetic algorithms provide an excellent tool for setting these parameters as a game progresses in response to a player's actions and the changing state of the game. If the genetic population is taken to be the set of control parameters for each of the Crogan ships, then we have the added advantage that individual Crogan ships will behave differently from each other, although their average behavior as a group will continually evolve so that, on average, the Crogan ships become more effective adversaries in changing game situations.

There are 8 (2 raised to the third power) possible strategies that each Crogan ship can use. Each Crogan ship has its own "chromosome," which is represented as three bits. If the first bit (gene) is equal to 1, then the ship will move in a straight line; if it is equal to 0, then the ship will zigzag toward a destination. If the second bit (gene) is equal to 1, then the Crogan ship will stay close to an asteroid, slowly absorbing energy; if it is equal to 0, then the ship will actively hunt for Processor and Player ships. If the third bit (gene) is equal to 1, then the ship will move quickly; if it is equal to 0, then the ship will move slowly.

Using Genetic Algorithms in Games

By using the C++ classes for genetic algorithms developed in Chapter 2, it is fairly easy to use this technology in the games that you write by following these steps:

1. Choose which game object will change its strategy in response to the game situation. This should ideally be a type of object that is replicated several times in the game.

2. Write a subroutine that will control the object. Define the actions of this control program to be a function of both the environment around the object and a few control parameters. These parameters will be encoded as a "chromosome" for each object in the "population."

3. Determine how many game cycles are executed before the chromosomes of each object in the population is evolved using crossover and mutation. This evolution process should not occur too frequently. For example, if there are 20 game cycles per second, and objects in the game have major interactions with each other every 2 seconds, it might be reasonable to evolve the chromosomes in the population every 200 game cycles (or every 10 seconds). All objects in the population will exhibit their new strategy immediately after their chromosomes are evolved.

Implementing the Crogan Ship Population

Our example game will contain a single instance of a new C++ class **Crogan**. This class is derived from the class **genetic** developed in Chapter 2. The storage for the control parameters will be the protected storage inherited from the base class. Additional private storage is defined to store the positions and current strategy plan for each Crogan ship in the population.

Figure 5.8 shows the Booch class diagram for the C++ class **Crogan**. This C++ class is unusual in that there can only be one instance of it in a program because the use of static (class) data. Listing 5.8 of file CROGAN.H shows the C++ class interface for **Crogan**.

The enumerated constant **Crogan::POPULATION_SIZE**, which indicates how many chromosomes are contained inside an instance of class **genetic**, determines how many Crogan ships are in the spaceship simulation. There is one chromosome for each Crogan ship. Differences in the chromosome population result in Crogan ships with different behavior. As seen in Figure 5.8, an instance of class **Crogan** contains one instance of class **game_object** for each simulated Crogan ship.

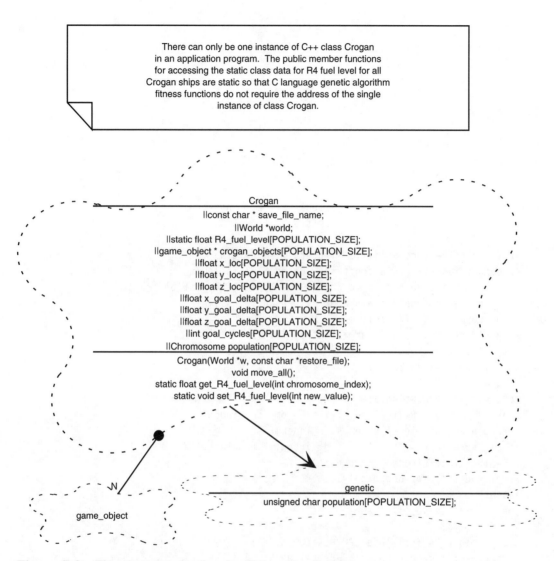

There can only be one instance of C++ class Crogan in an application program. The public member functions for accessing the static class data for R4 fuel level for all Crogan ships are static so that C language genetic algorithm fitness functions do not require the address of the single instance of class Crogan.

Crogan

||const char * save_file_name;
||World *world;
||static float R4_fuel_level[POPULATION_SIZE];
||game_object * crogan_objects[POPULATION_SIZE];
||float x_loc[POPULATION_SIZE];
||float y_loc[POPULATION_SIZE];
||float z_loc[POPULATION_SIZE];
||float x_goal_delta[POPULATION_SIZE];
||float y_goal_delta[POPULATION_SIZE];
||float z_goal_delta[POPULATION_SIZE];
||int goal_cycles[POPULATION_SIZE];
||Chromosome population[POPULATION_SIZE];

Crogan(World *w, const char *restore_file);
void move_all();
static float get_R4_fuel_level(int chromosome_index);
static void set_R4_fuel_level(int new_value);

game_object

genetic

unsigned char population[POPULATION_SIZE];

Figure 5.8 The class diagram for the C++ class **Crogan**.

Listing 5.8

```
// File: crogan.h
//
// Description: This file contains the C++ interface for
//              class 'Crogan', which is derived using
//              public inheritance from 'genetic'.
```

```
//
// Copyright 1995, Mark Watson.
//

#ifndef crogan_h
#define crogan_h

#include "genetic.h"
#include "world.h"
#include "geom_obj.h"

class Crogan : public genetic {   // only allow 1 instance
                                  // (see Section 5.3)
 public:
   // To make the code a little simpler, I am setting the
   // population size as a constant.  Change the following
   // constant and recompile to change the genetic population
   // size (which equals the number of Crogan ships):
   enum {POPULATION_SIZE=16};
   Crogan(World *w, const char * restore_file);
  ~Crogan(); // destructor over-writes restore_file
   enum {CHROMOSOME_SIZE=3};
   void move_all();
   void evolve_population();
   static float get_R4_fuel_level(int chromosome_index)
   { return R4_fuel_level[chromosome_index]; }
   static void set_R4_fuel_level(int index, float amount)
   { R4_fuel_level[index] = amount; }
   long count; // for debug only...
 private:
   const char * save_file_name;
   World *world;
   static float R4_fuel_level[POPULATION_SIZE];
   game_object * crogan_objects[POPULATION_SIZE];
   // coordinates of the Crogan ships:
   float x_loc[POPULATION_SIZE];
   float y_loc[POPULATION_SIZE];
   float z_loc[POPULATION_SIZE];
   // coordinates of movement goals of each Crogan ship:
   float x_goal_delta[POPULATION_SIZE];
   float y_goal_delta[POPULATION_SIZE];
   float z_goal_delta[POPULATION_SIZE];
   int goal_cycles[POPULATION_SIZE];
```

```
    // Note: The 2D array 'population' inherited from genetic is
    // used to store the state variables used for determining the
    // current strategy of each Crogan.
};


#endif
```

Figure 5.9 shows a Booch object diagram for instances of the classes **World** and **Crogan**. The single instance of class **Crogan** can

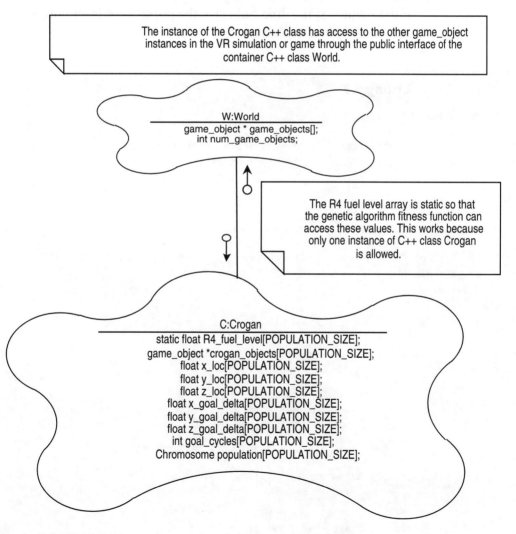

Figure 5.9   Booch object diagram for the C++ class **Crogan**.

access data for all instances of **game_object** through the public class interface of C++ class **World**. Listing 5.9 of file CROGAN.CPP shows the implementation of C++ class **Crogan**. The constructor for class **Crogan** first calls the base class constructor (C++ class **genetic**), which allocates an array of **Crogan::POPULATION_SIZE** chromosomes. The **Crogan** class constructor then creates **Crogan::POPULATION_SIZE** new instances of the class **game_object**. The constructor attempts to open an existing chromosome data file; if the requested file does not exist, the population is initialized with randomly calculated genes.

Listing 5.9

```
// File: crogan.cpp
//
// Description: This file contains the C++ implementation for
//              the class 'Crogan', which is derived using
//              public inheritance from 'genetic'.
//
// Copyright 1995, Mark Watson.
//

#include <iostream.h>
#include <fstream.h>
#include <stdlib.h>
#include <stdio.h>
#include <math.h>

#include "game_val.h"
#include "out_log.h"

#include "crogan.h"


float fitness_f(int chrom_index, int ch_size, unsigned char *chrom)
{
    return Crogan::get_R4_fuel_level(chrom_index);
}


Crogan::Crogan(World *w, const char * restore_file)
  : world(w),
```

```
      save_file_name(restore_file),
      genetic(CHROMOSOME_SIZE, POPULATION_SIZE, fitness_f)
{
    // Attempt to open restore_file.  If there is an error,
    // assume that the file does not exist, and simply
    // create a new random population.
    filebuf input_file;
    if (input_file.open(save_file_name, ios::in) != 0) {
        // File exists:
        istream in_strm(&input_file);
        in_strm >> chromosome_size;
        if (chromosome_size != CHROMOSOME_SIZE) {
#ifdef TEXT_MODE
            cerr << "Chromosome size in restore file="
                 << chromosome_size << ", but POPULATION_SIZE="
                 << CHROMOSOME_SIZE << "\n";
#endif
            exit(1);
        }
        in_strm >> num_chromosomes;
        int ii;
        for (int i=0; i<num_chromosomes; i++) {
            for (int j=0; j<chromosome_size; j++) {
                in_strm >> ii;
                population[i][j] = ii;;
            }
            R4_fuel_level[i] = 200;
        }
    } else {
#ifdef TEXT_MODE
        cerr << "No restore file; start with a new random population\n";
#endif
    }
    for (int c=0; c<POPULATION_SIZE; c++) {
        char * cp = new char[32];
        sprintf(cp,"crogan_%d", c);
        crogan_objects[c] =
            new game_object(w, cp, geometric_object::CUBE, 5);
        crogan_objects[c]->set_type(CROGAN);
        x_loc[c] = 50 + random(350);
        y_loc[c] = 50 + random(350);
        z_loc[c] = 50 + random(350);
        crogan_objects[c]->set_position(x_loc[c], y_loc[c], z_loc[c]);
```

```
        world->add_game_object(*crogan_objects[c]);
        R4_fuel_level[c] = 200;
        goal_cycles[c] = 0;
    }
}


Crogan::~Crogan() // destructor over-writes restore_file
{
    filebuf output_file;
    if (output_file.open(save_file_name, ios::out) != 0) {
        // File exists:
        ostream out_strm(&output_file);
        out_strm << chromosome_size << "\n";
        out_strm << num_chromosomes << "\n";
        for (int i=0; i<num_chromosomes; i++) {
            for (int j=0; j<chromosome_size; j++) {
                out_strm << (int)population[i][j] << "\n";
            }
        }
    } else {
#ifdef TEXT_MODE
        cerr << "Error opening output Crogan chromosome data file\n";
#endif
    }
}



void Crogan::move_all()
{
    // pre-calculate to speeds:
    float slow_delta = 1.5;  // 3D grid values per game cycle
    float fast_delta = 3.0;  // 3D grid values per game cycle

    for (int c=0; c<POPULATION_SIZE; c++) {
        if (R4_fuel_level[c] > 0) {

            int x_loc_ship = -1000;
            int y_loc_ship = -1000;
            int z_loc_ship = -1000;
            int distance_ship = 5000;
            float del_x_ship = 0;
            float del_y_ship = 0;
            float del_z_ship = 0;
```

```
int x_loc_asteroid = -1000;
int y_loc_asteroid = -1000;
int z_loc_asteroid = -1000;
int distance_asteroid = 5000;
float del_x_asteroid = 0;
float del_y_asteroid = 0;
float del_z_asteroid = 0;

int x, y, z;
crogan_objects[c]->get_position(x, y, z);
float dif_x, dif_y, dif_z;

// Define local variables for 3 state variables:
int move_in_straight_line = population[c][0];
int favor_asteroids = population[c][1];
int move_slowly = population[c][2];
float current_speed;
float fuel_use;
if (move_slowly) {
   current_speed = slow_delta;
   fuel_use = 0.01;
} else {
   current_speed = fast_delta;
   fuel_use = 0.02;
}
if (move_in_straight_line == 0)  current_speed *= 0.9;
OutputLog::write("\nCrogan #");
OutputLog::write(c);
OutputLog::write(" flags: move straight=");
OutputLog::write(move_in_straight_line);
OutputLog::write(", favor asteroids=");
OutputLog::write(favor_asteroids);
OutputLog::write(", move slowly=");
OutputLog::write(move_slowly);
OutputLog::write("\n");

OutputLog::write("   Position: ");
OutputLog::write(x_loc[c]);
OutputLog::write(" ");
OutputLog::write(y_loc[c]);
OutputLog::write(" ");
OutputLog::write(z_loc[c]);
OutputLog::write("\n");
```

```cpp
// Find the location of the nearest player or
// processor ship, and the nearest asteroid:
const int NUM_NEAR_OBJECTS = 12;
game_object *objs[NUM_NEAR_OBJECTS];
int distances[NUM_NEAR_OBJECTS];
int num;
num = world->return_nearby_objects(crogan_objects[c],
                                   NUM_NEAR_OBJECTS,
                                   objs,
                                   distances);
for (int k=0; k<num; k++) {

    if (objs[k]->get_type() == ASTEROID) {
        int distance = crogan_objects[c]->distance(*objs[k]);
        if (distance < 20) {
            OutputLog::write(" !! Crogan (");
            OutputLog::write(c);
            OutputLog::write(") absorbs energy from asteroid\n");
            R4_fuel_level[c] += 0.04;
        }
        if (distance < distance_asteroid) {
            distance_asteroid = distance;
            objs[k]->get_position(x_loc_asteroid,
                                  y_loc_asteroid,
                                  z_loc_asteroid);
        }
    }


    if (objs[k]->get_type() == PLAYER ||
        objs[k]->get_type() == PROCESSOR) {
        int distance = crogan_objects[c]->distance(*objs[k]);
        if (distance < 30) {
            OutputLog::write(" !! Crogan (");
            OutputLog::write(c);
            OutputLog::write(") absorbs energy from ship ");
            OutputLog::write(objs[k]->get_name());
            OutputLog::write("\n");
            R4_fuel_level[c] += 1.5;
        }
        if (distance < distance_ship) {
            distance_ship = distance;
            objs[k]->get_position(x_loc_ship,
                                  y_loc_ship,
```

```
                                          z_loc_ship);
            }
        }
    }

    // Special test for Crogans who favor slowly absorbing
    // energy from asteroids: If a ship passes very close by,
    // then set a goal to follow the ship:
    if (favor_asteroids == 1 && distance_ship < 25) {
        OutputLog::write("-- resetting asteroid favoring ");
        OutputLog::write("Crogan to follow nearby ship at ");
        OutputLog::write(x_loc_ship);
        OutputLog::write(" ");
        OutputLog::write(y_loc_ship);
        OutputLog::write(" ");
        OutputLog::write(z_loc_ship);
        OutputLog::write("\n");
        dif_x = x_loc_ship - x;
        dif_y = y_loc_ship - y;
        dif_z = z_loc_ship - z;
        float distance_before_move =
            sqrt(dif_x*dif_x + dif_y*dif_y + dif_z*dif_z);

        float scale_factor = 1.0 / (distance_before_move + 0.0001);
        x_goal_delta[c] = dif_x * scale_factor;
        y_goal_delta[c] = dif_y * scale_factor;
        z_goal_delta[c] = dif_z * scale_factor;

        goal_cycles[c] = (0.25 * distance_before_move)
                         / current_speed + 1;
        if (goal_cycles[c] > 6)  goal_cycles[c] = 6;
    }

    if (goal_cycles[c] < 1) {

        // No current plan, so develop one:

        OutputLog::write("New Crogan (");
        OutputLog::write(c);
        OutputLog::write(") goal ");
        if (favor_asteroids == 0) {
            OutputLog::write("ship at: ");
            OutputLog::write(x_loc_ship);
            OutputLog::write(", ");
```

```
        OutputLog::write(y_loc_ship);
        OutputLog::write(", ");
        OutputLog::write(z_loc_ship);
        // Set goal to move towards the nearest ship:
        dif_x = x_loc_ship - x;
        dif_y = y_loc_ship - y;
        dif_z = z_loc_ship - z;
    } else {
        OutputLog::write("asteroid at: ");
        OutputLog::write(x_loc_asteroid);
        OutputLog::write(", ");
        OutputLog::write(y_loc_asteroid);
        OutputLog::write(", ");
        OutputLog::write(z_loc_asteroid);
        // Set goal to move towards the nearest asteroid:
        dif_x = x_loc_asteroid - x;
        dif_y = y_loc_asteroid - y;
        dif_z = z_loc_asteroid - z;
    }

    float distance_before_move =
        sqrt(dif_x*dif_x + dif_y*dif_y + dif_z*dif_z);
    OutputLog::write(". Distance= ");
    OutputLog::write(distance_before_move);
    OutputLog::write("\n");

    float scale_factor = 1.0 / (distance_before_move + 0.0001);
    x_goal_delta[c] = dif_x * scale_factor;
    y_goal_delta[c] = dif_y * scale_factor;
    z_goal_delta[c] = dif_z * scale_factor;

    goal_cycles[c] = (0.25 * distance_before_move)
            / current_speed;
    if (goal_cycles[c] > 6)  goal_cycles[c] = 6;

}


// Move according to current goal/plan:
x_loc[c] += current_speed * x_goal_delta[c];
y_loc[c] += current_speed * y_goal_delta[c];
z_loc[c] += current_speed * z_goal_delta[c];
if (move_in_straight_line == 0) {
    x_loc[c] += random(5) - 2;
```

```
            y_loc[c] += random(5) - 2;
            z_loc[c] += random(5) - 2;
        }
        R4_fuel_level[c] -= fuel_use;
        goal_cycles[c] -= 1;
        OutputLog::write("Crogan (");
        OutputLog::write(c);
        OutputLog::write(") new pos: ");
        OutputLog::write(x_loc[c]);
        OutputLog::write(" ");
        OutputLog::write(y_loc[c]);
        OutputLog::write(" ");
        OutputLog::write(z_loc[c]);
        OutputLog::write(", fuel=");
        OutputLog::write(R4_fuel_level[c]);
        OutputLog::write(", remaining goal cycles=");
        OutputLog::write(goal_cycles[c]);
        OutputLog::write("\n");

        crogan_objects[c]->set_position((int)x_loc[c],
                                        (int)y_loc[c],
                                        (int)z_loc[c]);


    }
  }
}


void Crogan::evolve_population()
{
    sort_by_fitness();
    do_mutations();
    do_crossovers();
    // reposition ships to the center of the asteroid field:
#if 0
    for (int c=0; c<POPULATION_SIZE; c++) {
      crogan_objects[c]->set_position(50 + random(350),
                                      50 + random(350),
                                      50 + random(350));
    }
#endif
}

float Crogan::R4_fuel_level[Crogan::POPULATION_SIZE];
```

The **Crogan** class constructor uses the base class (**genetic**) constructor to initialize the inherited data for genetic algorithms. The constructor tries to initialize the chromosome population by reading a restore file. This restore file name is saved in private class data; the class destructor writes the current chromosome population to the same file when the single instance of class **Crogan** is destroyed.

The public class member function **Crogan::move_all** updates the positions of all Crogan ships with the following behavior for each ship:

1. Use the chromosome for this ship to set strategy flags for moving in a straight line or zigzagging, favoring asteroids or chasing enemy ships, and moving at a slow fuel-efficient speed or moving quickly.
2. Write current strategy flags and position to the output log file.
3. Calculate energy bonus if very close to an enemy ship or an asteroid.
4. Find the objects nearest to the Crogan ship. Based on strategy flags and environment, create a movement goal.
5. Move according to the current movement goal.

The public member function **Crogan::evolve_population** is called occasionally (such as, a few times a minute during game play) to update the chromosome population by:

1. Sorting the chromosomes in order of fitness.
2. Applying the mutation operation to a very small percentage of the chromosomes.
3. Applying the crossover operation.

For the Crogan ships, we simply calculate the current fitness value for a chromosome by the amount of R4 fuel that it has. When the chromosome population is evolved, the new chromosomes are instantaneously assigned to the Crogan ships; when this happens, you may see a Crogan ship that has been favoring the location of an asteroid suddenly take off after an enemy ship.

The use of genetic programming in this simple example simulation shows how easy it is to adjust the strategy of game agents. This programming strategy is scaleable to a much larger number of strategy control variables. Here, we have only 8 possible states (2 raised to the third power). If, for example, you have written a game agent control program that uses 10 tuning parameters (each with an ON/OFF binary value), then you have 1,024 possible control states (this is 2 raised to the tenth power). The C++ class **genetic** developed in Chapter 2 can easily handle this size of problem. The last line in Listing 5.9 allocates storage for **Crogan::R4_fuel_level**.

The Future: Emergent Complex Behavior with Genetic Algorithms and Recurrent Neural Networks

One of my favorite areas of research is in the field of emergent complex behavior. (See Watson, 1994 for a discussion of using genetic algorithms to train recurrent neural networks such as the back-propagation neural networks that we developed in Chapter 2, with added feedback loops so that the network can recognize temporal patterns as well as spatial patterns.) In preparing this book, I spent over 100 hours trying to adapt my previous work to the current problem of creating Crogan ships that adapt to their environments dynamically using recurrent neural networks. Unfortunately, the learning time for this operation is definitely not real time, so this interesting technique fails the hard test of practicality. Still, I will briefly discuss in this section how a recurrent neural network works, and how we can train them (but not in real time).

The C++ class **Crogan** that we developed earlier used a genetic algorithm to set in real game time the values of three state variables that control the strategy of each Crogan ship. Since the genes were represented as a single bit of information, these chromosomes containing three genes each represent a possible search space of only 2 raised to the third power, or 8. In the following test code for producing Crogan ships that can learn to navigate, the search space is much larger:

```
enum {POPULATION_SIZE=100};
enum {GENE_SIZE=4};
enum {NUM_INPUTS=3, NUM_HIDDEN_1=3, NUM_HIDDEN_2=3, NUM_OUTPUTS=3};
enum {CHROMOSOME_SIZE=(NUM_INPUTS*NUM_HIDDEN_1 +
                        NUM_HIDDEN_1*NUM_HIDDEN_2 +
                        NUM_HIDDEN_2 * NUM_OUTPUTS +
                        NUM_OUTPUTS * NUM_HIDDEN_2 +
                        NUM_OUTPUTS * NUM_HIDDEN_1 +
                        NUM_OUTPUTS * NUM_INPUTS) * GENE_SIZE};
enum {CHROMOSOME_SIZE=(NUM_INPUTS * NUM_OUTPUTS) * GENE_SIZE};
```

Here, the search space is 2 raised to the 216 power, a large number indeed! Two raised to the 216 power is:

$$105312291668557186697918027683670432318895095400549111254310977536$$

This number represents the number of possible states in our search space. We are asking the genetic algorithm to find a good solution in this large search space. A good solution is any set of weights for the recurrent network that efficiently control the Crogan ships.

The activations and weights for this neural network can be allocated:

```
// because we are using a recurrent neural network, we need
// to save the activation values from the last time step:
float inputs[POPULATION_SIZE][NUM_INPUTS];
float hidden_1[POPULATION_SIZE][NUM_HIDDEN_1];
float hidden_2[POPULATION_SIZE][NUM_HIDDEN_2];
float outputs[POPULATION_SIZE][NUM_OUTPUTS];

// Weights:
float I_to_H1[NUM_INPUTS][NUM_HIDDEN_1];
float H1_to_H2[NUM_HIDDEN_1][NUM_HIDDEN_2];
float H2_to_O[NUM_HIDDEN_2][NUM_OUTPUTS];
float O_to_H2[NUM_OUTPUTS][NUM_HIDDEN_2];
float O_to_H1[NUM_OUTPUTS][NUM_HIDDEN_1];
float O_to_I[NUM_OUTPUTS][NUM_INPUTS];
```

Now, since the Crogan class is derived from the class **genetic**, the following protected data is also inherited:

```
typedef unsigned char gene;
enum {MAX_CHROMOSOMES=100};
gene * population[MAX_CHROMOSOMES];
```

The constructor for class **genetic**, which is called before the constructor for class **Crogan**, will allocate an array of 216 unsigned char, or gene, values for each chromosome in the population. In order to use the recurrent neural network, we need to convert the 54 4-bit weight values into floating point numbers:

```
int i, j, k;
int count = 0;
int ival;
static int powers_of_2[13] =
    {1,2,4,8,16,32,64,128,256,512,1024,2048,4096};
for (i=0; i<NUM_INPUTS; i++) {
    for (j=0; j<NUM_HIDDEN_1; j++) {
        float val = 0;
        ival = 0;
        for (k=0; k<GENE_SIZE; k++) {
            ival += population[pop_index][count++] * powers_of_2[k];
        }
        val = INVERSE_GRAY_CODE[ival];
        I_to_H1[i][j] =  (val - HALF) * SCALE_FACTOR;
    }
}

for (i=0; i<NUM_HIDDEN_1; i++) {
    for (j=0; j<NUM_HIDDEN_2; j++) {
        float val = 0;
        ival = 0;
        for (k=0; k<GENE_SIZE; k++) {
            ival += population[pop_index][count++] * powers_of_2[k];
        }
        val = INVERSE_GRAY_CODE[ival];
        H1_to_H2[i][j] =  (val - HALF) * SCALE_FACTOR;
    }
}

for (i=0; i<NUM_HIDDEN_2; i++) {
    for (j=0; j<NUM_OUTPUTS; j++) {
        float val = 0;
        ival = 0;
        for (k=0; k<GENE_SIZE; k++) {
            ival += population[pop_index][count++] * powers_of_2[k];
        }
```

```
      val = INVERSE_GRAY_CODE[ival];
      H2_to_O[i][j] =  (val - HALF) * SCALE_FACTOR;
   }
}


for (i=0; i<NUM_OUTPUTS; i++) {
   for (j=0; j<NUM_HIDDEN_2; j++) {
      float val = 0;
      ival = 0;
      for (k=0; k<GENE_SIZE; k++) {
         ival += population[pop_index][count++] * powers_of_2[k];
      }
      val = INVERSE_GRAY_CODE[ival];
      O_to_H2[i][j] =  (val - HALF) * SCALE_FACTOR;
   }
}



for (i=0; i<NUM_OUTPUTS; i++) {
   for (j=0; j<NUM_HIDDEN_1; j++) {
      float val = 0;
      ival = 0;
      for (k=0; k<GENE_SIZE; k++) {
         ival += population[pop_index][count++] * powers_of_2[k];
      }
      val = INVERSE_GRAY_CODE[ival];
      O_to_H1[i][j] =  (val - HALF) * SCALE_FACTOR;
   }
}

for (i=0; i<NUM_OUTPUTS; i++) {
   for (j=0; j<NUM_INPUTS; j++) {
      float val = 0;
      ival = 0;
      for (k=0; k<GENE_SIZE; k++) {
         ival += population[pop_index][count++] *
                 powers_of_2[k];
      }
      val = INVERSE_GRAY_CODE[ival];
      O_to_I[i][j] =  (val - HALF) * SCALE_FACTOR;
   }
}
```

Here, we could have simply treated 4-bit integers as numbers between 0 and 15, and scaled these to small floating-point values for each weight. However, if you randomly change a bit in a 4-bit number (during crossover or mutation), you drastically change the value of the weight. Here we use Gray coding to order the integers from 0 through 15 so that changing a single bit only changes the value of the number by 1 (see Goldberg, 1989). Here are the Gray codes that I used:

```
static int GRAY_CODE[16] = {
    0, 1, 3, 2, 6, 7, 5, 4, 12, 13, 15, 14, 10, 11, 9, 8};
static int INVERSE_GRAY_CODE[16] = {
    0, 1, 3, 2, 7, 6, 4, 5, 15, 14, 12, 13, 8, 9, 11, 10};
```

The following constants define the range of the converted floating point weights:

```
const int HALF = 7.0;
static float SCALE_FACTOR = 0.50;
```

If we assume that three input values for each recurrent neural network are the:

1. scaled difference in x coordinate between this Crogan ship and the nearest Processor ship,
2. scaled difference in y coordinate between this Crogan ship and the nearest Processor ship,
3. scaled difference in z coordinate between this Crogan ship and the nearest Processor ship,

then the three output values are interpreted as:

1. new velocity in x direction,
2. new velocity in y direction, and
3. new velocity in z direction.

I also experimented with seven inputs, but the size of the recurrent network was far too large to train in a reasonable amount of time. Here, the seven inputs were:

1. scaled difference in x coordinate between this Crogan ship and the nearest Processor ship,
2. scaled difference in y coordinate between this Crogan ship and the nearest Processor ship,
3. scaled difference in z coordinate between this Crogan ship and the nearest Processor ship,
4. scaled difference in x coordinate between this Crogan ship and the nearest asteroid,
5. scaled difference in y coordinate between this Crogan ship and the nearest asteroid,
6. scaled difference in z coordinate between this Crogan ship and the nearest asteroid,
7. scaled amount of R4 fuel for this Crogan ship.

Even though emergent adaptive behavior for complex systems is outside the realm of practical application using today's technology, I believe that in the near future, advances in computer hardware and, more important, in our understanding of how biological systems evolve to meet changing environments, will make it possible to use something similar to my experiments with genetic algorithms controlling the evolution of recurrent neural networks for complex emergent behavior.

The following example code shows how I use a single recurrent network after defining the weights from a chromosome in the Crogan genetic population. I assume that the three input values are in the array **input_vals** and that the results for controlling the ship's velocity are stored in the array **output_vals**.

```
for (i=0; i<NUM_INPUTS; i++) {
    inputs[pop_index][i] = input_vals[i];
}
for (i=0; i<NUM_HIDDEN_1; i++) {
    hidden_1[pop_index][i] = 0;
    for (j=0; j<NUM_INPUTS; j++) {
        hidden_1[pop_index][i] +=
            inputs[pop_index][j] * I_to_H1[j][i];
    }
    for (j=0; j<NUM_OUTPUTS; j++) {
```

```
            hidden_1[pop_index][i] +=
                outputs[pop_index][j] * O_to_H1[j][i];
        }
        hidden_1[pop_index][i] = Sigmoid(hidden_1[pop_index][i]);
    }
    for (i=0; i<NUM_HIDDEN_2; i++) {
        hidden_2[pop_index][i] = 0;
        for (j=0; j<NUM_HIDDEN_1; j++) {
            hidden_2[pop_index][i] +=
                hidden_1[pop_index][j] * H1_to_H2[j][i];
        }
        for (j=0; j<NUM_OUTPUTS; j++) {
            hidden_2[pop_index][i] +=
                outputs[pop_index][j] * O_to_H2[j][i];
        }
        hidden_2[pop_index][i] = Sigmoid(hidden_2[pop_index][i]);
    }
    for (i=0; i<NUM_OUTPUTS; i++) {
        outputs[pop_index][i] = 0;
        for (j=0; j<NUM_HIDDEN_2; j++) {
            outputs[pop_index][i] +=
                hidden_2[pop_index][j] * H2_to_O[j][i];
        }
        outputs[pop_index][i] = Sigmoid(outputs[pop_index][i]);
        // Copy the final output values to the output_vals
        // array:
        output_vals[i] = outputs[pop_index][i];
    }
```

In order to evolve a population of chromosomes that, when converted to weights for our recurrent network, effectively control the movement of Crogan ships, it is necessary to randomly test the population by simulating hundreds of game cycles from randomly constructed game scenarios. After hundreds of simulations, the population is rated and sorted by effectiveness (that is, how much R4 fuel they have), and mutation is used to create new chromosomes from the most fit members of the previous population. This process must be repeated thousands of times to evolve a fit population. It does not make sense to use crossover operations to evolve the population for recurrent neural networks.

Testing Three Ship Types in a Simulated Asteroid Field

The interaction of intelligent software agents with even relatively simple game environments can be infinitely complex. My strategy for writing the agents to control the three ship types (Player, Processor, and Crogan) was to unit test the utility class components (genetic algorithm, neural network, expert system rule functions, and plan manager rule functions) before integrating these components. The text-based simulation program listed in this section is the first integration test of these software agents. In practice, the combination of this text-based simulation, observations of the 3D simulations developed in Chapters 6 and 7, and the 2D game version of the simulation developed in Chapters 8, 9, and 10 are required to tune the software agents.

The agents for controlling the three ship types are simple, but they provide an example for using the VR Agent Toolkit in your own programs. Listing 5.10 shows file TXT_GAME.CPP, which is used for testing all three ship types.

Listing 5.10

```
// File: txt_game.cpp
//
// Description: This file contains a text mode test
//              program for the C++ Intelligent Agent classes:
//
//                   ExpertSystem
//                   PlanManager
//                   Neural
//                   genetic
//                   geometric_object
//                   game_object
//                   Agent
//                   World
//
// Copyright 1995, Mark Watson

#include "world.h"
#include "agent.h"
```

```
#include "expert.h"
#include "genetic.h"
#include "crogan.h"

#include "out_log.h"
#include "game_val.h"

#include <stdio.h>
#include <stdlib.h>
#include <time.h>

// Protoype for single function in setup.cpp:
void world_setup(World *w);

static void test(int open_log)
{
   OutputLog *ol;
   if (open_log) {
      ol = new OutputLog("test.log");
      OutputLog::write("Text mode version or Intelligent agent space game\n");
   }

   World world;
   world_setup(&world);
   // Add in the Crogans:
   Crogan crogan_population(&world, "crogan.dat");

   const int NUM_ITERS = 4;
   crogan_population.count = 0;
   for (int iter=0; iter<NUM_ITERS; iter++) {
      for (int nn=0; nn<Crogan::POPULATION_SIZE; nn++)
         Crogan::set_R4_fuel_level(nn, 50);
      cerr << "Starting cycle " << iter << " of " << NUM_ITERS << "\n";
      // NOTE: In order to optimize training, we want to frequently
      // randomize the positions of the Processor ships, to allow each
      // generation of Crogans to have the opportunity to be tested
      // with many nearby Processor ships:
      int num = world.number_of_game_objects();
      for (int n=0; n<num; n++) {
         if ((world.get_game_object(n)).get_type() == PROCESSOR) {
            (world.get_game_object(n)).set_position(50+random(300),
                                                    50+random(300),
                                                    50+random(300));
```

```
        }
    }
    for (int j=0; j<20; j++) {
        world.update_all_game_objects();
        crogan_population.move_all();
    }
    cerr << "\n* * * Evolving Crogan population\n";
    crogan_population.evolve_population();
    }
    OutputLog::write("\n");
    if (open_log)    delete ol;

}

void main()
{
    // randomize the stdlib random number generator:
    long t = time(NULL) % 1117;
    for (int d=0; d<t; d++)  random(4);

    // For testing with no output to log file:
#if 0
    test(0);
#else
    test(1);
#endif
}
```

In Listing 5.10, the function **test(int open_log)** sets up the **World** data object and sample ships, then runs the simulation by calling the member functions **World::update_all_game_objects()** and **Crogan::move_all()**. If the integer argument to function test is nonzero, then an output log file is created. Every 20 simulation cycles, the Crogan chromosome population is updated by calling the member function **Crogan::evolve_population()**.

Listing 5.11 is a partial execution log file, TEST.LOG, created using C++ class **OutputLog** in the sample program given in Listing 5.10. As usual, the listing text is printed using a monospace font; while comments are added in a regular serif font.

Listing 5.11

```
Text mode version or Intelligent agent space game
Entering constructor for class World
Entering game_object constructor
Entering game_object constructor
Entering game_object constructor
Entering game_object constructor
Entering game_object constructor
Entering constructor for Agent class
Entering game_object constructor
Entering constructor for Agent class
Entering game_object constructor
Entering constructor for Agent class
Entering game_object constructor
Entering constructor for Agent class
Entering game_object constructor
Entering constructor for Agent class
Entering game_object constructor
Entering constructor for Agent class
Entering game_object constructor
Entering game_object constructor
```

Here, there are a few hundred lines of output from the class constructors for **World, PlayerShip, ProcessorShip,** and **Crogan**. The **Crogan** class contains static data for using a genetic algorithm to evolve a population of chromosomes used to specify the strategy of the Crogan ships. A game object is also created for each **Crogan** class instance in the class constructor of C++ class **Crogan**.

```
Position of processor ship #0: x: 161, y: 58, z: 332 vel: 0 0 0

Closest objects:
0 : crogan_10, x: 224, y: 84, z: 324, distance = 68
1 : crogan_4, x: 103, y: 118, z: 247, distance = 119
2 : crogan_14, x: 260, y: 111, z: 233, distance = 149
3 : crogan_11, x: 113, y: 81, z: 189, distance = 152
Entered test function for pr_ship fuel use
    new R4 level=305
Entered rule function for motion correction for processor ship #0
    setting course back to asteroid field
```

Here, we have entered the main event loop for the text-based 3D space simulation. All spaceship objects are moved; in this case, Processor ship number 0 is currently at rest, and fairly far from the center of the asteroid field. With nothing better to do, the ship heads back toward the center of the asteroid field.

```
Position of processor ship #4: x: 176, y: 136, z: 198 vel: 0 0 0

Closest objects:
0 : crogan_11, x: 113, y: 81, z: 189, distance = 84
1 : crogan_4, x: 103, y: 118, z: 247, distance = 89
2 : crogan_14, x: 260, y: 111, z: 233, distance = 94
3 : crogan_2, x: 185, y: 188, z: 103, distance = 108
Entered test function for pr_ship fuel use
    new R4 level=289
Entered rule function for motion correction for processor ship #4
  Stopped ship (0 0 0): setting small random velocity
```

This output shows Processor ship number 4 starting to move slowly in a random direction, since it has a small or 0 velocity, it is already near the asteroids, and there are no trading partners nearby.

```
Position of player_ship: x: 120, y: 350, z: 390 vel: 0 0 0

Closest objects:
0 : crogan_5, x: 168, y: 361, z: 354, distance = 61
1 : asteroid4, x: 60, y: 400, z: 400, distance = 78
2 : processor ship #2, x: 134, y: 294, z: 320, distance = 90
3 : asteroid3, x: 200, y: 350, z: 320, distance = 106
## entered plan pre test rule
.. pre test rule: low supply of Magnozate
```

This output shows the initial condition of the Player ship. Since the Player ship has a good supply of fuel, but no Magnozate ore, the **PlanManager** object selected the plan to set a constant velocity toward the nearest asteroid. Remember that each plan contained in a **PlanManager** instance is defined by three functions: preconditions test, execute plan, and plan termination test. Once this plan is in effect, its execute plan function will be called every simulation time step until the plan termination function returns a nonzero value, thus terminating the plan.

```
Position of player_ship: x: 117, y: 351, z: 390 vel: -0.7620007 0.6350006 0.1270001

Closest objects:
0 : crogan_5, x: 165, y: 360, z: 355, distance = 59
1 : asteroid4, x: 60, y: 400, z: 400, distance = 75
2 : processor ship #2, x: 136, y: 296, z: 318, distance = 92
3 : asteroid3, x: 200, y: 350, z: 320, distance = 108
Entered test function for fuel use in player ship
    new R4 level=639.954
```

Here, in the next simulation time step, the Player ship has a velocity moving toward an asteroid.

```
Position of player_ship: x: 59, y: 401, z: 400 vel: -0.7743735 0.6637487 0.1106248

Closest objects:
0 : asteroid4, x: 60, y: 400, z: 400, distance = 1
1 : crogan_5, x: 113, y: 372, z: 382, distance = 63
2 : asteroid3, x: 200, y: 350, z: 320, distance = 169
3 : processor ship #2, x: 57, y: 227, z: 341, distance = 183
Entered test function for fuel use in player ship
    new R4 level=639.068
Entered rule function for moving back to asteroid field
Entered rule function for trading
Entered rule function for mining asteroid
  ..mining asteroid
```

In this output, the plan for moving toward an asteroid has terminated, and the Player ship is close enough to an asteroid for the expert system rule function **mining asteroid** to be triggered.

The following two fragments from the output log show information on the Crogan ships early in the simulation, and a short time later, after two cycles of evolving the chromosomes that control the strategies of the Crogan ships.

```
Crogan #0 flags: move straight=1, favor asteroids=0, move slowly=1
    Position: 309.838 144.979 228.475
Crogan (0) new pos: 309.806 146.175 227.57, fuel=49.94, remaining goal cycles=0

Crogan #1 flags: move straight=1, favor asteroids=0, move slowly=1
    Position: 146.787 230.653 142.574
Crogan (1) new pos: 147.144 229.384 143.289, fuel=49.94, remaining goal cycles=0
```

```
Crogan #2 flags: move straight=1, favor asteroids=0, move slowly=1
    Position: 184.243 184.283 109.47
Crogan (2) new pos: 184.091 183.54 110.764, fuel=49.94, remaining goal cycles=0


Crogan #3 flags: move straight=1, favor asteroids=0, move slowly=1
    Position: 355.235 115.727 361.108
Crogan (3) new pos: 354.682 116.473 359.93, fuel=49.94, remaining goal cycles=0


Crogan #4 flags: move straight=1, favor asteroids=0, move slowly=1
    Position: 109.031 119.359 242.753
Crogan (4) new pos: 110.237 119.631 241.904, fuel=49.94, remaining goal cycles=0


Crogan #5 flags: move straight=1, favor asteroids=0, move slowly=1
    Position: 162.052 359.665 358.37
Crogan (5) new pos: 160.863 359.398 359.244, fuel=49.94, remaining goal cycles=0


Crogan #6 flags: move straight=1, favor asteroids=0, move slowly=1
    Position: 374.482 240.547 147.001
Crogan (6) new pos: 373.579 239.656 147.802, fuel=49.94, remaining goal cycles=0


Crogan #7 flags: move straight=1, favor asteroids=0, move slowly=1
    Position: 159.104 65.1057 124.382
Crogan (7) new pos: 159.325 66.1269 125.458, fuel=49.94, remaining goal cycles=0


Crogan #8 flags: move straight=1, favor asteroids=0, move slowly=1
    Position: 255.921 77.2136 180.243
Crogan (8) new pos: 254.706 78.0563 180.492, fuel=49.94, remaining goal cycles=0


Crogan #9 flags: move straight=1, favor asteroids=0, move slowly=0
    Position: 345.505 293.73 108.261
Crogan (9) new pos: 344.806 291.475 110.113, fuel=49.88, remaining goal cycles=0


Crogan #10 flags: move straight=1, favor asteroids=0, move slowly=0
    Position: 210.207 78.3076 325.533
New Crogan (10) goal ship at: 166, 63, 327. Distance= 46.5296
Crogan (10) new pos: 207.37 77.3405 325.662, fuel=49.88, remaining goal cycles=2


Crogan #11 flags: move straight=1, favor asteroids=0, move slowly=1
    Position: 118.634 85.8951 189.739
Crogan (11) new pos: 119.761 86.8741 189.887, fuel=49.94, remaining goal cycles=0


Crogan #12 flags: move straight=1, favor asteroids=0, move slowly=1
    Position: 209.89 381.021 85.4854
Crogan (12) new pos: 210.468 379.825 86.1824, fuel=49.94, remaining goal cycles=0
```

```
Crogan #13 flags: move straight=1, favor asteroids=0, move slowly=1
    Position: 203.009 101.248 96.8725
Crogan (13) new pos: 202.611 101.698 98.247, fuel=49.94, remaining goal cycles=0

Crogan #14 flags: move straight=1, favor asteroids=0, move slowly=1
    Position: 264.269 116.663 230.56
Crogan (14) new pos: 265.123 117.796 230.073, fuel=49.94, remaining goal cycles=0

Crogan #15 flags: move straight=1, favor asteroids=0, move slowly=1
    Position: 353.188 304.774 359.161
Crogan (15) new pos: 353.025 303.329 358.794, fuel=49.94, remaining goal cycles=0
```

This output shows both the state of the chromosomes controlling Crogan ship strategy and the physical data associated with each Crogan ship. Remember that each Crogan ship uses a different chromosome in the genetic population to control its strategy. The following output shows the same Crogan ships much later in the simulation.

```
Crogan #0 flags: move straight=1, favor asteroids=0, move slowly=1
    Position: 274.63 146.543 234.722
Crogan (0) new pos: 275.501 146.721 235.931, fuel=49.81, remaining goal cycles=1

Crogan #1 flags: move straight=0, favor asteroids=0, move slowly=1
    Position: 143.263 234.53 165.36
New Crogan (1) goal ship at: 198, 275, 153. Distance= 69.6419
Crogan (1) new pos: 142.329 235.325 163.128, fuel=49.81, remaining goal cycles=5

Crogan #2 flags: move straight=1, favor asteroids=0, move slowly=1
    Position: 203.964 200.76 138.925
New Crogan (2) goal ship at: 198, 275, 153. Distance= 76.6486
Crogan (2) new pos: 203.866 202.227 139.218, fuel=49.81, remaining goal cycles=5

Crogan #3 flags: move straight=1, favor asteroids=0, move slowly=1
    Position: 320.589 161.689 302.97
 !! Crogan (3) absorbs energy from ship processor ship #2
New Crogan (3) goal ship at: 317, 155, 297. Distance= 8.3666
Crogan (3) new pos: 320.051 160.613 302.074, fuel=64.81, remaining goal cycles=0

Crogan #4 flags: move straight=1, favor asteroids=0, move slowly=1
    Position: 156.396 170.684 210.685
New Crogan (4) goal ship at: 198, 275, 153. Distance= 126.641
Crogan (4) new pos: 156.893 171.927 210.01, fuel=49.81, remaining goal cycles=5
```

```
Crogan #5 flags: move straight=1, favor asteroids=0, move slowly=1
   Position: 73.2028 367.93 380.215
 !! Crogan (5) absorbs energy from ship player_ship
Crogan (5) new pos: 73.6994 367.061 379.098, fuel=76.81, remaining goal cycles=0

Crogan #6 flags: move straight=1, favor asteroids=0, move slowly=1
   Position: 322.865 226.977 164.659
New Crogan (6) goal ship at: 320, 257, 273. Distance= 113.34
Crogan (6) new pos: 322.839 227.387 166.102, fuel=49.81, remaining goal cycles=5

Crogan #7 flags: move straight=1, favor asteroids=0, move slowly=1
   Position: 196.087 132.772 138.449
New Crogan (7) goal ship at: 198, 275, 153. Distance= 143.798
Crogan (7) new pos: 196.108 134.263 138.605, fuel=49.81, remaining goal cycles=5

Crogan #8 flags: move straight=1, favor asteroids=0, move slowly=1
   Position: 236.093 136.037 153.169
New Crogan (8) goal ship at: 198, 275, 153. Distance= 144.101
Crogan (8) new pos: 235.697 137.484 153.169, fuel=49.81, remaining goal cycles=5

Crogan #9 flags: move straight=1, favor asteroids=0, move slowly=1
   Position: 278.716 243.535 134.579
New Crogan (9) goal ship at: 198, 275, 153. Distance= 88.2327
Crogan (9) new pos: 277.356 244.079 134.902, fuel=49.81, remaining goal cycles=5

Crogan #10 flags: move straight=1, favor asteroids=0, move slowly=1
   Position: 214.815 130.464 273.291
New Crogan (10) goal ship at: 317, 155, 297. Distance= 108.674
Crogan (10) new pos: 216.237 130.809 273.622, fuel=49.81, remaining goal cycles=5

Crogan #11 flags: move straight=1, favor asteroids=0, move slowly=1
   Position: 154.955 162.281 195.307
Crogan (11) new pos: 155.454 163.605 194.808, fuel=49.81, remaining goal cycles=4

Crogan #12 flags: move straight=1, favor asteroids=0, move slowly=1
   Position: 197.296 310.631 151.874
New Crogan (12) goal ship at: 198, 275, 153. Distance= 35.0714
Crogan (12) new pos: 197.339 309.134 151.959, fuel=49.81, remaining goal cycles=4

Crogan #13 flags: move straight=1, favor asteroids=0, move slowly=1
   Position: 218.479 147.68 126.115
New Crogan (13) goal ship at: 198, 275, 153. Distance= 132.337
Crogan (13) new pos: 218.253 149.131 126.421, fuel=49.81, remaining goal cycles=5
```

```
Crogan #14 flags: move straight=1, favor asteroids=0, move slowly=1
   Position: 261.627 127.82 237.718
New Crogan (14) goal ship at: 317, 155, 297. Distance= 86.7179
Crogan (14) new pos: 262.596 128.304 238.755, fuel=49.81, remaining goal cycles=5

Crogan #15 flags: move straight=0, favor asteroids=0, move slowly=1
   Position: 318.925 247.743 297.944
 !! Crogan (15) absorbs energy from ship processor ship #4
Crogan (15) new pos: 320.108 247.11 298.658, fuel=54.31, remaining goal cycles=3
```

It is interesting to compare the chromosome population between these two time periods. When the text-based simulation started, it used an existing population data file with only 2 of the 8 possible control strategies in the population:

- Fourteen chromosomes that cause a Crogan ship to move straight (rather than zigzag), favor following ships (rather than asteroids), and to move slowly, conserving fuel (rather than moving quickly to keep up with the Player ship).

- Two chromosomes that cause a Crogan ship to move straight (rather than zigzag), favor following ships (rather than staying near asteroids), and to move quickly.

In the later population, we see a similar distribution:

- Fourteen chromosomes that cause a Crogan ship to move straight (rather than zigzag), favor following ships (rather than asteroids), and to move slowly, conserving fuel (rather than moving quickly to keep up with the Player ship).

- Two chromosomes that cause a Crogan ship to zigzag (rather than move straight), favor following ships (rather than staying near asteroids), and to move quickly.

It is also interesting to delete the Crogan chromosome data file (CROGAN.DAT) before running the simulation. Then you will see an initial random distribution of control strategies. In the 3D simulations and the 2D games in Chapters 6 through 10, the Crogan chromosomes are evolved a few times a minute to adjust for changing game situations.

Space Simulation Implemented with 3D Graphics for RenderWare

Chapter 5 contained the design and implementation of a space simulation program with three types of computer-controlled ships. In this chapter, we will use the 3D graphics library RenderWare, from Criterion Software (a Canon subsidiary), to add 3D graphics to the simulation of three types of computer-controlled ships in an asteroid field. This program supports dynamically changing the viewing position in 3D space while the simulation is running. The computer-controlled space ships are free to move in three dimensions in the simulation. In later chapters, all three types of ships, and the asteroids, are constrained to lie in a two-dimensional plane, and the space simulation is turned into a game by adding optional user control of the Player ship. This game is implemented for Microsoft Windows, Apple Macintosh, and UNIX X Windows in Chapters 8, 9, and 10. Figure 6.1 shows a view of the RenderWare-based 3D spaceship simulation. The right mouse button is used to rotate the

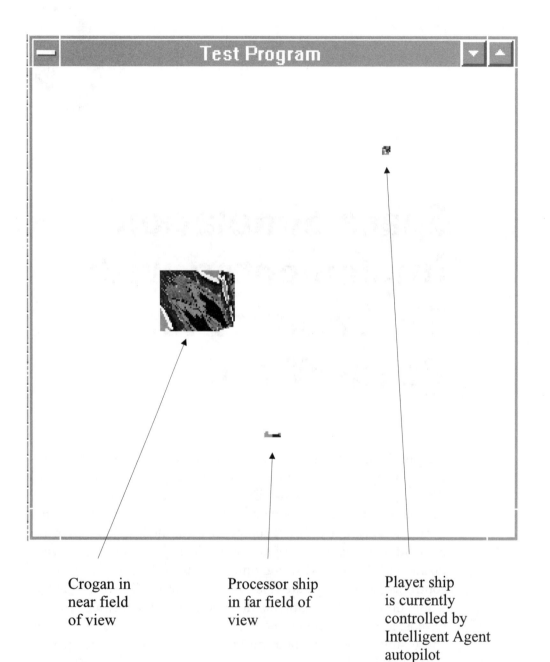

Crogan in
near field
of view

Processor ship
in far field of
view

Player ship
is currently
controlled by
Intelligent Agent
autopilot

Figure 6.1   RenderWare-based 3D spaceship simulation showing a Crogan ship in the foreground.

viewpoint in the 3D world and to zoom in and out by holding down the right mouse button while dragging the mouse cursor horizontally or vertically. An executable version of this program is on the CD-ROM in file SRC\RW\WIN_GUI.CPP. The RenderWare-specific source code is in file SRC\WIN_GUI.CPP. You must have the environment variable RWSHAPEPATH set to the location of the Render-Ware script files used by the sample program (set RWSHAPEPATH D:\RENDWARE\SCRIPTS;D:\RENDWARE\TEXTURES).

Figure 6.2 shows a Harel state transition diagram (Booch 1994) of the RenderWare-based spaceship simulation program developed in this chapter.

As seen in Figure 6.2, when the program starts, a data setup function is called that creates an instance of C++ class **World**, a set of contained instances of class **game_object**, and the instances of classes derived from C++ class **Agent** to control the instances of class **game_object**. The real-time behavior of this graphics-based simulation is implemented by calling the following two update functions each time step before redrawing the graphics:

World::update_all_game_objects()

Crogan::move_all()

The member function **World::update_all_game_objects()** simply calls the functions **game_object::run_all_agents()** and **game_object::update_position()** for each instance of class **game_object** contained in the **World** data object.

The Crogan ships are handled differently. The C++ class **Crogan** is derived, using public inheritance, from the C++ class **genetic** developed in Chapter 2. Class **Crogan** uses static class data to maintain control parameters for each Crogan ship; these control parameters are encoded in chromosomes, and evolved using a genetic algorithm. The chromosomes controlling the behavior of the Crogan ships are modified periodically by the simulation, so that the Crogan ships can optimize their strategy for the current game situation. Figure 6.3 shows a view of the RenderWare-based 3D spaceship simulation.

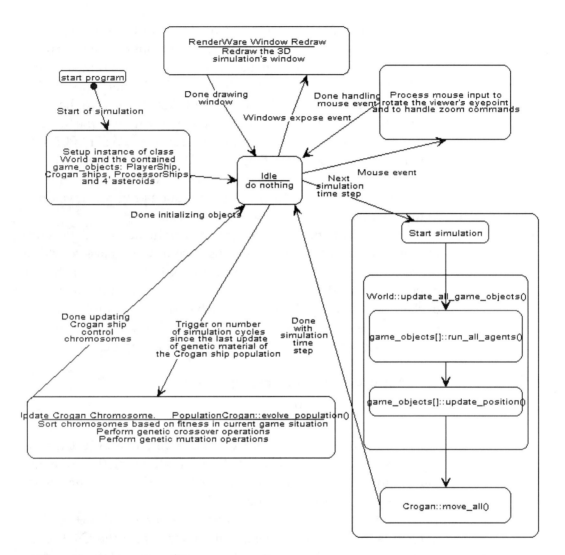

Figure 6.2   Harel state transition diagram showing the event-ordered behavior of the RenderWare-based 3D spaceship simulation program.

In order to add 3D graphics to our spaceship simulation, we replace the C++ source file TXT_GAME.CPP (in the SRC\TXT_GAME directory) with the file WIN_GUI.CPP (in directory SRC\RW) shown in Listing 6.1. The RenderWare version of the 3D simulation was partially derived from the viewer example program supplied with the RenderWare developer's kit.

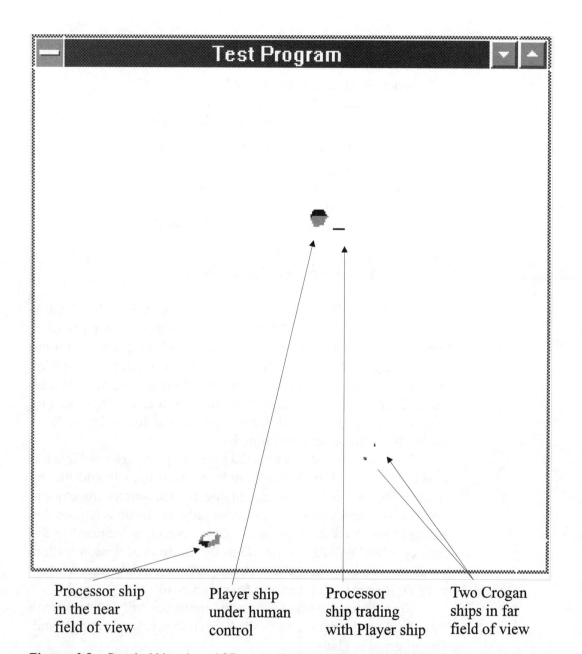

Figure 6.3   RenderWare-based 3D spaceship simulation showing a Processor ship trading with the Player ship. The right mouse button is used to rotate the viewpoint in the 3D world and to zoom in and out.

You can get more information on RenderWare by contacting, in the United States and Canada:

Criterion Software, (408) 749-0493
E-mail: rw-info@csl.com, ftp: ftp.csl.com
WEB: http://www/csl.com/csl/cslhome.html

European readers can contact Criterion software at:

Criterion Software, +441-483-448833
E-mail: rw-info@criterion.canon.co.uk
FTP: ftp.canon.co.uk
WEB: http://www.canon.co.uk/csl/cslhome.html

Japanese readers can contact:

Canon Sales Co. Inc. +81-43-211-9152

Criterion Software Ltd., is a subsidiary of Canon Inc., and is the leader in interactive 3D graphics software tools for personal computers. Criterion develops, markets, and supports computer products and technologies that expand the interactive 3D graphics frontiers on the desktop. The company licenses its products and technology to major developers worldwide through its offices in Sunnyvale, California; Guildford, England; and Tokyo, Japan. RenderWare is a trademark of Canon Inc.

There are several excellent 3D graphics packages available for desktop systems, but RenderWare is my favorite. I would like to thank Criterion Software for supplying an evaluation copy of RenderWare for developing the example program in this chapter. An example RenderWare application, Cyber Street, is included in directory \RENDWARE on the CD-ROM. Additional demonstration programs can be obtained directly from Criterion Software's Internet FTP sites at ftp.csl.com and ftp.canon.co.uk.

Since RenderWare is a proprietary graphics API, I will summarize the most important API calls here so that you can understand the program in Listing 6.1:

- **RwCreateCamera(int maxWidth, int MaxHeight, (void *)NULL)**: Creates a camera viewport.

- **RwSetCameraBackColor(RwCamers *c, RPARAM red, RPARAM green, RPARAM blue)**: Sets the RGB background color for a camera.

- **RwTiltCamera(RwCamera *c, RPARAM angle)**: Rotates the camera about the X axis.

- **RwVCMoveCamera(RwCamera *c, RPARAM x, RPARAM y, RPARAM z)**: Moves the camera a delta of (x,y,z) in camera units.

- **RwSetCameraViewwindow(RwCamera *c, RPARAM width, RPARAM height)**: Sets the relative size of a camera's view window; larger values give a wide angle field of view.

- **RwCreateScene()**: Creates a new empty scene that can hold 3D models.

- **RwDestroyCamera(RwCamera *c)**: Frees data associated with a camera object.

- **RwClose()**: This function must be called before exiting a RenderWare application.

- **RwCreateLight(RwLightType lt, RPARAM x, RPARAM y, RPARAM z, RPARAM intensity)**: Creates a new light source at position (x,y,z).

- **RwAddLightToScene(RwScene *scene, RwLight *light)**: Adds a light source to a scene object.

- **RwBeginCameraUpdate(RwCamera *c)**: Uses a specified camera for subsequent rendering operations.

- **RwClearCameraViewport(RwCamera *c)**: Clears a camera's image buffer.

- **RwRenderScene(RwScene *scene)**: Renders all objects contained in a scene object into the current camera's image buffer.

- **RwEndCameraUpdate(RwCamera *c)**: Cleans up internal data structures after the rendering into a camera's image buffer is complete.

- **RwShowCameraImage(RwCamera *c, void *param)**: Copies modified regions of the camera's image buffer to the current viewport.

- **RwReadShape(char *file_name)**: Reads a file containing a 3D object clump from a RenderWare script file, and returns a **RwClump** pointer.

- **RwAddClumpToScene(RwScene *scene, RwClump *clump)**: Adds a 3D clump object to a specified scene.

- **RwGetClumpMatrix(RwClump *clump, RwMatrix4D *matrix)**: Gets a specified clump's modeling matrix.

- **RwTranslateMatrix(RwMatrix4D *matrix, RPARAM delta_x, RPARAM delta_y, RPARAM delta_z, RwCombineOperation op)**: Used to move a 3D clump object.

- **RwTransformClump(RwClump *clump, RwMatrix4d *matrix, RwCombineOperation op)**: Applies a specified transformation matrix to a clump's modeling matrix.

- **RwScratchMatrix()**: Returns the address of a scratch pad matrix that can be used for temporary operations.

There are many more functions in the RenderWare library that I did not use in the example program in Listing 6.1.

Listing 6.1

```
// File : win_gui.c
//
// Description: This file uses the Intelligent Agent C++ classes
//              and the RenderWare 3D graphics library from
//              Criterion Software.
//

//

// un-comment out the following define to generate a detailed log
// file to GAME.LOG:
// #define GENERATE_LOG
```

```c
#include "world.h"
#include "agent.h"
#include "expert.h"
#include "genetic.h"
#include "game_val.h"
#include "crogan.h"
#include "pr_ship.h"
#include "player.h"

#include "out_log.h"

// Protoype for single function in setup.cpp:
void world_setup(World *w);

#define  INCLUDE_SHELLAPI_H
#include <windows.h>

#include <stdlib.h>
#include <stdio.h>

#include "rwlib.h"
#include "rwwin31.h"

#define RWVIEW_CLASS_NAME        "RwTest"
#define ERROR_DIALOG_TITLE       "RenderWare(tm) Test Error"
#define DEFAULT_WINDOW_WIDTH     400
#define DEFAULT_WINDOW_HEIGHT    400
#define MAXIMUM_WINDOW_WIDTH     512
#define MAXIMUM_WINDOW_HEIGHT    512
#define DEFAULT_CAMERA_DISTANCE CREAL(-10.0)

// Storage for pointers to RenderWare clumps for each ship:

static RwClump    *CroganClumps[NUM_CROGAN];
static RwClump    *ProcessorClumps[NUM_PROCESSOR];
static RwClump    *PlayerClump;
static RwClump    *AsteroidClumps[NUM_ASTEROIDS];

// Pointer to game World object:
World *world;

// Pointer to the Crogan genetic population object:
Crogan *crogan;
```

```
/* PROTOTYPES */

LRESULT CALLBACK MainWndProc(HWND window, UINT message,
                WPARAM wParam, LPARAM lParam);

typedef enum
{
    MMNoAction,
    MMPanAndZoomCamera,
    MMTiltCamera
} MouseMode;


static HANDLE      AppInstance;
static RwScene     *Scene  = NULL;
static RwCamera    *Camera = NULL;
static RwLight     *Light  = NULL;
static RwLight     *Light2 = NULL;
static RwLight     *Light3 = NULL;
static RwClump     *PickedClump = NULL; /* last clump selected */
static RwMatrix4d  *SpinMatrix = NULL;
static MouseMode   MouseMoveMode = MMNoAction;
static int         LastX; /* last mouse X */
static int         LastY; /* last mouse Y */
static RwReal      CameraDistance = DEFAULT_CAMERA_DISTANCE;
static RwReal      CameraTilt = CREAL(0.0);
static int         FrameNumber = 0; /* animation frame number */
static BOOL        ThreeDInitialized = FALSE;

static BOOL InitApplication(HANDLE instance)
{
    WNDCLASS windowClass;

    windowClass.style         = CS_BYTEALIGNWINDOW;
    windowClass.lpfnWndProc   = (WNDPROC)MainWndProc;
    windowClass.cbClsExtra    = 0;
    windowClass.cbWndExtra    = 0;
    windowClass.hInstance     = instance;
    windowClass.hIcon         = NULL;
    windowClass.hCursor       = LoadCursor(NULL, IDC_ARROW);
    windowClass.hbrBackground = NULL;
    windowClass.lpszMenuName  = NULL;
    windowClass.lpszClassName = RWVIEW_CLASS_NAME;
```

```
        return RegisterClass(&windowClass);
}

static HWND InitInstance(HANDLE instance)
{
    return
      CreateWindow(RWVIEW_CLASS_NAME,
                   "RenderWare version of Space Ship Simulation",
                   WS_OVERLAPPEDWINDOW,
                   CW_USEDEFAULT, CW_USEDEFAULT,
                   DEFAULT_WINDOW_WIDTH, DEFAULT_WINDOW_HEIGHT,
                   NULL, NULL, instance, NULL);
}

static BOOL Init3D(HWND window)
{
    char windowText[128];
    char version[30];
    long isDebug;
    long depth;

    if (!RwOpen("MSWindows", NULL)) {
       MessageBox(window,
         "Error opening the RenderWare(tm) library",
         ERROR_DIALOG_TITLE, MB_OK | MB_ICONSTOP | MB_APPLMODAL);
       return FALSE;
    }

    Camera = RwCreateCamera(MAXIMUM_WINDOW_WIDTH,
                            MAXIMUM_WINDOW_HEIGHT, NULL);
    if (Camera == NULL) {
       // Check for insufficient memory:
       if (RwGetError() == E_RW_NOMEM) {
          MessageBox(window,
            "Insufficient memory to create the RenderWare(tm) camera",
            ERROR_DIALOG_TITLE, MB_OK | MB_ICONSTOP | MB_APPLMODAL);
       } else {
          MessageBox(window,
            "Error creating the RenderWare(tm) camera",
            ERROR_DIALOG_TITLE, MB_OK | MB_ICONSTOP | MB_APPLMODAL);
       }
       RwClose();
```

```
      return FALSE;
}

RwSetCameraBackColor(Camera, CREAL(0.0), CREAL(0.0), CREAL(0.0));

RwTiltCamera(Camera, CameraTilt);
RwVCMoveCamera(Camera, CREAL(0.0), CREAL(0.0), CameraDistance);

RwSetCameraViewwindow(Camera, CREAL(0.8), CREAL(0.8));

Scene = RwCreateScene();
if (Scene == NULL) {
   RwDestroyCamera(Camera);
   RwClose();
   MessageBox(window,
     "Error creating the RenderWare(tm) scene",
     ERROR_DIALOG_TITLE, MB_OK | MB_ICONSTOP | MB_APPLMODAL);
   return FALSE;
}


Light = RwCreateLight(rwPOINT, CREAL(-9.0), CREAL(-9.0),
                      CREAL(-9.0), CREAL(25.0));
if (Light == NULL) {
   RwDestroyScene(Scene);
   RwDestroyCamera(Camera);
   RwClose();
   MessageBox(window,
     "Error creating the RenderWare(tm) light",
     ERROR_DIALOG_TITLE, MB_OK | MB_ICONSTOP | MB_APPLMODAL);
   return FALSE;
}

Light2 = RwCreateLight(rwPOINT, CREAL(8.0), CREAL(8.0),
         CREAL(-8.0), CREAL(25.0));
if (Light2 == NULL) {
   RwDestroyScene(Scene);
   RwDestroyCamera(Camera);
   RwClose();
   MessageBox(window,
     "Error creating the RenderWare(tm) light",
     ERROR_DIALOG_TITLE, MB_OK | MB_ICONSTOP | MB_APPLMODAL);
   return FALSE;
}
```

```
      Light3 = RwCreateLight(rwPOINT, CREAL(8.0), CREAL(-8.0),
                             CREAL(8.0), CREAL(25.0));
      if (Light3 == NULL) {
         RwDestroyScene(Scene);
         RwDestroyCamera(Camera);
         RwClose();
         MessageBox(window,
           "Error creating the RenderWare(tm) light",
           ERROR_DIALOG_TITLE, MB_OK | MB_ICONSTOP | MB_APPLMODAL);
         return FALSE;
      }


      RwAddLightToScene(Scene, Light);
      RwAddLightToScene(Scene, Light2);
      RwAddLightToScene(Scene, Light3);

      SpinMatrix = RwCreateMatrix();
      if (SpinMatrix == NULL) {
         RwDestroyScene(Scene);
         RwDestroyCamera(Camera);
         RwClose();
         MessageBox(window,
           "Error creating the RenderWare(tm) matrix",
           ERROR_DIALOG_TITLE, MB_OK | MB_ICONSTOP | MB_APPLMODAL);
         return FALSE;
      }


      ThreeDInitialized = TRUE;

      return TRUE;
}

static void TidyUp3D(void)
{
      RwDestroyMatrix(SpinMatrix);
      RwDestroyScene(Scene);
      if (RwGetCameraBackdrop(Camera)) {
        RwDestroyRaster(RwGetCameraBackdrop(Camera));
        RwSetCameraBackdrop(Camera, NULL);
      }
      RwDestroyCamera(Camera);
      RwClose();
}
```

```
static void RenderScene(HWND window, HDC dc)
{
    RwBeginCameraUpdate(Camera);
    RwClearCameraViewport(Camera);
    RwRenderScene(Scene);
    RwEndCameraUpdate(Camera);
 #ifdef WIN32
    RwShowCameraImage(Camera, (void*)dc);
#else
    RwShowCameraImage(Camera, (void*)(MAKELONG(window, dc)));
#endif
}

static void HandleSize(HWND window, int width, int height)
{
    HDC dc;
    RwSetCameraViewport(Camera, 0, 0, width, height);
    RwSetCameraBackdropViewportRect(Camera, 0, 0, width, height);
    dc = GetDC(window);
    RenderScene(window, dc);
    ReleaseDC(window, dc);
}


static void HandleRightButtonDown(HWND window, int x, int y, WPARAM vKeys)
{
    POINT pos;

    MouseMoveMode = MMPanAndZoomCamera;
    if (MouseMoveMode != MMNoAction) {
      SetCapture(window);
      pos.x = x;
      pos.y = y;
      ClientToScreen(window, &pos);
      LastX = pos.x;
      LastY = pos.y;
    }
}

static void HandleMouseMove(HWND window, int x, int y)
{
    HDC        dc;
    RwClump    *parent;
```

```
RwMatrix4d *tmpMatrix;
RwMatrix4d *worldToLocal;
RwV3d      up;
RwV3d      right;
RwV3d      at;
RwReal     xDelta;
RwReal     yDelta;
RwReal     xAngle;
RwReal     yAngle;
POINT      pos;
int        xOffset;
int        yOffset;

pos.x = x;
pos.y = y;
ClientToScreen(window, &pos);

switch (MouseMoveMode) {
   case MMNoAction:
       break;

   case MMPanAndZoomCamera:
       RwVCMoveCamera(Camera, CREAL(0.0),
                   CREAL(0.0), -CameraDistance);
       RwTiltCamera(Camera, -CameraTilt);
       RwPanCamera(Camera, INT2REAL(LastX - pos.x));
       CameraDistance =
         RAdd(CameraDistance,
             RDiv(INT2REAL(LastY - pos.y),
             CREAL(10.0)));
       RwTiltCamera(Camera, CameraTilt);

       RwVCMoveCamera(Camera, CREAL(0.0),
                   CREAL(0.0), CameraDistance);
       break;

   case MMTiltCamera:
       RwVCMoveCamera(Camera, CREAL(0.0), CREAL(0.0),
                   -CameraDistance);
       RwTiltCamera(Camera, -CameraTilt);
       CameraTilt = RAdd(CameraTilt, INT2REAL(LastY - pos.y));
       RwTiltCamera(Camera, CameraTilt);
```

```
                RwVCMoveCamera(Camera, CREAL(0.0), CREAL(0.0),
                            CameraDistance);
            break;
        }


    if (MouseMoveMode != MMNoAction)  {
        dc = GetDC(window);
        RenderScene(window, dc);
        ReleaseDC(window, dc);
        LastX = pos.x;
        LastY = pos.y;
    }
}



static void HandleRightButtonUp(void)
{
    if (MouseMoveMode != MMNoAction) {
        MouseMoveMode = MMNoAction;
        ReleaseCapture();
    }
}

static void HandlePaint(HWND window)
{
    HDC dc;
    PAINTSTRUCT paintStruct;

    dc = BeginPaint(window, &paintStruct);
    RwInvalidateCameraViewport(Camera);
#ifdef WIN32
    RwShowCameraImage(Camera, (void*)dc);
#else
    RwShowCameraImage(Camera, (void*)MAKELONG(window, dc));
#endif
    EndPaint(window, &paintStruct);
}



static void HandleTimer(HWND window)
{
    HDC dc;
```

```cpp
// Move the game objects, and periodically
// update the crogan population:
world->update_all_game_objects();
crogan->move_all();

static int crogan_update_count = 0;
if (crogan_update_count++ > 100) {
   crogan_update_count = 0;
   crogan->evolve_population();
}

const float scale = 0.06;
const int offset = 250;  // text game objects are
                         // centered around (250,250,250)

int x_lookat = 150;
int y_lookat = 150;
int z_lookat = 150;

// Loop through all instances of game_object in
// the game world:
int num_objects = world->number_of_game_objects();
int count_pr_ship = 0;
int count_crogan = 0;
int count_asteroid = 0;
for (int g=0; g<num_objects; g++) {
   game_object * g_obj = &(world->get_game_object(g));
   int x, y, z;
   g_obj->get_position(x, y, z);

   OutputLog::write("Moving object ");

   PickedClump = NULL;
   if (g_obj->get_type() == PROCESSOR) {
       PickedClump = ProcessorClumps[count_pr_ship++];
       OutputLog::write("(processor ship) ");
   }
   if (g_obj->get_type() == PLAYER) {
       PickedClump = PlayerClump;
       OutputLog::write("(player ship) ");
   }
   if (g_obj->get_type() == CROGAN) {
       PickedClump = CroganClumps[count_crogan++];
```

```
            OutputLog::write("(Crogan ship) ");
        }
        if (g_obj->get_type() == ASTEROID) {
            PickedClump = AsteroidClumps[count_asteroid++];
            OutputLog::write("(asteroid) ");
        }
        OutputLog::write(x);
        OutputLog::write(", ");
        OutputLog::write(y);
        OutputLog::write(", ");
        OutputLog::write(z);
        OutputLog::write("\n");
        if (PickedClump != NULL) {
            x -= offset;
            y -= offset;
            z -= offset;
            x *= scale;
            y *= scale;
            z *= scale;
            RwPushScratchMatrix();
            RwGetClumpMatrix(PickedClump, RwScratchMatrix());
            RwTranslateMatrix(RwScratchMatrix(),CREAL(x),
                            CREAL(y), CREAL(z), rwREPLACE);
            RwTransformClump(PickedClump, RwScratchMatrix(),
                            rwREPLACE);
            RwPopScratchMatrix();
        }
    }


    // Re-render the scene and copy the results
    // to the display:
    dc = GetDC(window);
    RenderScene(window, dc);
    ReleaseDC(window, dc);
}

LRESULT CALLBACK MainWndProc(HWND window,
                            UINT message,
                            WPARAM wParam,
                            LPARAM lParam)
{
#ifdef WIN32
    POINTS point;
```

```
#else
    POINT point;
#endif

    switch (message) {
        case WM_CREATE:
            SetTimer(window, 1, 20, NULL);
            return 0L;

        case WM_SIZE:
            if (ThreeDInitialized)
                HandleSize(window, LOWORD(lParam),
                        HIWORD(lParam));
            return 0L;

        case WM_RBUTTONDOWN:
            if (ThreeDInitialized) {
#ifdef WIN32
                point = MAKEPOINTS(lParam);
#else
                point = MAKEPOINT(lParam);
#endif
                HandleRightButtonDown(window, point.x,
                                    point.y, wParam);
            }
            return 0L;

        case WM_MOUSEMOVE:
            if (ThreeDInitialized) {
                if (MouseMoveMode != MMNoAction) {
#ifdef WIN32
                point = MAKEPOINTS(lParam);
#else
                point = MAKEPOINT(lParam);
#endif
                HandleMouseMove(window, point.x, point.y);
                }
            }
            return 0L;

        case WM_RBUTTONUP:
            if (ThreeDInitialized)
                HandleRightButtonUp();
            return 0L;
```

```
        case WM_PAINT:
            if (ThreeDInitialized)
                HandlePaint(window);
            return OL;

        case WM_TIMER:
            if (ThreeDInitialized)
                HandleTimer(window);
            return OL;

        case WM_DESTROY:
            DragAcceptFiles(window, FALSE);
            KillTimer(window, 1);
            PostQuitMessage(O);
            return OL;
    }
    return DefWindowProc(window, message, wParam, lParam);
}

int PASCAL WinMain(HINSTANCE instance, HINSTANCE prevInstance,
                LPSTR cmdLine, int cmdShow)
{
    MSG  message;
    HWND window;
    RwClump *clump;

    AppInstance = instance;

    if (prevInstance) {
        MessageBox(NULL,
            "One copy of program is already running",
            ERROR_DIALOG_TITLE,
            MB_OK | MB_APPLMODAL | MB_ICONSTOP);
        return FALSE;
    }

    /* Register the window class */
    if (!InitApplication(instance)) {
        return FALSE;
    }

    /* Create the window: */
    window = InitInstance(instance);
```

```
    if (window == NULL) {
       return FALSE;
    }

    if (!Init3D(window))  {
       DestroyWindow(window);
       return FALSE;
    }

    // Create an output log file:
#ifdef GENERATE_LOG
    OutputLog *outLog = new OutputLog("game.log");
#endif

    OutputLog::write("Creating Crogan RenderWare clumps...\n");
    for (int c=0; c<NUM_CROGAN; c++) {
        CroganClumps[c] = RwReadShape("crogan.rwx");
        if (CroganClumps[c])
            RwAddClumpToScene(Scene, CroganClumps[c]);
    }
    OutputLog::write("Creating clumps for processor ships...\n");
    for (int pr=0; pr<NUM_PROCESSOR; pr++) {
       ProcessorClumps[pr] =
       RwReadShape("pr_ship.rwx");
       if (ProcessorClumps[pr])
          RwAddClumpToScene(Scene, ProcessorClumps[pr]);
    }
    OutputLog::write("Creating clumps for asteroids...\n");
    for (int a=0; a<NUM_ASTEROIDS; a++) {
       AsteroidClumps[a] =
       RwReadShape("asteroid.rwx");
       if (AsteroidClumps[a])
          RwAddClumpToScene(Scene, AsteroidClumps[a]);
    }
    OutputLog::write("Creating play ship RenderWare clump...\n");
    PlayerClump = RwReadShape("player.rwx");
    if (PlayerClump)
       RwAddClumpToScene(Scene, PlayerClump);

    ShowWindow(window, cmdShow);
    UpdateWindow(window);

    // Create the test game objects
```

```
    OutputLog::write("Creating instance of C++ class 'World'...\n");

    world = new World();
    OutputLog::write(" ... placing objects in the world...\n");
    world_setup(world);
    // Add in the Crogans
    OutputLog::write("Creating Crogans...\n");
    crogan = new Crogan(world, "crogan.dat");

    OutputLog::write("\nEntering Windows event loop...\n");

    while (GetMessage(&message, NULL, 0U, 0U)) {
        TranslateMessage(&message);
        DispatchMessage(&message);
    }
    TidyUp3D();

#ifdef GENERATE_LOG
    delete outLog;
#endif

    return message.wParam;
}
```

The file WIN_GUI.CPP is located in the SRC\RW directory on the CD-ROM. This directory is set up for building a RenderWare application (you must own the RenderWare software development software to do this) using the Watcom 10.0 C++ compiler. The directory SRC\RW_NT is set up for building an NT executable of this same program using Microsoft Visual C++ 2.0.

The sample program in Listing 6.1 uses the following include files for defining the interface for the C++ VR Agent Toolkit:

world.h

agent.h

expert.h

genetic.h

out_log.h

The following include files are specific to this sample program:

game_val.h

crogan.h

pr_ship.h

player.h

In RenderWare programs, 3D models are read from script files into data structures named clumps. The following clump pointers are initialized in function **WinMain()** by reading script files:

```
static RwClump    *CroganClumps[NUM_CROGAN];
static RwClump    *ProcessorClumps[NUM_PROCESSOR];
static RwClump    *PlayerClump;
static RwClump    *AsteroidClumps[NUM_ASTEROIDS];
```

Function **InitApplication(HANDLE instance)** sets up Windows-specific data for the sample program in Listing 6.1. The function **InitInstance(HANDLE instance)** creates a window for the sample program. The function **Init3D()** initializes the RenderWare environment by:

- Creating a viewing camera.

- Setting the background color for the graphics window.

- Setting the initial camera viewing angle.

- Creating a RenderWare scene data structure that will hold all clump data objects.

- Creating three point light sources.

The function **TidyUp3D()** is called when the sample program terminates to free up RenderWare data structures. The function **RenderScene(HWND window, HDC dc)** renders all 3D clumps in the current scene; the position of all clumps should be set before calling this function. The function **HandleSize(HWND window, int width, int height)**, derived from the RenderWare VIEWER.EXE example program, is called when the sample program receives a window resize message.

The right mouse button is used to zoom and pan the camera viewpoint while running the 3D spaceship simulation. The function **HandleRightButtonDown()**, derived from the RenderWare VIEWER.EXE example program, records the position of the mouse cursor when the right mouse button is pressed. In order to zoom the graphics window, the right mouse button is held down while the mouse cursor is moved up and down the screen. The camera angle is rotated around the origin by holding down the right mouse button and moving the mouse cursor horizontally on the display screen. Functions **HandleMouseMove()** and **HandleRightButtonUp()** (derived from the RenderWare VIEWER.EXE example program) handle mouse movement and right button up messages.

The function **HandlePaint(HWND window)** is called to update the contents of the graphics window when it is invalidated. The positions of the spaceship simulation objects and the RenderWare clump data structures are updated in the Windows Timer callback function **HandleTimer(HWND window)**. Function **HandleTimer** first updates the state of all simulation objects:

```
// Move the game objects, and periodically
// update the crogan population:
world->update_all_game_objects();
crogan->move_all();

static int crogan_update_count = 0;
if (crogan_update_count++ > 100) {
   crogan_update_count = 0;
   crogan->evolve_population();
}
```

The positions of all simulation objects are copied into the RenderWare clump data structures for each simulation object. The object's position is stored in the variables x, y, and z. The clump pointer **PickedClump** is set to each simulation object's clump data structure, and the clump data is updated:

```
x -= offset;
y -= offset;
z -= offset;
```

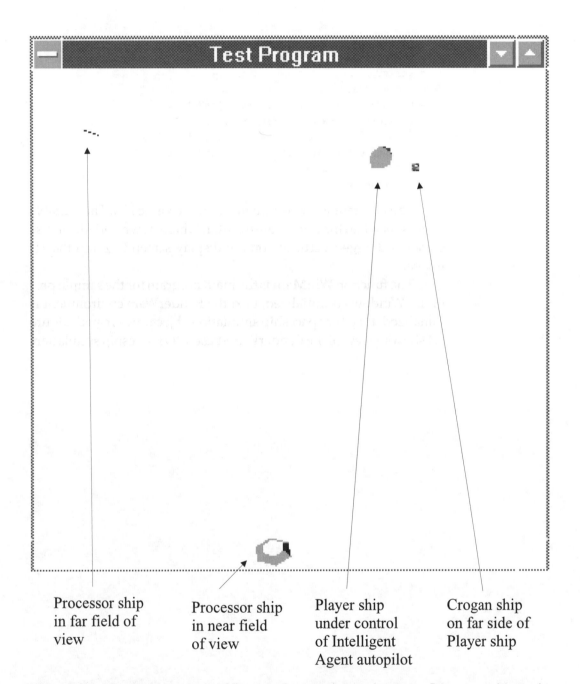

Processor ship in far field of view

Processor ship in near field of view

Player ship under control of Intelligent Agent autopilot

Crogan ship on far side of Player ship

Figure 6.4 RenderWare-based 3D spaceship simulation showing a Processor ship in the foreground. The right mouse button is used to rotate the viewpoint in the 3D world and to zoom in and out.

```
x *= scale;
y *= scale;
z *= scale;
RwPushScratchMatrix();
RwGetClumpMatrix(PickedClump, RwScratchMatrix());
RwTranslateMatrix(RwScratchMatrix(),CREAL(x),
                  CREAL(y), CREAL(z), rwREPLACE);
RwTransformClump(PickedClump, RwScratchMatrix(),
                  rwREPLACE);
RwPopScratchMatrix();
```

The constant **offset** is initialized to the value 250. The variable scale is set when the right mouse button is held down and the mouse cursor is dragged vertically on the display screen to zoom the 3D image.

The function **WinMain** is the main program for the sample program. Windows is initialized, next the RenderWare environment is initialized, then the spaceship simulation objects are created. Figure 6.4 shows a view of the RenderWare-based 3D spaceship simulation.

Space Simulation Implemented with 3D Graphics for OpenGL

Chapter 5 contained the design and implementation of a space simulation program with three types of computer-controlled ships. In this chapter, we will use the 3D graphics library OpenGL (created originally by Silicon Graphics and added to Windows NT 3.5 by Microsoft) to add 3D graphics to the simulation of three types of computer-controlled ships in an asteroid field. This program supports dynamically changing the viewing position in 3D space while the simulation is running. The computer-controlled spaceships are free to move in three dimensions in the simulation. In later chapters, all three types of ships, and the asteroids, are constrained to lie in a two-dimensional plane, and the space simulation is turned into a game by adding optional user control of the Player ship. This game is implemented for Microsoft Windows, Apple Macintosh, and UNIX X Windows in Chapters 8, 9, and 10.

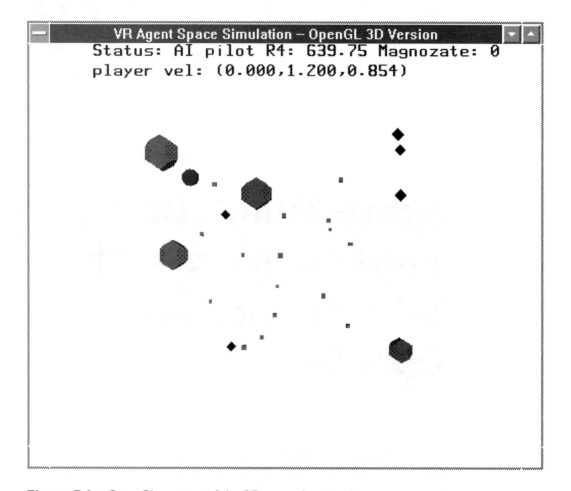

Figure 7.1   OpenGL version of the 3D spaceship simulation program.

Figure 7.1 shows a screen image of the OpenGL 3D spaceship simulation program. Asteroids appear as large Octohedrons. The Player ship is a red sphere. The Crogan ships are small green cubes, and the Processor ships are blue solid diamonds. The arrow keys on the keyboard are used to change the viewpoint. The z key zooms in the display, while the o key zooms out the display. Figure 7.2 shows a Harel state transition diagram (Booch, 1994) of the OpenGL-based spaceship simulation program developed in this chapter.

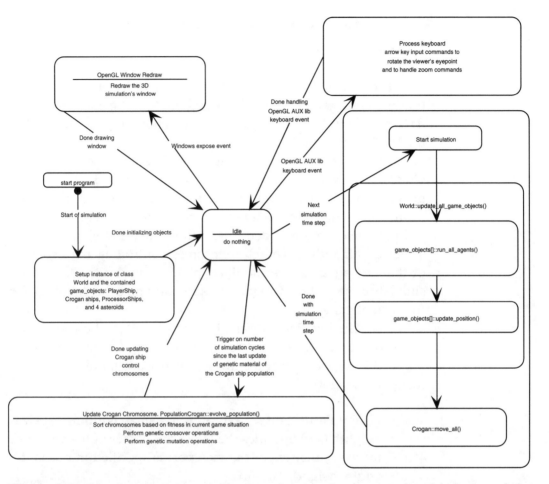

Figure 7.2 Harel state transition diagram showing the event-ordered behavior of the OpenGL-based 3D spaceship simulation program.

As seen in Figure 7.2, when the program starts, a data setup function is called that creates an instance of C++ class **World**, a set of contained instances of class **game_object**, and the instances of classes derived from C++ class **Agent** to control the instances of class **game_object**. The real-time behavior in the OpenGL-based simulation occurs because an idle work function is called several times per second to update the state of all game objects; this idle work function calls the following two update functions each time step:

World::update_all_game_objects()

Crogan::move_all()

The function **World::update_all_game_objects()** simply calls the functions **game_object::run_all_agents()** and **game_object::update_position()** for each instance of class **game_object** contained in the **World** data object.

The Crogan ships are handled differently. The C++ class **Crogan** is derived, using public inheritance, from the C++ class **genetic** developed in Chapter 2. Class **Crogan** uses static class data to maintain control parameters for each Crogan ship; these control parameters are encoded in chromosomes, and evolved using a genetic algorithm. The chromosomes controlling the behavior of the Crogan ships are modified periodically by the text-based simulation, so that the Crogan ships can optimize their strategy for the current game situation.

OpenGL, like RenderWare, is a high-level graphics API (Neider, Davis, and Woo 1992, 1993). The following OpenGL API calls are used in the example three-dimensional space simulation implemented in Listing 7.1:

- **glViewPort(GLint x, GLint y, GLsizei widthm GLsizei height)**: (x,y) Specifies the lower left corner of the viewport in pixels; the size of the viewport is specified in pixels (by width, height).

- **glMatrixMode(GLenum mode)**: Specifies which matrix is the current mode matrix (from a choice of model view, projection, or texture).

- **glPushMatrix()**: Saves the current matrix on the matrix stack.

- **glPopMatrix()**: Restores a previous graphics state by popping the current matrix off of the matrix stack.

- **glPushAttrib(GLbitfield mask)**: The input mask specifies which state variables have their values saved onto the attribute stack.

- **glPopAttrib()**: Restores state from the attribute stack.

- **glMaterialfv(GLenum face, GLenum property_name, GLfloat *parameters)**: Applies a material property to a specified property name and face (front or back face).

- **glTranslatef(GLfloat x, GLfloat y, GLfloat z)**: Multiplies the current matrix by a translation matrix; this is used to move objects.

- **glLightfv(GLenum light, GLenum property_name, GLfloat *parameters)**: Sets the parameters for the specified light source.

Most implementations of OpenGL supply a standard auxiliary library (functions beginning with aux). Some of these library functions, given here, are used in Listing 7.1:

- **auxSolidSphere(GLdouble radius)**: Draws a solid sphere with the current material properties and position of size specified by the input parameter radius.

- **auxSolidCube(GLdouble size)**: Draws a solid cube with the current material properties and position of size specified by the input parameter radius.

- **auxSolidOctahedron(GLdouble radius)**: Draws a solid octohedron with the current material properties and position of size specified by the input parameter radius.

- **auxSolidDodecahedron(GLdouble radius)**: Draws a solid dodecahedron with the current material properties and position of size specified by the input parameter radius.

- **auxInitPosition(GLint x, GLint y, GLsizei width, GLsizei height)**: (x,y) Specifies the lower left corner of the window in pixels on the display screen; specifies the size of the window in pixels (width, height).

- **auxInitDisplayMode(GLbitfield mask)**: Sets attributes for RGB mode, double buffering, and so on.

- **auxInitWindow(GLbyte *window_title)**: Opens a window for performing OpenGL graphics.

- **auxReshapeFunc(void (*function)(GLsizei width, GLsizei height))**: Specifies a callback function that is called whenever the OpenGL window is resized; this allows an application program to accommodate dynamic changes in window size.

- **auxKeyFunc(GLint keyboard_character, void (*function)())**: Specifies a callback function to be called whenever the specified key on the keyboard is pressed.

- **auxMouseFunc(GLint button, GLint mode, void (*mouse_function)(AUX_EVENTREC *))**: Specifies a function in the application that is to be called when the indicated type of mouse event occurs.

- **auxIdleFunc(void (*func)())**: Specifies a function in the application to be called whenever the OpenGL system has nothing to do (that is, when all rendering operations are complete).

- **auxMainLoop(void (*display_function)())**: Specifies both a display function to be called when the graphics window needs to be redrawn (such as when part of the window is uncovered), and serves as a main loop in an OpenGL application that uses the auxiliary library.

- **auxSwapBuffers()**: Swaps buffers when in double buffer mode.

The OpenGL library also includes utility functions in a GLU library. One of these functions is used in Listing 7.1:

- **gluPerspective(GLdouble field_of_view_y, GLdouble aspect_ratio, GLdouble zNear_clipping_plane, GLdouble zFar_clipping_plane)**: Sets the projection parameters in the projection matrix.

Listing 7.1

```
// File: test_gl.cpp
//
// Description: A 3D interface to space simulation using OpenGL.
//              Uses the OpenGL AUX library.
//
```

```cpp
#include <iostream.h>
#include <stdlib.h>
#include <time.h>

//              Intelligent Agent Space Simulation Data:


// un-comment out the following #define to generate a detailed
// log file to GAME.LOG:
// #define GENERATE_LOG

#include "world.h"
#include "agent.h"
#include "expert.h"
#include "genetic.h"
#include "game_val.h"
#include "crogan.h"
#include "pr_ship.h"
#include "player.h"

#include "out_log.h"

// Protoype for single function in setup.cpp:
void world_setup(World *w);

// Pointer to game World object:
static World *world;

// Pointer to the Crogan genetic population object:
static Crogan *crogan;

// Pointer to the Player ship object:

static PlayerShip *player_ship = NULL;

// Velocity of the player ship (for display):
static float x_vel = 0.0;
static float y_vel = 0.0;
static float z_vel = 0.0;

// Flag for human player, or Ai assistant control of player ship:

static int AUTOMATIC_MODE = 1;  // start with AI assistant control
```

```
//              OpenGL Setup:

#include "glos.h"

#include <GL\gl.h>
#include <GL\glu.h>
#include <GL\glaux.h>

void CALLBACK draw(void);
void change_viewpoint(GLdouble, GLdouble, GLdouble);



GLfloat latitude, longitude, radius;

const float INITIAL_RADIUS = 5.0;

void CALLBACK resize(GLsizei width, GLsizei height)
{
    GLfloat aspect;

    glViewport(0, 0, width, height);

    aspect = (GLfloat) width / height;

    glMatrixMode(GL_PROJECTION);
    glLoadIdentity();
    gluPerspective(45.0, aspect, 3.0, 7.0);
    glMatrixMode(GL_MODELVIEW);
}


static GLfloat whiteAmbient[] = {0.3, 0.3, 0.3, 1.0};
static GLfloat whiteDiffuse[] = {1.0, 1.0, 1.0, 1.0};
static GLfloat whiteSpecular[] = {1.0, 1.0, 1.0, 1.0};
static GLfloat PLAYER_Ambient[] = {0.3, 0.1, 0.1, 1.0};
static GLfloat PLAYER_Diffuse[] = {1.0, 0.0, 0.0, 1.0};
static GLfloat PLAYER_Specular[] = {1.0, 0.0, 0.0, 1.0};
static GLfloat CROGAN_Ambient[] = {0.1, 0.3, 0.1, 1.0};
static GLfloat CROGAN_Diffuse[] = {0.0, 1.0, 0.0, 1.0};
static GLfloat CROGAN_Specular[] = {0.0, 1.0, 0.0, 1.0};
static GLfloat PR_SHIP_Ambient[] = {0.1, 0.1, 0.3, 1.0};
static GLfloat PR_SHIP_Diffuse[] = {0.0, 0.0, 1.0, 1.0};
static GLfloat PR_SHIP_Specular[] = {0.0, 0.0, 1.0, 1.0};
```

```
static GLfloat ASTEROID_Ambient[] = {0.2, 0.2, 0.2, 0.05};
static GLfloat ASTEROID_Diffuse[] = {0.2, 0.2, 0.2, 0.05};
static GLfloat ASTEROID_Specular[] = {0.3, 0.4, 0.4, 0.05};

const float SCALE = 1.0 / 180.0;

void plot_player(int x, int y, int z)
{
float xx = x - 250;
float yy = y - 250;
float zz = z - 250;
xx *= SCALE;
yy *= SCALE;
zz *= SCALE;

    glPushAttrib(GL_LIGHTING_BIT);

        glMaterialfv(GL_FRONT, GL_AMBIENT, PLAYER_Ambient);
        glMaterialfv(GL_FRONT, GL_DIFFUSE, PLAYER_Diffuse);
        glMaterialfv(GL_FRONT, GL_SPECULAR, PLAYER_Specular);
        glMaterialfv(GL_BACK, GL_AMBIENT, PLAYER_Ambient);
        glMaterialfv(GL_BACK, GL_DIFFUSE, PLAYER_Diffuse);
        glMaterialfv(GL_BACK, GL_SPECULAR, PLAYER_Specular);
        glMaterialf(GL_FRONT, GL_SHININESS, 75.0);

        glPushMatrix();
            glTranslatef(xx, yy, zz);
            auxSolidSphere(0.07);
        glPopMatrix();

    glPopAttrib();

}


void plot_crogan(int x, int y, int z)
{
float xx = x - 250;
float yy = y - 250;
float zz = z - 250;
xx *= SCALE;
yy *= SCALE;
zz *= SCALE;
    glPushAttrib(GL_LIGHTING_BIT);
```

```
        glMaterialfv(GL_FRONT, GL_AMBIENT, CROGAN_Ambient);
        glMaterialfv(GL_FRONT, GL_DIFFUSE, CROGAN_Diffuse);
        glMaterialfv(GL_FRONT, GL_SPECULAR, CROGAN_Specular);
        glMaterialfv(GL_BACK, GL_AMBIENT, CROGAN_Ambient);
        glMaterialfv(GL_BACK, GL_DIFFUSE, CROGAN_Diffuse);
        glMaterialfv(GL_BACK, GL_SPECULAR, CROGAN_Specular);
        glMaterialf(GL_FRONT, GL_SHININESS, 65.0);

        glPushMatrix();
            glTranslatef(xx, yy, zz);
            auxSolidCube(0.04);
        glPopMatrix();

    glPopAttrib();


}


void plot_pr_ship(int x, int y, int z)
{
    float xx = x - 250;
    float yy = y - 250;
    float zz = z - 250;
    xx *= SCALE;
    yy *= SCALE;
    zz *= SCALE;
    glPushAttrib(GL_LIGHTING_BIT);

        glMaterialfv(GL_FRONT, GL_AMBIENT, PR_SHIP_Ambient);
        glMaterialfv(GL_FRONT, GL_DIFFUSE, PR_SHIP_Diffuse);
        glMaterialfv(GL_FRONT, GL_SPECULAR, PR_SHIP_Specular);
        glMaterialfv(GL_BACK, GL_AMBIENT, PR_SHIP_Ambient);
        glMaterialfv(GL_BACK, GL_DIFFUSE, PR_SHIP_Diffuse);
        glMaterialfv(GL_BACK, GL_SPECULAR, PR_SHIP_Specular);
        glMaterialf(GL_FRONT, GL_SHININESS, 75.0);

        glPushMatrix();
            glTranslatef(xx, yy, zz);
            auxSolidOctahedron(0.06);
        glPopMatrix();

    glPopAttrib();


}
```

```
void plot_asteroid(int x, int y, int z)
{
    float xx = x - 250;
    float yy = y - 250;
    float zz = z - 250;
    xx *= SCALE;
    yy *= SCALE;
    zz *= SCALE;
    glPushAttrib(GL_LIGHTING_BIT);

        glMaterialfv(GL_FRONT, GL_AMBIENT, ASTEROID_Ambient);
        glMaterialfv(GL_FRONT, GL_DIFFUSE, ASTEROID_Diffuse);
        glMaterialfv(GL_FRONT, GL_SPECULAR, ASTEROID_Specular);
        glMaterialfv(GL_BACK, GL_AMBIENT, ASTEROID_Ambient);
        glMaterialfv(GL_BACK, GL_DIFFUSE, ASTEROID_Diffuse);
        glMaterialfv(GL_BACK, GL_SPECULAR, ASTEROID_Specular);
        glMaterialf(GL_FRONT, GL_SHININESS, 15.0);

        glPushMatrix();
            glTranslatef(xx, yy, zz);
            auxSolidDodecahedron(0.15);
        glPopMatrix();

    glPopAttrib();

}

void print_string(int x, int y, char *str, int len);


void CALLBACK draw(void)
{
    // For text output display:

    static int special_message_count = 0;
    static char special_message[80];

    static char *trade_status[] = {"trade not accepted"," ",
                                    "trade accepted"};
    static char *mining_status[] = {" ", "mining Magnozate"};
    static char *pilot_status[] = {"Human pilot", "AI pilot"};

    game_object *g_obj;
```

```
glClear(GL_COLOR_BUFFER_BIT | GL_DEPTH_BUFFER_BIT);

glPushMatrix();

    // Print text before changing the viewpoint:
    glTranslated(0.0, 0.0, -INITIAL_RADIUS);
    glRotated(0.0, 0.0, 0.0, 1.0);
    // Print out the status line:
    static char status_buf[131], accel_buf[90];
    sprintf(accel_buf,"player vel: (%5.3f,%5.3f,%5.3f)",
            x_vel, y_vel, z_vel);

    float R4;
    int magnozate;
    int trade_type, mining_type;
    if (player_ship != NULL) {
        trade_type = player_ship->get_trading_flag() + 1;
        if (trade_type == 2)  cerr << (char)7;
        mining_type = player_ship->get_mining_flag();
        if (mining_type == 1) cerr << (char)7;;
        R4 = player_ship->get_R4();
        magnozate = player_ship->get_Magnozate();
        player_ship->get_velocity(x_vel, y_vel, z_vel);
    } else {
        trade_type = 1;
        mining_type = 0;
        R4 = 0;
        magnozate = 0;
    }
    sprintf(status_buf,
            "Status: %s R4: %6.2f Magnozate: %d",
            pilot_status[AUTOMATIC_MODE], R4, magnozate);
    print_string(14, 10, status_buf, strlen(status_buf));
    print_string(14, 70, accel_buf, strlen(accel_buf));
    if (special_message_count < 1) {
        if (trade_type != 1) {
            special_message_count = 15;
            sprintf(special_message,"Trading:  %s",
                    trade_status[trade_type]);
        }
        if (mining_type != 0) {
            special_message_count = 15;
            sprintf(special_message,"%s", mining_status[mining_type]);
```

```
        }
    }
    if (special_message_count-- > 0) {
        print_string(15, 130, special_message,
                    strlen(special_message));
    }
    if (special_message_count < 0) special_message_count = 0;

glPopMatrix();

glPushMatrix();

    change_viewpoint(radius, latitude, longitude);

    // Loop through all instances of game_object in the game world:
    int num_objects = world->number_of_game_objects();
    for (int g=0; g<num_objects; g++) {
        g_obj = &(world->get_game_object(g));
        int x, y, z;
        g_obj->get_position(x, y, z);

        OutputLog::write("Moving object ");

        if (g_obj->get_type() == PROCESSOR) {
            plot_pr_ship(x, y, z);
            OutputLog::write("(processor ship) ");
        }
        if (g_obj->get_type() == PLAYER) {
            plot_player(x, y, z);
            OutputLog::write("(player ship) ");
            player_ship = (PlayerShip *)g_obj;
        }
        if (g_obj->get_type() == CROGAN) {
            plot_crogan(x, y, z);
            OutputLog::write("(Crogan ship) ");
        }
        if (g_obj->get_type() == ASTEROID) {
            plot_asteroid(x, y, z);
            OutputLog::write("(asteroid) ");
        }
        OutputLog::write(x);
        OutputLog::write(", ");
        OutputLog::write(y);
```

```
            OutputLog::write(", ");
            OutputLog::write(z);
            OutputLog::write("\n");
        }

    glPopMatrix();

    auxSwapBuffers();
}

void initialize_OpenGL_graphics(void)
{
    GLfloat aspect;
    GLsizei width, height;

    // Light values from SGI/Microsoft example program:
    GLfloat ambientProperties[] = {0.7, 0.7, 0.7, 1.0};
    GLfloat diffuseProperties[] = {0.8, 0.8, 0.8, 1.0};
    GLfloat specularProperties[] = {1.0, 1.0, 1.0, 1.0};

    width = 500.0;
    height = 400.0;

    auxInitPosition(80, 80, width, height);

    auxInitDisplayMode(AUX_RGBA | AUX_DEPTH | AUX_DOUBLE);

    auxInitWindow("VR Agent Space Simulation -- OpenGL 3D Version");

    auxReshapeFunc(resize);

    glClearColor(0.0, 0.0, 0.0, 1.0);
    glClearDepth(1.0);

    glEnable(GL_DEPTH_TEST);

    glEnable(GL_LIGHTING);

    glLightfv(GL_LIGHT0, GL_AMBIENT, ambientProperties);
    glLightfv(GL_LIGHT0, GL_DIFFUSE, diffuseProperties);
    glLightfv(GL_LIGHT0, GL_SPECULAR, specularProperties);
    glLightModelf(GL_LIGHT_MODEL_TWO_SIDE, 1.0);

    glEnable(GL_LIGHT0);
```

```
    glMatrixMode(GL_PROJECTION);
    aspect = (GLfloat) width / height;
    gluPerspective(45.0, aspect, 0.5, 20.0);
    glMatrixMode(GL_MODELVIEW);

    radius = INITIAL_RADIUS;

    latitude = 0.0;
    longitude = 0.0;


}

void change_viewpoint(GLdouble radius, GLdouble latitude,
        GLdouble longitude)
{
    glTranslated(0.0, 0.0, -radius);
    glRotated(0.0, 0.0, 0.0, 1.0);
    glRotated(-latitude, 1.0, 0.0, 0.0);
    glRotated(longitude, 0.0, 0.0, 1.0);

}


static void CALLBACK Key_left_arrow()
{
    longitude -= 2.5;
}

static void CALLBACK Key_right_arrow()
{
    longitude += 2.5;
}
static void CALLBACK Key_up_arrow()
{
    latitude += 4.0;
}
static void CALLBACK Key_down_arrow()
{
    latitude -= 4.0;
}
static void CALLBACK Key_Z()
{
```

```c
    radius *= 0.9;
}
static void CALLBACK Key_O()
{
    radius *= 1.1;
}
static void CALLBACK Key_P()
{
    // Toggle between automatic play mode for player ship
    // and manual mode:
    AUTOMATIC_MODE = 1 - AUTOMATIC_MODE;
}


void CALLBACK do_simulation(void)
{
    // Run the Intelligent Agent 3D Space Simulation:

    // Move the game objects, and periodically update
    // the crogan population:
    world->update_all_game_objects();
    crogan->move_all();

    static int crogan_update_count = 0;
    if (crogan_update_count++ > 100) {
        crogan_update_count = 0;
        crogan->evolve_population();
    }

    // Update graphics display:
    draw();
}


void font_init(void);

void main(void)
{
    // Use the current time to randomize the state of the world:
    // randomize the stdlib random number generator:
    long t = time(NULL) % 1117;
    for (int d=0; d<t; d++)  random(4);

    initialize_OpenGL_graphics();
    font_init();
```

```
    // Create an output log file:
#ifdef GENERATE_LOG
    OutputLog *outLog = new OutputLog("game.log");
#endif
    OutputLog::write("Creating instance of C++ class 'World'...\n");

    world = new World();
    OutputLog::write(" ... placing objects in the world...\n");
    world_setup(world);
    // Add in the Crogans
    OutputLog::write("Creating Crogans...\n");
    crogan = new Crogan(world, "crogan.dat");

auxKeyFunc(AUX_LEFT,  Key_left_arrow);
auxKeyFunc(AUX_RIGHT, Key_right_arrow);
auxKeyFunc(AUX_UP,    Key_up_arrow);
auxKeyFunc(AUX_DOWN,  Key_down_arrow);
auxKeyFunc(AUX_z,     Key_Z);
auxKeyFunc(AUX_o,     Key_O);
auxKeyFunc(AUX_p,     Key_P);
auxKeyFunc(AUX_Z,     Key_Z);
auxKeyFunc(AUX_O,     Key_O);
auxKeyFunc(AUX_P,     Key_P);

    auxIdleFunc(do_simulation);

    auxMainLoop(draw);
}
```

The main program at the end of Listing 7.1 calls function **initialize_OpenGL_graphics()** to create a graphics window; set up a callback function for handling window resizing, enabling Z buffer depth sorting; set up parameters for a single light source; and set up the parameters for perspective. The global variables latitude and longitude are initialized to 0; these variables are modified by the following keyboard event callback functions:

Key_left_arrow()

Key_right_arrow()

Key_up_arrow()

Key_down_arrow()

The window drawing callback function **draw** uses the values of latitude and longitude to set the viewing eye point. The global variable radius is used to set the distance of the viewing eye point from the origin (0, 0, 0). The value of the global variable radius is modified by the following keyboard event callback functions:

Key_Z() // zoom in

Key_O() // zoom out

The function **draw** prints text messages at the top of the OpenGL display window indicating the current state of the space-ship simulation, then loops over all instances of class **game_object** contained in the instance of class **World**. Depending on the type of object, function **draw** calls one of the following functions to render a 3D object:

plot_pr_ship(int x, int y, int z)

plot_player(int x, int y, int z)

plot_crogan(int x, int y, int z)

plot_asteroid(int x, int y, int z)

The coordinates (x, y, z) specify the object's location in the simulated asteroid field. When function **draw** is done drawing all the game objects, it calls the OpenGL auxiliary library function **auxSwapBuffers()** to show the current scene. This example program uses double graphics buffering; while one graphics buffer is displayed, the program renders objects into the other graphics buffer. Figure 7.3 shows the open GL graphics window.

Listing 7.2 shows a utility from Silicon Graphics Inc., the original designer of OpenGL, to create OpenGL display lists for a simple font. It is not necessary to understand the operation of function **print_string** in this listing in order to use the example program in Listing 7.1; it is included for completeness.

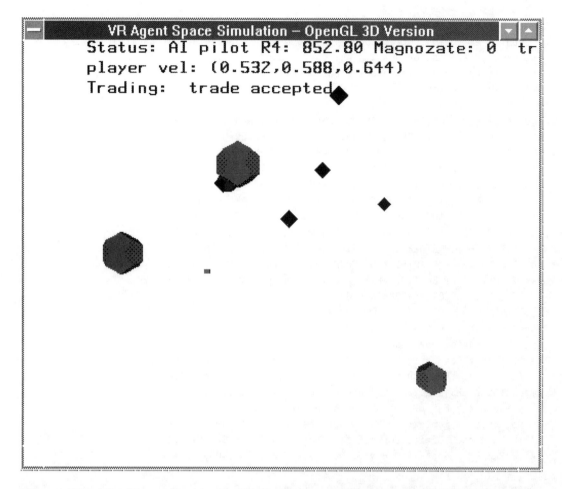

Figure 7.3   The Player ship has just finished mining Magnozate ore at the asteroid at the upper center of the display. Almost immediately, the Player ship traded this Magnozate ore with the Processor ship just below the asteroid in the display.

Listing 7.2

```
/*
 * (c) Copyright 1993, Silicon Graphics, Inc.

Disclaimer for Sample Applications that contain SGI copyright notice


ALL RIGHTS RESERVED
Permission to use, copy, modify, and distribute this software for
any purpose and without fee is hereby granted, provided that the above
```

```
 */
#include "glos.h"

#include <GL/gl.h>
#include <GL/glu.h>
#include <GL/glaux.h>

void myinit(void);
void makeRasterFont(void);
void printString(char *s);
```

```
GLubyte rasters[][13] = {
{0x00,0x00,0x00,0x00,0x00,0x00,0x00,0x00,0x00,0x00,0x00,0x00,0x00},
{0x00,0x00,0x18,0x18,0x00,0x00,0x18,0x18,0x18,0x18,0x18,0x18,0x18},
{0x00,0x00,0x00,0x00,0x00,0x00,0x00,0x00,0x00,0x36,0x36,0x36,0x36},
{0x00,0x00,0x00,0x66,0x66,0xff,0x66,0x66,0xff,0x66,0x66,0x00,0x00},
{0x00,0x00,0x18,0x7e,0xff,0x1b,0x1f,0x7e,0xf8,0xd8,0xff,0x7e,0x18},
{0x00,0x00,0x0e,0x1b,0xdb,0x6e,0x30,0x18,0x0c,0x76,0xdb,0xd8,0x70},
{0x00,0x00,0x7f,0xc6,0xcf,0xd8,0x70,0x70,0xd8,0xcc,0xcc,0x6c,0x38},
{0x00,0x00,0x00,0x00,0x00,0x00,0x00,0x00,0x00,0x18,0x1c,0x0c,0x0e},
{0x00,0x00,0x0c,0x18,0x30,0x30,0x30,0x30,0x30,0x30,0x30,0x18,0x0c},
{0x00,0x00,0x30,0x18,0x0c,0x0c,0x0c,0x0c,0x0c,0x0c,0x0c,0x18,0x30},
{0x00,0x00,0x00,0x00,0x99,0x5a,0x3c,0xff,0x3c,0x5a,0x99,0x00,0x00},
{0x00,0x00,0x00,0x18,0x18,0x18,0xff,0xff,0x18,0x18,0x18,0x00,0x00},
{0x00,0x00,0x30,0x18,0x1c,0x1c,0x00,0x00,0x00,0x00,0x00,0x00,0x00},
{0x00,0x00,0x00,0x00,0x00,0x00,0xff,0xff,0x00,0x00,0x00,0x00,0x00},
{0x00,0x00,0x00,0x38,0x38,0x00,0x00,0x00,0x00,0x00,0x00,0x00,0x00},
{0x00,0x60,0x60,0x30,0x30,0x18,0x18,0x0c,0x0c,0x06,0x06,0x03,0x03},
{0x00,0x00,0x3c,0x66,0xc3,0xe3,0xf3,0xdb,0xcf,0xc7,0xc3,0x66,0x3c},
{0x00,0x00,0x7e,0x18,0x18,0x18,0x18,0x18,0x18,0x18,0x78,0x38,0x18},
{0x00,0x00,0xff,0xc0,0xc0,0x60,0x30,0x18,0x0c,0x06,0x03,0xe7,0x7e},
{0x00,0x00,0x7e,0xe7,0x03,0x03,0x07,0x7e,0x07,0x03,0x03,0xe7,0x7e},
{0x00,0x00,0x0c,0x0c,0x0c,0x0c,0x0c,0xff,0xcc,0x6c,0x3c,0x1c,0x0c},
{0x00,0x00,0x7e,0xe7,0x03,0x03,0x07,0xfe,0xc0,0xc0,0xc0,0xc0,0xff},
{0x00,0x00,0x7e,0xe7,0xc3,0xc3,0xc7,0xfe,0xc0,0xc0,0xc0,0xe7,0x7e},
{0x00,0x00,0x30,0x30,0x30,0x30,0x18,0x0c,0x06,0x03,0x03,0x03,0xff},
{0x00,0x00,0x7e,0xe7,0xc3,0xc3,0xe7,0x7e,0xe7,0xc3,0xc3,0xe7,0x7e},
{0x00,0x00,0x7e,0xe7,0x03,0x03,0x03,0x7f,0xe7,0xc3,0xc3,0xe7,0x7e},
{0x00,0x00,0x00,0x38,0x38,0x00,0x00,0x38,0x38,0x00,0x00,0x00,0x00},
{0x00,0x00,0x30,0x18,0x1c,0x1c,0x00,0x00,0x1c,0x1c,0x00,0x00,0x00},
{0x00,0x00,0x06,0x0c,0x18,0x30,0x60,0xc0,0x60,0x30,0x18,0x0c,0x06},
{0x00,0x00,0x00,0x00,0xff,0xff,0x00,0xff,0xff,0x00,0x00,0x00,0x00},
{0x00,0x00,0x60,0x30,0x18,0x0c,0x06,0x03,0x06,0x0c,0x18,0x30,0x60},
{0x00,0x00,0x18,0x00,0x00,0x18,0x18,0x0c,0x06,0x03,0xc3,0xc3,0x7e},
{0x00,0x00,0x3f,0x60,0xcf,0xdb,0xd3,0xdd,0xc3,0x7e,0x00,0x00,0x00},
{0x00,0x00,0xc3,0xc3,0xc3,0xc3,0xff,0xc3,0xc3,0xc3,0x66,0x3c,0x18},
{0x00,0x00,0xfe,0xc7,0xc3,0xc3,0xc7,0xfe,0xc7,0xc3,0xc3,0xc7,0xfe},
{0x00,0x00,0x7e,0xe7,0xc0,0xc0,0xc0,0xc0,0xc0,0xc0,0xc0,0xe7,0x7e},
{0x00,0x00,0xfc,0xce,0xc7,0xc3,0xc3,0xc3,0xc3,0xc3,0xc7,0xce,0xfc},
{0x00,0x00,0xff,0xc0,0xc0,0xc0,0xc0,0xfc,0xc0,0xc0,0xc0,0xc0,0xff},
{0x00,0x00,0xc0,0xc0,0xc0,0xc0,0xc0,0xc0,0xfc,0xc0,0xc0,0xc0,0xff},
{0x00,0x00,0x7e,0xe7,0xc3,0xc3,0xcf,0xc0,0xc0,0xc0,0xc0,0xe7,0x7e},
{0x00,0x00,0xc3,0xc3,0xc3,0xc3,0xc3,0xff,0xc3,0xc3,0xc3,0xc3,0xc3},
{0x00,0x00,0x7e,0x18,0x18,0x18,0x18,0x18,0x18,0x18,0x18,0x18,0x7e},
```

```
{0x00,0x00,0x7c,0xee,0xc6,0x06,0x06,0x06,0x06,0x06,0x06,0x06,0x06},
{0x00,0x00,0xc3,0xc6,0xcc,0xd8,0xf0,0xe0,0xf0,0xd8,0xcc,0xc6,0xc3},
{0x00,0x00,0xff,0xc0,0xc0,0xc0,0xc0,0xc0,0xc0,0xc0,0xc0,0xc0,0xc0},
{0x00,0x00,0xc3,0xc3,0xc3,0xc3,0xc3,0xc3,0xdb,0xff,0xff,0xe7,0xc3},
{0x00,0x00,0xc7,0xc7,0xcf,0xcf,0xdf,0xdb,0xfb,0xf3,0xf3,0xe3,0xe3},
{0x00,0x00,0x7e,0xe7,0xc3,0xc3,0xc3,0xc3,0xc3,0xc3,0xc3,0xe7,0x7e},
{0x00,0x00,0xc0,0xc0,0xc0,0xc0,0xc0,0xfe,0xc7,0xc3,0xc3,0xc7,0xfe},
{0x00,0x00,0x3f,0x6e,0xdf,0xdb,0xc3,0xc3,0xc3,0xc3,0xc3,0x66,0x3c},
{0x00,0x00,0xc3,0xc6,0xcc,0xd8,0xf0,0xfe,0xc7,0xc3,0xc3,0xc7,0xfe},
{0x00,0x00,0x7e,0xe7,0x03,0x03,0x07,0x7e,0xe0,0xc0,0xc0,0xe7,0x7e},
{0x00,0x00,0x18,0x18,0x18,0x18,0x18,0x18,0x18,0x18,0x18,0x18,0xff},
{0x00,0x00,0x7e,0xe7,0xc3,0xc3,0xc3,0xc3,0xc3,0xc3,0xc3,0xc3,0xc3},
{0x00,0x00,0x18,0x3c,0x3c,0x66,0x66,0xc3,0xc3,0xc3,0xc3,0xc3,0xc3},
{0x00,0x00,0xc3,0xe7,0xff,0xff,0xdb,0xdb,0xc3,0xc3,0xc3,0xc3,0xc3},
{0x00,0x00,0xc3,0x66,0x66,0x3c,0x3c,0x18,0x3c,0x3c,0x66,0x66,0xc3},
{0x00,0x00,0x18,0x18,0x18,0x18,0x18,0x18,0x3c,0x3c,0x66,0x66,0xc3},
{0x00,0x00,0xff,0xc0,0xc0,0x60,0x30,0x7e,0x0c,0x06,0x03,0x03,0xff},
{0x00,0x00,0x3c,0x30,0x30,0x30,0x30,0x30,0x30,0x30,0x30,0x30,0x3c},
{0x00,0x03,0x03,0x06,0x06,0x0c,0x0c,0x18,0x18,0x30,0x30,0x60,0x60},
{0x00,0x00,0x3c,0x0c,0x0c,0x0c,0x0c,0x0c,0x0c,0x0c,0x0c,0x0c,0x3c},
{0x00,0x00,0x00,0x00,0x00,0x00,0x00,0x00,0x00,0xc3,0x66,0x3c,0x18},
{0xff,0xff,0x00,0x00,0x00,0x00,0x00,0x00,0x00,0x00,0x00,0x00,0x00},
{0x00,0x00,0x00,0x00,0x00,0x00,0x00,0x00,0x00,0x18,0x38,0x30,0x70},
{0x00,0x00,0x7f,0xc3,0xc3,0x7f,0x03,0xc3,0x7e,0x00,0x00,0x00,0x00},
{0x00,0x00,0xfe,0xc3,0xc3,0xc3,0xc3,0xfe,0xc0,0xc0,0xc0,0xc0,0xc0},
{0x00,0x00,0x7e,0xc3,0xc0,0xc0,0xc0,0xc3,0x7e,0x00,0x00,0x00,0x00},
{0x00,0x00,0x7f,0xc3,0xc3,0xc3,0xc3,0x7f,0x03,0x03,0x03,0x03,0x03},
{0x00,0x00,0x7f,0xc0,0xc0,0xfe,0xc3,0xc3,0x7e,0x00,0x00,0x00,0x00},
{0x00,0x00,0x30,0x30,0x30,0x30,0x30,0xfc,0x30,0x30,0x30,0x33,0x1e},
{0x7e,0xc3,0x03,0x03,0x7f,0xc3,0xc3,0xc3,0x7e,0x00,0x00,0x00,0x00},
{0x00,0x00,0xc3,0xc3,0xc3,0xc3,0xc3,0xc3,0xfe,0xc0,0xc0,0xc0,0xc0},
{0x00,0x00,0x18,0x18,0x18,0x18,0x18,0x18,0x18,0x00,0x00,0x18,0x00},
{0x38,0x6c,0x0c,0x0c,0x0c,0x0c,0x0c,0x0c,0x0c,0x00,0x00,0x0c,0x00},
{0x00,0x00,0xc6,0xcc,0xf8,0xf0,0xd8,0xcc,0xc6,0xc0,0xc0,0xc0,0xc0},
{0x00,0x00,0x7e,0x18,0x18,0x18,0x18,0x18,0x18,0x18,0x18,0x18,0x78},
{0x00,0x00,0xdb,0xdb,0xdb,0xdb,0xdb,0xdb,0xfe,0x00,0x00,0x00,0x00},
{0x00,0x00,0xc6,0xc6,0xc6,0xc6,0xc6,0xc6,0xfc,0x00,0x00,0x00,0x00},
{0x00,0x00,0x7c,0xc6,0xc6,0xc6,0xc6,0xc6,0x7c,0x00,0x00,0x00,0x00},
{0xc0,0xc0,0xc0,0xfe,0xc3,0xc3,0xc3,0xc3,0xfe,0x00,0x00,0x00,0x00},
{0x03,0x03,0x03,0x7f,0xc3,0xc3,0xc3,0xc3,0x7f,0x00,0x00,0x00,0x00},
{0x00,0x00,0xc0,0xc0,0xc0,0xc0,0xc0,0xe0,0xfe,0x00,0x00,0x00,0x00},
{0x00,0x00,0xfe,0x03,0x03,0x7e,0xc0,0xc0,0x7f,0x00,0x00,0x00,0x00},
{0x00,0x00,0x1c,0x36,0x30,0x30,0x30,0x30,0xfc,0x30,0x30,0x30,0x00},
{0x00,0x00,0x7e,0xc6,0xc6,0xc6,0xc6,0xc6,0xc6,0x00,0x00,0x00,0x00},
```

```
{0x00,0x00,0x18,0x3c,0x3c,0x66,0x66,0xc3,0xc3,0x00,0x00,0x00,0x00},
{0x00,0x00,0xc3,0xe7,0xff,0xdb,0xc3,0xc3,0xc3,0x00,0x00,0x00,0x00},
{0x00,0x00,0xc3,0x66,0x3c,0x18,0x3c,0x66,0xc3,0x00,0x00,0x00,0x00},
{0xc0,0x60,0x60,0x30,0x18,0x3c,0x66,0x66,0xc3,0x00,0x00,0x00,0x00},
{0x00,0x00,0xff,0x60,0x30,0x18,0x0c,0x06,0xff,0x00,0x00,0x00,0x00},
{0x00,0x00,0x0f,0x18,0x18,0x18,0x38,0xf0,0x38,0x18,0x18,0x18,0x0f},
{0x18,0x18,0x18,0x18,0x18,0x18,0x18,0x18,0x18,0x18,0x18,0x18,0x18},
{0x00,0x00,0xf0,0x18,0x18,0x18,0x1c,0x0f,0x1c,0x18,0x18,0x18,0xf0},
{0x00,0x00,0x00,0x00,0x00,0x00,0x06,0x8f,0xf1,0x60,0x00,0x00,0x00}
};

GLuint fontOffset;

void makeRasterFont(void)
{
    GLuint i;
    glPixelStorei(GL_UNPACK_ALIGNMENT, 1);

    fontOffset = glGenLists (128);
    for (i = 32; i < 127; i++) {
       glNewList(i+fontOffset, GL_COMPILE);
       glBitmap(8, 13, 0.0, 2.0, 10.0, 0.0, rasters[i-32]);
       glEndList();
    }
}

void font_init(void)
{
    glShadeModel (GL_FLAT);
    makeRasterFont();
}

static GLfloat white_color[3] = {1.0, 1.0, 1.0};

void print_string(int x, int y, char *str, int len)
{
   float xx = (((float)x) - 600.0) / 300.0;
   float yy = ((600.0 - (float)y)) / 300.0;

   glRasterPos2f(xx, yy);
   glPushAttrib(GL_LIST_BIT);
     glColor3fv(white_color);
     glListBase(fontOffset);
```

```
    glCallLists(len, GL_UNSIGNED_BYTE, (GLubyte *)str);
  glPopAttrib();
  glFlush();
}
```

Figure 7.4 shows the spaceship simulation running an Open GL window.

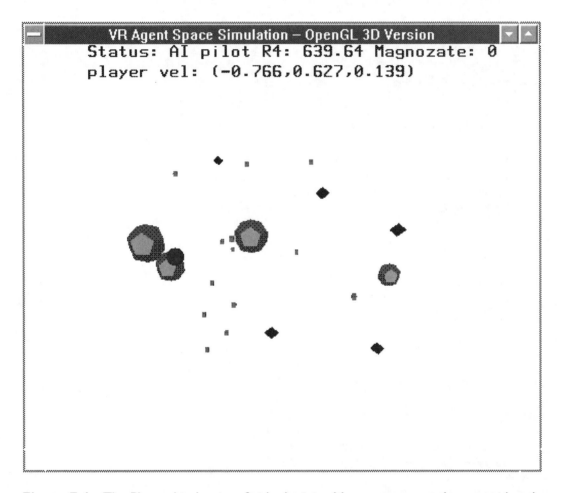

Figure 7.4   The Player ship has just finished mining Magnozate ore at the asteroid at the left center of the display. Compared with Figure 7.3, the viewing angle has been rotated using the keyboard arrow keys.

Space Game Implemented with 2D Graphics for Windows

Chapter 5 contained the design and implementation of a space simulation program with three types of computer-controlled ships. In this chapter, we constrain the spaceship and asteroid positions to lie on a two-dimensional plane, and add control logic so that a human player can take over control of the Player ship from the AI agent. Figure 8.1 shows a screen image of the Windows version of the 2D spaceship sample game.

In the game shown in Figure 8.1, the human player can take control of the Player ship by pressing the P key on the keyboard (either upper- or lowercase works). When in the manual play mode, the arrow keys can be used to move between asteroids and Processor ships, avoiding Crogan ships if possible. As a game, this example program is not very challenging, but it serves to bring together three important themes in this book:

237

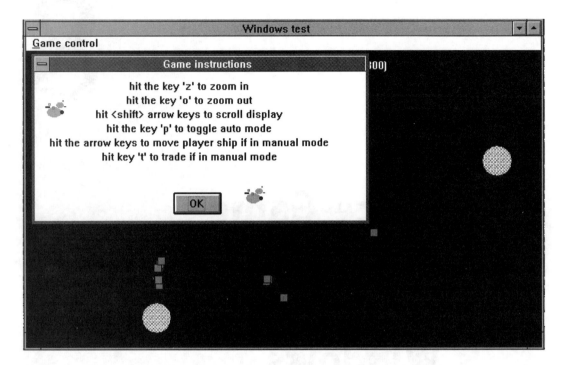

Figure 8.1   Two-dimensional spaceship sample game for Microsoft Windows 3.1. Asteroids appear as large textured circles. The Player ship is a small red circle, the Crogan ships appear as green squares, and the Processor ships appear as blue rectangles. The help screen overlaying the game window shows the available keyboard commands. The Player ship is obscured here by the dialog box.

- Creating C++ VR Agent Toolkit game objects that maintain state (position, velocity, acceleration, quantity of fuel on hand) and that use software agents created with the AI utility classes developed in Chapter 2.

- Real-time graphics display (the Windows timer is used to update the graphics window).

- Changing the state of the game world by interaction with the game player.

I anticipate that the first thing that many readers of this book will want to try is to retrofit an existing game that they have written using at least the AI C++ classes developed in Chapter 2, and possibly the complete VR Agent Toolkit to manage both the state and behavior of game objects. If this is intent, then the simple program shown in Listing 8.1 will serve as an example of using the VR Agent Toolkit in game implementations. Figure 8.2 shows a Harel state transition diagram for the Windows 3.1 version of the example spaceship game.

As seen in Figure 8.2, when the program starts, the application initialization for the Microsoft Windows environment is performed, then a data setup function is called that creates an instance of C++ class **World**, a set of contained instances of class **game_object**, and the instances of classes derived from C++ class **Agent** to control the

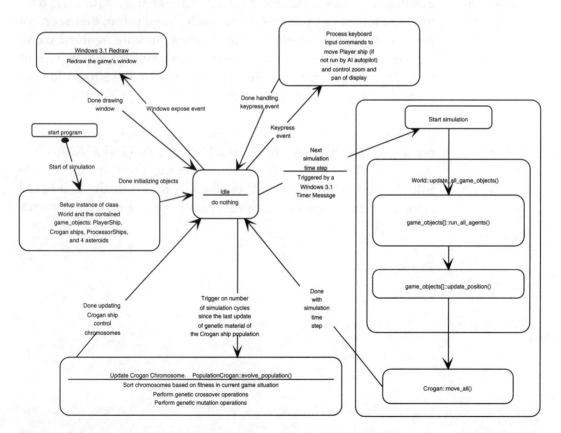

Figure 8.2 Harel state transition diagram for the Windows 3.1 version of the example spaceship game.

instances of class **game_object**. The following two update functions are called each time step:

World::update_all_game_objects()

Crogan::move_all()

The function **World::update_all_game_objects()** simply calls the functions **game_object::run_all_agents()** and **game_object::update_position()** for each instance of class **game_object** contained in the **World** data object.

The Crogan ships are handled differently. The C++ class **Crogan** is derived, using public inheritance, from the C++ class **genetic** developed in Chapter 2. Class **Crogan** uses static class data to maintain control parameters for each Crogan ship; these control parameters are encoded in chromosomes, and are evolved using a genetic algorithm. The chromosomes controlling the behavior of the Crogan ships are modified periodically by the simulation, so that the Crogan ships can optimize their strategy for the current game situation.

The 2D space game developed in this chapter is created by replacing the file TXT_GAME.CPP (file SRC\TXT_GAME\TXT_GAME.CPP on the CD-ROM) with the file TEST_WIN.CPP (file SRC\WIN31\TEST_WIN.CPP on the CD-ROM) in the text-based simulation developed in Chapter 5. Listing 8.1 shows the contents of TEST_WIN.CPP.

Listing 8.1

```
// File: test_win.cpp
//
// Description: This file uses the C++ classes:
//
//                ExpertSystem
//                Neural
//                genetic
//                Agent
//                World
//
// Copyright 1995, Mark Watson
//
```

```
#include "world.h"
#include "agent.h"
#include "expert.h"
#include "genetic.h"
#include "game_val.h"
#include "crogan.h"
#include "pr_ship.h"
#include "player.h"

#include "out_log.h"

#include <stdlib.h>
#include <string.h>
#include <time.h>

// For debug output to log file:
#define GENERATE_LOG

OutputLog *outLog = NULL;

// GLOBAL flag to control automatic/manual mode for player ship:
static int AUTOMATIC_MODE = 1;

// Pointer to game World object:
World *world;

// Pointer to the Crogan genetic population object:
Crogan *crogan;

// Pointer to the player's ship:
PlayerShip *player_ship = NULL;

// x and y acceleration components for manual mode player ship operation:
static float x_acc;
static float y_acc;

// x and y velocity components for manual mode player ship operation:
static float x_vel;
static float y_vel;

// Protoype for single function in setup.cpp:
void world_setup(World *w);
```

```c
#include <windows.h>
#include <stdio.h>
#include <malloc.h>
#include "test_win.h"

HANDLE hInstance;

static void HandleTimer(HWND window)
{
    HDC dc;
    static float direction = 0.01;
    static float x = 0.0;
    static int count = 0;
    float xa, ya, za, dummy;

    if (AUTOMATIC_MODE == 0) {
        if (player_ship->get_R4() < 1) {
            x_acc = y_acc = 0;
            player_ship->set_velocity(0.0, 0.0, 0.0);
            player_ship->set_acceleration(0.0, 0.0, 0.0);
        } else {
            player_ship->set_automatic_flag(0);
            player_ship->get_acceleration(xa, ya, za);
            xa += x_acc;
            ya += y_acc;
            x_acc = y_acc = 0.0;

            // Set Z coordinate to center of asteroid field for 2D game:
            za = Z_CENTER;

            // modification: it is too difficult for human pilots
            //               to navigate using real physics, so
            //               use the arrow keys as "thrusters"
            //               which have a momentary effect only
            //               (i.e., no conservation of momentum here!):
            xa *= 0.95;
            ya *= 0.95;
            player_ship->set_acceleration(xa, ya, za);
            x_acc = 0;
            y_acc = 0;
            player_ship->get_velocity(x_vel, y_vel, dummy);
            x_vel *= 0.95;
            y_vel *= 0.95;
```

```
            player_ship->set_velocity(x_vel, y_vel, 0.0);
        }
    } else {
        player_ship->set_automatic_flag(1);
        player_ship->get_velocity(x_vel, y_vel, dummy);
    }

    // Move the game objects, and periodically update
    // the crogan population:
    world->update_all_game_objects();
    crogan->move_all();

    static int crogan_update_count = 0;
    if (crogan_update_count++ > 100) {
        crogan_update_count = 0;
        crogan->evolve_population();
    }
}


BOOL FAR PASCAL AboutDlgProc(HWND hwnd, WORD msg,
                             WORD wparam, LONG lparam)
{

    switch(msg) {
    case WM_INITDIALOG:
        return(TRUE);

    case WM_COMMAND:
        if(LOWORD(wparam) == IDOK) {
            EndDialog(hwnd, TRUE);
            return(TRUE);
        }
        break;
    }
    return(FALSE);

}


LONG _EXPORT FAR PASCAL WindowProc(HWND hwnd, unsigned msg,
                                   UINT wparam, LONG lparam)
{
```

```
FARPROC             proc;
HDC                 hdc;
PAINTSTRUCT         ps;
RECT                rect;
HBRUSH              brush;

static FARPROC lpfnAboutDlgProc;

static int first_call = 1;
static HBRUSH background_brush;
static HBRUSH crogan_brush;
static HBRUSH pr_ship_brush;
static HBRUSH player_brush;
static HBRUSH asteroid_brush;

static float scale = 1.0;
static int x_offset = 120;
static int y_offset = 90;

int num_objects;
int count_pr_ship;
int count_crogan;
int count_asteroid;
int g;

static int special_message_count = 0;
static char special_message[80];

static char *trade_status[] =
     {"trade not accepted"," ", "trade accepted"};
static char *mining_status[] = {" ", "mining Magnozate"};
static char *pilot_status[] = {"Human pilot", "AI pilot"};
game_object * g_obj;

switch(msg) {
case WM_CREATE:

    lpfnAboutDlgProc =
        MakeProcInstance((FARPROC)AboutDlgProc, hInstance);
    background_brush = CreateSolidBrush(RGB(0, 0, 0));
    crogan_brush     = CreateSolidBrush(RGB(0, 255, 0));
    pr_ship_brush    = CreateSolidBrush(RGB(0, 0, 255));
```

```
        player_brush    = CreateSolidBrush(RGB(255, 0, 0));
        asteroid_brush  = CreateSolidBrush(RGB(200, 210, 220));

        // Create all game objects *before* setting up
        // the Windows timer:

        // Create an output log file:
#ifdef GENERATE_LOG
        outLog = new OutputLog("game.log");
#endif

        OutputLog::write("Creating instance of C++ class 'World'...\n");

        world = new World();
        OutputLog::write(" ... placing objects in the world...\n");
        world_setup(world);
        // Add in the Crogans
        OutputLog::write("Creating Crogans...\n");
        crogan = new Crogan(world, "crogan.dat");

        OutputLog::write("\nEntering Windows event loop...\n");

        // Now, set up the Window's timer:
        SetTimer(hwnd, 1, 20, NULL);
        return 0L;

    case WM_COMMAND:
        switch(LOWORD(wparam)) {
        case MENU_1:
            DialogBox(hInstance, "Directions", hwnd, lpfnAboutDlgProc);
            break;
        case ZOOM_IN:
            scale *= 1.3;
            break;
        case ZOOM_OUT:
            scale /= 1.3;
            break;
        case TOGGLE:
            // Toggle between automatic play mode for player ship
            // and manual mode:
            AUTOMATIC_MODE = 1 - AUTOMATIC_MODE;
            break;
```

```
        }
    break;

case WM_KEYDOWN:
    switch (LOWORD(wparam)) {
        case VK_UP:
            if (GetKeyState(VK_SHIFT) > -1) {
                y_acc -= 0.05;
            } else {
                y_offset -= 10;
            }
            break;
        case VK_DOWN:
            if (GetKeyState(VK_SHIFT) > -1) {
                y_acc += 0.05;
            } else {
                y_offset += 10;
            }
            break;
        case VK_RIGHT:
            if (GetKeyState(VK_SHIFT) > -1) {
                x_acc += 0.05;
            } else {
                x_offset += 10;
            }
            break;
        case VK_LEFT:
            if (GetKeyState(VK_SHIFT) > -1) {
                x_acc -= 0.05;
            } else {
                x_offset -= 10;
            }
            break;
        default:
            break;
    }
case WM_TIMER:
    HandleTimer(hwnd);
    InvalidateRect(hwnd, NULL, FALSE);
    return 0L;

case WM_DESTROY:
    PostQuitMessage(0);
    break;
```

```
case WM_PAINT:

    hdc = BeginPaint (hwnd, &ps);
    // Erase the window:
    FillRect(hdc, &ps.rcPaint, background_brush);

    // Print out the status line:
    static char status_buf[131], accel_buf[90];
    sprintf(accel_buf,"player vel: (%5.3f,%5.3f)",
            x_vel, y_vel);

    float R4;
    int magnozate;
    int trade_type, mining_type;
    if (player_ship != NULL) {
        trade_type = player_ship->get_trading_flag() + 1;
        if (trade_type == 2)  MessageBeep(0);
        mining_type = player_ship->get_mining_flag();
        if (mining_type == 1)   MessageBeep(0);
        R4 = player_ship->get_R4();
        magnozate = player_ship->get_Magnozate();
    } else {
        trade_type = 1;
        mining_type = 0;
        R4 = 0;
        magnozate = 0;
    }
    sprintf(status_buf,
            "Status: %s R4: %6.2f Magnozate: %d  %s %s %s",
            pilot_status[AUTOMATIC_MODE], R4, magnozate,
            trade_status[trade_type],
            mining_status[mining_type], accel_buf);
    SetTextColor(hdc, RGB(255, 255, 255));
    SetBkColor(hdc, RGB(0, 0, 0));
    TextOut(hdc, 15, 10, status_buf, strlen(status_buf));
    if (special_message_count < 1) {
        if (trade_type != 1) {
            special_message_count = 15;
            sprintf(special_message,"Trading:  %s",
                    trade_status[trade_type]);
        }
        if (mining_type != 0) {
            special_message_count = 15;
```

```
            sprintf(special_message,"%s", mining_status[mining_type]);
      }
}
if (special_message_count-- > 0) {
   TextOut(hdc, 15, 26, special_message,
            strlen(special_message));
}
if (special_message_count < 0) special_message_count = 0;


// Loop through all instances of game_object in the game world:
num_objects = world->number_of_game_objects();
count_pr_ship = 0;
count_crogan = 0;
count_asteroid = 0;
for (g=0; g<num_objects; g++) {
   g_obj = &(world->get_game_object(g));
   int x, y, z;
   g_obj->get_position(x, y, z);
   g_obj->set_position(x, y, 0);
   x += x_offset;
   y += y_offset;
   x *= scale;
   y *= scale;

   OutputLog::write("Moving object ");

   int crogan_scale, pr_ship_scale,
       player_scale, asteroid_scale;
   crogan_scale = 5 * scale;
   pr_ship_scale = 4 * scale;
   player_scale = 7 * scale;
   asteroid_scale = 20 * scale;

   if (g_obj->get_type() == PROCESSOR) {
       SelectObject(hdc, pr_ship_brush);
       Rectangle(hdc, x -  2 * pr_ship_scale,
                    y - pr_ship_scale,
                    x + 2 * pr_ship_scale + 1,
                    y + pr_ship_scale + 1);
       OutputLog::write("(processor ship) ");
   }
```

```
            if (g_obj->get_type() == PLAYER) {
                SelectObject(hdc, player_brush);
                Ellipse(hdc, x - player_scale, y - player_scale,
                             x + player_scale + 1, y + player_scale + 1);
                OutputLog::write("(player ship) ");
                player_ship = (PlayerShip *)g_obj;
            }
            if (g_obj->get_type() == CROGAN) {
                SelectObject(hdc, crogan_brush);
                Rectangle(hdc, x- crogan_scale, y - crogan_scale,
                          x + crogan_scale + 1, y + crogan_scale + 1);
                OutputLog::write("(Crogan ship) ");
            }
            if (g_obj->get_type() == ASTEROID) {
                SelectObject(hdc, asteroid_brush);
                Ellipse(hdc, x - asteroid_scale, y - asteroid_scale,
                             x + asteroid_scale, y + asteroid_scale);
                OutputLog::write("(asteroid) ");
            }
            OutputLog::write(x);
            OutputLog::write(", ");
            OutputLog::write(y);
            OutputLog::write(", ");
            OutputLog::write(z);
            OutputLog::write("\n");
        }


        EndPaint(hwnd, &ps);
        break;



    default:
        return(DefWindowProc(hwnd, msg, wparam, lparam));
    }
    return(0L);


}


static BOOL setup_windows_attributes(HANDLE this_inst)
{
    WNDCLASS    wc;
    BOOL        rc;
```

```
    /*
     * set up and register window class
     */
    wc.style = CS_HREDRAW | CS_VREDRAW;
    wc.lpfnWndProc = WindowProc;
    wc.cbClsExtra = 0;
    wc.cbWndExtra = sizeof(DWORD);
    wc.hInstance = this_inst;
    wc.hIcon = LoadIcon(this_inst, "test_winIcon");
    wc.hCursor = LoadCursor(NULL, IDC_ARROW);
    wc.hbrBackground = GetStockObject(WHITE_BRUSH);
    wc.lpszMenuName = "test_winMenu";
    wc.lpszClassName = "test_win";
    rc = RegisterClass(&wc);
    return(rc);


}

int PASCAL WinMain(HANDLE this_inst, HANDLE prev_inst, LPSTR cmdline,
                   int cmdshow)
{
    MSG     msg;
    HANDLE hAccel;

    // Use the current time to randomize the state of the world:
    // randomize the stdlib random number generator:
    long t = time(NULL) % 1117;
    for (int d=0; d<t; d++)  random(4);

    hAccel = LoadAccelerators(this_inst, "GameAccelerators");
    hInstance = this_inst;
    if(!prev_inst) {
        if(!setup_windows_attributes(this_inst)) return(FALSE);
    }


    HWND        hwnd;

    // Create main window:
    hwnd = CreateWindow(
        "test_win",             /* class */
        "Windows test",          /* caption */
        WS_OVERLAPPEDWINDOW,     /* style */
        CW_USEDEFAULT,           /* init. x pos */
```

```
            CW_USEDEFAULT,        /* init. y pos */
            CW_USEDEFAULT,        /* init. x size */
            CW_USEDEFAULT,        /* init. y size */
            NULL,                 /* parent window */
            NULL,                 /* menu handle */
            this_inst,            /* program handle */
            NULL                  /* create parms */
        );

    if(!hwnd) return(FALSE);

    // Display window:

    ShowWindow(hwnd, cmdshow);
    UpdateWindow(hwnd);

    while(GetMessage(&msg, NULL, NULL, NULL)) {
        if (!TranslateAccelerator(hwnd, hAccel, &msg)) {
            TranslateMessage(&msg);
            DispatchMessage(&msg);
        }

    }
    delete outLog;
    return(msg.wParam);
}
```

The example game program in Listing 8.1 requires the following include files for using the entire VR Agent Toolkit:

```
world.h
agent.h
expert.h
genetic.h
out_log.h
```

The following include files were defined in Chapter 5 and are specific to the spaceship simulation:

```
game_val.h
crogan.h
pr_ship.h
player.h
```

The statement:

```
#define GENERATE\_LOG
```

should usually be commented out, since a multimegabyte log file can be created very quickly when playing the game with logging turned on. The global variable AUTOMATIC_MODE is used to enable or disable the software agent that can operate the Player ship. The prototype for function **world_setup()** prevents a forward reference for the call to this function (which is defined in the file TXT_GAME\SETUP.CPP) in the main program.

The real-time graphics display is triggered indirectly by a Windows timer event, which causes the simulation to run about 18 times a second. The spaceship simulation is performed in function **HandleTimer()**; the code in function **WindowProc()**, which handles timer messages, invalidates the entire window after calling **Handle-Timer()**. Invalidating the window causes a WM_PAINT message to be sent to the application. The code in function **WindowProc()**, which handles WM_PAINT messages, displays text at the top of the window, providing a summary of the state of the game, then paints the graphics window with an image of each game object.

The Microsoft Windows application setup is fairly standard. See Watson (1995) for additional information on Windows programming. Listing 8.2 shows the contents of file SRC\WIN31\TEST _WIN.RC on the CD-ROM.

Listing 8.2

```
#include "windows.h"
#include "test_win.h"

test_winIcon ICON test_win.ico
test_winMenu MENU
BEGIN
    POPUP "&Game control"
    BEGIN
        MENUITEM "Directions", MENU_1
    END
END

Directions DIALOG 22, 17, 218, 95
STYLE DS_MODALFRAME | WS_CAPTION | WS_SYSMENU
```

```
CAPTION "Game instructions"
BEGIN
    CTEXT "hit the key 'z' to zoom in", -1, 0,  5, 203, 8
    CTEXT "hit the key 'o' to zoom out", -1, 0, 14, 203, 8
    CTEXT "hit <shift> arrow keys to scroll display", -1, 0, 23, 203, 8
    CTEXT "hit the key 'p' to toggle auto mode", -1, 0, 32, 203, 8
    CTEXT "hit the arrow keys to move player ship if in manual mode",
        -1, 0, 41, 203, 8
    CTEXT "hit key 't' to trade if in manual mode", -1, 0, 50, 203, 8
    DEFPUSHBUTTON "OK", IDOK, 91, 77, 32, 14, WS_GROUP
    ICON "test_winIcon", -1, 5,15,40,40
    ICON "test_winIcon", -1, 136,70,40,40
END
```

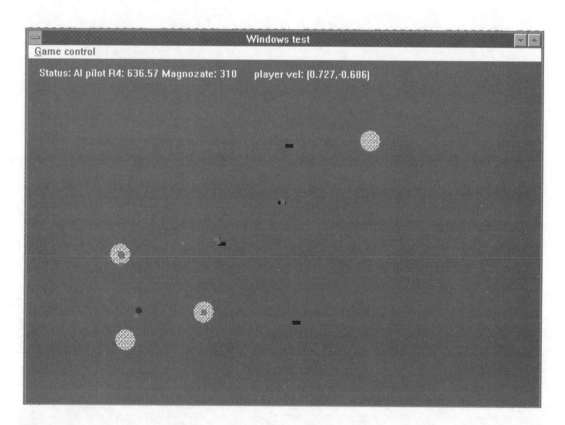

Figure 8.3 Crogan ships clustered around the Player ship and two asteroids in the lower left corner of the game display window.

```
GameAccelerators ACCELERATORS
{
    "z", ZOOM_IN
    "o", ZOOM_OUT
    "t", TRADE
    "p", TOGGLE
}
```

Space Game Implemented with 2D Graphics for Macintosh

Chapter 5 contained the design and implementation of a space simulation program with three types of computer-controlled ships. In this chapter, we constrain the spaceship and asteroid positions to lie on a two-dimensional plane, and add control logic so that a human player can take over control of the Player ship from the AI agent. I developed the Macintosh version of the 2D test program using the Symantec C++ compiler, version 6.0. I would like to thank Symantec for providing this compiler.

Figure 9.1 shows the Harel state transition diagram for the Macintosh version of the two-dimensional example spaceship game. Note in this figure that the example Macintosh game program starts by creating instances of VR Agent Toolkit classes **World**, **game_object**, **genetic**, **ExpertSystem**, and **PlanManager**. The program also creates instances of the class **NavigationAgent**, which is derived from the VR Agent Toolkit class **Agent**. After Macintosh-

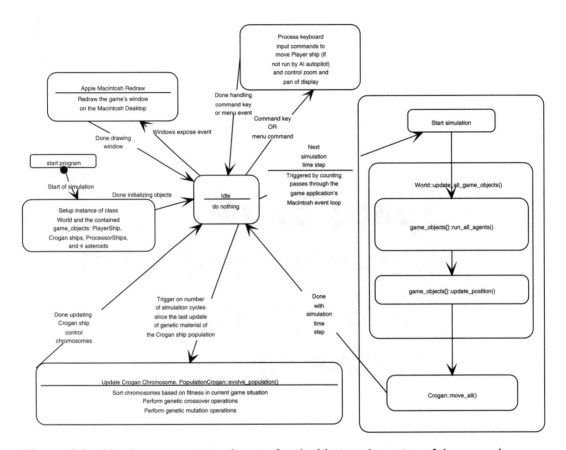

Figure 9.1 Harel state transition diagram for the Macintosh version of the example space-ship game.

specific setup is complete, the example program detailed in Listing 9.1 enters a standard Macintosh event loop (see Watson 1995).

A Macintosh application typically waits for some user interaction (via menus, keyboard, and mouse), which the program processes. When a Macintosh application is not redrawing an application window (due to an expose event) or responding to user interaction, it runs in an idle loop. The example game shown in Listing 9.1 is an atypical application because it continually runs the spaceship simulation while waiting for user interaction. The main program executes a continuous loop performing the following tasks:

- Checks for Macintosh mouse and keyboard events; processes any events.

- Runs the spaceship simulation; this is the same simulation that was developed in Chapter 5 except that all spaceships are constrained to lie in the X-Y plane (the Z coordinate is clamped to a zero value).

- Draws all game objects in the Macintosh document window.

Figure 9.2 shows the two-dimensional space game running on a Macintosh. In the game shown in this figure, the human player can take control of the Player ship by using the Toggle human/Agent control item on the Control menu. When in the manual play mode, other Control menu options allow you to maneuver between asteroids and Processor ships, avoiding Crogan ships if possible. As a game, this example program is not very challenging, but it serves to bring together three important themes in this book:

- Creating C++ VR Agent Toolkit game objects that maintain state (position, velocity, acceleration, quantity of fuel on hand) and that use software agents created with the AI utility classes developed in Chapter 2.

- Real-time graphics display (the graphics window is redrawn every time through the Macintosh event loop).

- Changing the state of the game world by interaction with the game player.

I anticipate that the first thing that many readers of this book will want to try is to retrofit an existing game that they have written using at least the AI C++ classes developed in Chapter 2, and possibly the complete VR Agent Toolkit to manage both the state and behavior of game objects. If this is the intent, then the sample program shown in Listing 9.1 will serve as an example of using the VR Agent Toolkit in game implementations. I would like to thank Symantec for providing the C++ compiler used to build the application shown in this listing. The window and menu setup code

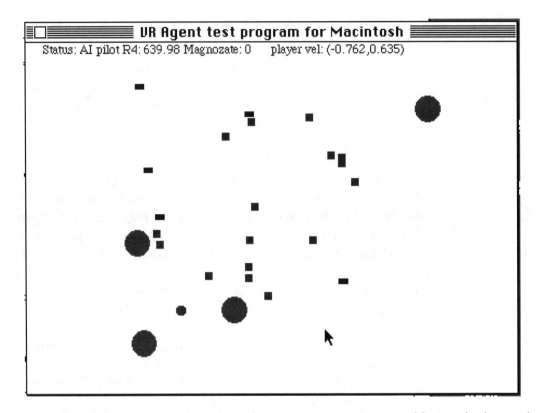

Figure 9.2 Two-dimensional version of space game running on a Macintosh. Asteroids appear as large pink solid circles, Crogan ships appear as small green squares, Processor ships appear as blue rectangles, and the Player ship appears as a small red-filled circle. The Apple Macintosh menu bar does not show in this figure. Menu items allow the player to control the Player ship, and zoom and pan the display.

for the Macintosh were derived from several of the programming examples provided with Symantec C++ version 6.

The 2D space game developed in this chapter is created by replacing the file TXT_GAME.CPP (file SRC\TXT_GAME\TXT_GAME.CPP on the CD-ROM) with the file MAC_GUI.CPP (file SRC\MAC\MAC_GUI.CPP on the CD-ROM). Listing 9.1 shows the contents of MAC_GUI.CPP.

Listing 9.1

```cpp
// File: GUI_MAC.CPP
//


#include "world.h"
#include "agent.h"
#include "expert.h"
#include "genetic.h"
#include "game_val.h"
#include "crogan.h"
#include "pr_ship.h"
#include "player.h"

#include "out_log.h"

#include <stdlib.h>
#include <string.h>

static int keep_running = 1;

// For debug output to log file:
//#define GENERATE_LOG

OutputLog *outLog = NULL;

// GLOBAL flag to control automatic/manual mode for player ship:
static int AUTOMATIC_MODE = 1;

// For scaling the graphics during "zoom in" and "zoom out":
static float scale = 0.6;



// Pointer to game World object:
static World *world;

// Pointer to the Crogan genetic population object:
Crogan *crogan;

// Pointer to the player's ship:
PlayerShip *player_ship = NULL;
```

```cpp
// x and y acceleration components for manual mode player ship operation:
static float x_acc;
static float y_acc;

// x and y velocity components for manual mode player ship operation:
static float x_vel;
static float y_vel;

// Protoype for single function in setup.cpp:
void world_setup(World *w);

// Utility to do periodic simlation calculations:

static void do_simulation()
{
    float xa, ya, za, dummy;

    if (AUTOMATIC_MODE == 0) {
        if (player_ship->get_R4() < 1) {
            x_acc = y_acc = 0;
            player_ship->set_velocity(0.0, 0.0, 0.0);
            player_ship->set_acceleration(0.0, 0.0, 0.0);
        } else {
            player_ship->set_automatic_flag(0);
            player_ship->get_acceleration(xa, ya, za);
            xa += x_acc;
            ya += y_acc;
            x_acc = y_acc = 0.0;
            za = 0.0;
            // modification: it is too difficult for human pilots
            //               to navigate using real physics, so
            //               use the arrow keys as "thrusters"
            //               which have a momentary effect only
            //               (i.e., no conservation of momentum here!):
            xa *= 0.95;
            ya *= 0.95;
            player_ship->set_acceleration(xa, ya, za);
            x_acc = 0;
            y_acc = 0;
            player_ship->get_velocity(x_vel, y_vel, dummy);
            x_vel *= 0.95;
            y_vel *= 0.95;
            player_ship->set_velocity(x_vel, y_vel, 0.0);
```

```
      }
   } else {
      player_ship->set_automatic_flag(1);
      player_ship->get_velocity(x_vel, y_vel, dummy);
   }

   // Move the game objects, and periodically update
   // the crogan population:
   world->update_all_game_objects();
   crogan->move_all();
   static int crogan_update_count = 0;
   if (crogan_update_count++ > 100) {
      crogan_update_count = 0;
      crogan->evolve_population();
   }
}


WindowPtr gui_macWindow;
Rect dragRect;
Rect windowBounds = { 45, 45, 360, 500 };


void Drawgui_mac()
{
   Rect myRect;
   int    color = true;

    static int x_offset = 120;
    static int y_offset = 50;

    int num_objects;
    int count_pr_ship;
    int count_crogan;
    int count_asteroid;
    int g;

    static int special_message_count = 0;
    static char special_message[80];

    static char *trade_status[] =
         {"trade not accepted"," ", "trade accepted"};
    static char *mining_status[] = {" ", "mining Magnozate"};
```

```c
static char *pilot_status[] = {"Human pilot", "AI pilot"};
game_object * g_obj;

SetPort(gui_macWindow);
EraseRect(&gui_macWindow->portRect);

// Print out the status line:
static char status_buf[131], accel_buf[90];
sprintf(accel_buf,"player vel: (%5.3f,%5.3f)",
        x_vel, y_vel);

float R4;
int magnozate;
int trade_type, mining_type;
if (player_ship != NULL) {
    trade_type = player_ship->get_trading_flag() + 1;
    if (trade_type == 2)  SysBeep(2);
    mining_type = player_ship->get_mining_flag();
    if (mining_type == 1) SysBeep(1);
    R4 = player_ship->get_R4();
    magnozate = player_ship->get_Magnozate();
} else {
    trade_type = 1;
    mining_type = 0;
    R4 = 0;
    magnozate = 0;
}
sprintf(status_buf,
        "Status: %s R4: %6.2f Magnozate: %d  %s %s %s",
        pilot_status[AUTOMATIC_MODE], R4, magnozate,
        trade_status[trade_type],
        mining_status[mining_type], accel_buf);

MoveTo(15, 10);
DrawText(status_buf, 0, strlen(status_buf));
if (special_message_count < 1) {
   if (trade_type != 1) {
      special_message_count = 15;
      sprintf(special_message,"Trading:  %s",
              trade_status[trade_type]);
   }
   if (mining_type != 0) {
```

```
        special_message_count = 15;
        sprintf(special_message,"%s", mining_status[mining_type]);
    }
}
if (special_message_count-- > 0) {
    MoveTo(15, 26);
    DrawText(special_message, 0, strlen(special_message));
}
if (special_message_count < 0) special_message_count = 0;



// Loop through all instances of game_object in the game world:
num_objects = world->number_of_game_objects();
count_pr_ship = 0;
count_crogan = 0;
count_asteroid = 0;
for (g=0; g<num_objects; g++) {
    g_obj = &(world->get_game_object(g));
    int x, y, z;
    g_obj->get_position(x, y, z);
    g_obj->set_position(x, y, 0);
    x += x_offset;
    y += y_offset;
    x *= scale;
    y *= scale;

    OutputLog::write("Moving object ");

    int crogan_scale, pr_ship_scale, player_scale, asteroid_scale;
    crogan_scale = 5 * scale;
    pr_ship_scale = 4 * scale;
    player_scale = 7 * scale;
    asteroid_scale = 20 * scale;

    if (g_obj->get_type() == PROCESSOR) {
      ForeColor(blueColor);
      SetRect(&myRect, x -  2 * pr_ship_scale,
                       y - pr_ship_scale,
                       x + 2 * pr_ship_scale + 1,
                       y + pr_ship_scale + 1);
      FillRect(&myRect, black);
      OutputLog::write("(processor ship) ");
    }
```

```
        if (g_obj->get_type() == PLAYER) {
          SetRect(&myRect, x - player_scale,
                           y - player_scale,
                           x + player_scale + 1,
                           y + player_scale + 1);
          ForeColor(redColor);
          FillOval(&myRect, black);
           OutputLog::write("(player ship) ");
           player_ship = (PlayerShip *)g_obj;
        }
        if (g_obj->get_type() == CROGAN) {
          SetRect(&myRect, x- crogan_scale,
                           y - crogan_scale,
                           x + crogan_scale + 1,
                           y + crogan_scale + 1);
          ForeColor(greenColor);
          FillRect(&myRect, black);
           OutputLog::write("(Crogan ship) ");
        }
        if (g_obj->get_type() == ASTEROID) {
          SetRect(&myRect, x - asteroid_scale,
                           y - asteroid_scale,
                           x + asteroid_scale,
                           y + asteroid_scale);
          ForeColor(magentaColor);
          FillOval(&myRect, black);
           OutputLog::write("(asteroid) ");
        }
        OutputLog::write(x);
        OutputLog::write(", ");
        OutputLog::write(y);
        OutputLog::write(", ");
        OutputLog::write(z);
        OutputLog::write("\n");
    }

}

void InitMac(void)
{
   MaxApplZone();
   InitGraf(&thePort);
```

```
   InitFonts();
   FlushEvents(everyEvent, 0);
   InitWindows();
   InitMenus();
   TEInit();
   InitDialogs(OL);
   InitCursor();

}


// Menu support:

MenuHandle appleMenu, fileMenu, controlMenu;
enum {appleID=1, fileID=2, controlID=3, quitItem=4};
enum {UP=10, DOWN=11, LEFT=12, RIGHT=13, ZOOM_IN=14,
      ZOOM_OUT=15, TOGGLE=16};

void SetUpMenu(void)
{
   InsertMenu(appleMenu = NewMenu(appleID, "\p\024"), 0);
   InsertMenu(fileMenu = NewMenu(fileID, "\pFile"), 0);
   InsertMenu(controlMenu = NewMenu(controlID, "\pControl"), 0);
   DrawMenuBar();
   AddResMenu(appleMenu, 'DRVR');
   AppendMenu(fileMenu, "\pQuit/Q");
   AppendMenu(controlMenu,"\pMove up/U");
   AppendMenu(controlMenu,"\pMove down/D");
   AppendMenu(controlMenu,"\pMove left/L");
   AppendMenu(controlMenu,"\pMove right/R");
   AppendMenu(controlMenu,"\pZoom in/Z");
   AppendMenu(controlMenu,"\pZoom out/O");
   AppendMenu(controlMenu,"\pToggle human/AI agent control/P");
}



void HandleMenu(long mSelect)
{
   int      menuID = HiWord(mSelect);
   int      menuItem = LoWord(mSelect);
   Str255   name;
   GrafPtr  savePort;
   WindowPeekfrontWindow;
```

```
switch(menuID)
  {
  case  appleID:
   GetPort(&savePort);
   GetItem(appleMenu, menuItem, name);
   OpenDeskAcc(name);
   SetPort(savePort);
   break;

  case  fileID:
   keep_running = 0;;
   break;

  case controlID:
    switch (menuItem + UP - 1) {
       case UP:
          y_acc -= 0.05;
         break;
       case DOWN:
          y_acc += 0.05;
         break;
       case RIGHT:
          x_acc += 0.05;
         break;
       case LEFT:
          x_acc -= 0.05;
         break;
       case ZOOM_IN:
         scale *= 1.3;
          break;
       case ZOOM_OUT:
         scale /= 1.3;
         break;
       case TOGGLE:
         // Toggle between automatic play mode for player ship
          // and manual mode:
          AUTOMATIC_MODE = 1 - AUTOMATIC_MODE;
          break;
     }
    InvalRect(&gui_macWindow->portRect);
    EraseRect(&gui_macWindow->portRect);
    break;
```

```
    }
}
void HandleMouseDown(EventRecord *theEvent)
{
    WindowPtr theWindow;
    int windowCode = FindWindow(theEvent->where, &theWindow);

    switch(windowCode) {
     case inSysWindow:
       SystemClick(theEvent, theWindow);
       break;

     case inMenuBar:
       HandleMenu(MenuSelect(theEvent->where));
       break;

     case inGoAway:
      if(theWindow == gui_macWindow &&
        TrackGoAway(gui_macWindow, theEvent->where))
       HideWindow(gui_macWindow);
       break;
     case inDrag:
      if(theWindow == gui_macWindow)
        DragWindow(gui_macWindow, theEvent->where, &dragRect);
        break;
     case inContent:
      if(theWindow == gui_macWindow)
        {
        if(theWindow != FrontWindow())
         SelectWindow(gui_macWindow);
        else
         InvalRect(&gui_macWindow->portRect);
        }
      break;
    }
}

void SetUpWindow(void)
{
    dragRect = screenBits.bounds;
```

```c
    gui_macWindow = NewWindow(0L, &windowBounds,
                              "\pVR Agent test program for Macintosh",
                              true, noGrowDocProc,(WindowPtr) -1L,
                              true, 0);
    SetPort(gui_macWindow);
}

void HandleEvent(void)
{
    int         ok;
    EventRecord theEvent;

    HiliteMenu(0);
    SystemTask();     /* Handle desk accessories */

    ok = GetNextEvent(everyEvent, &theEvent);
     if(ok)
       switch(theEvent.what)
         {
       case mouseDown:
          HandleMouseDown(&theEvent);
          break;

       case keyDown:
       case autoKey:
          if((theEvent.modifiers & cmdKey) != 0) {
          HandleMenu(MenuKey((char)(theEvent.message & charCodeMask)));
          }
         break;

       case updateEvt:
          BeginUpdate(gui_macWindow);
          Drawgui_mac();
          EndUpdate(gui_macWindow);
          break;

       case activateEvt:
          InvalRect(&gui_macWindow->portRect);
          break;
          }

}
```

```
void main( void)
{
    InitMac();
    SetUpMenu();
    SetUpWindow();
    // Create an output log file:
#ifdef GENERATE_LOG
    outLog = new OutputLog("game.log");
#endif
    OutputLog::write("Creating instance of C++ class 'World'...\n");

    world = new World();
    OutputLog::write(" ... placing objects in the world...\n");
    world_setup(world);
    // Add in the Crogans
    OutputLog::write("Creating Crogans...\n");
    crogan = new Crogan(world, "crogan.dat");

    OutputLog::write("\nEntering Windows event loop...\n");

    while (keep_running) {
      HandleEvent();
      // run the simulation:
      do_simulation();
      Drawgui_mac();
    }
#ifdef GENERATE_LOG
    delete outLog;
#endif
}
```

In Listing 9.1, we use the following include files from the VR Agent Toolkit:

```
world.h
agent.h
expert.h
genetic.h
out_log.h
```

The following include files were defined in Chapter 5 and are specific to the spaceship simulation:

```
game_val.h
crogan.h
pr_ship.h
player.h
```

The C style define statement:

```
#define GENERATE_LOG
```

should usually be commented out. Defining the constant GENER-ATE_LOG turns on debug output to the file GAME.LOG.

The function **do_simulation()** handles the simulation of all game objects through the public C++ class interfaces of the classes in the VR Agent Toolkit. If the player has turned off the software agent that usually controls the Player ship, function **do_simulation()** uses these global variables:

x_acc // acceleration in the X direction

y_acc // acceleration in the Y direction

x_vel // velocity in the X direction

y_vel // velocity in the Y direction

to update the motion of the Player ship. The global variables x_acc and y_acc are set in function **HandleMenu()**. The variables x_vel and y_vel are set so the function **Drawgui_mac()** can display the velocity of the Player ship in the graphics window (see Figure 9.2).

Function **do_simulation()**, regardless of the mode the Player ship is in, calls the public member function **World::update_all_game_objects()** to move all objects based on their current state (position, velocity, and acceleration). The state of the Crogan ships is updated with a call to the public member function **Crogan::move_all()**. The Crogan chromosome population (for controlling the strategy of the Crogan ships) is updated every 100 simulation cycles by calling the public member function **Crogan::evolve_population()**.

The function **Drawgui_mac()** prints a text message, indicating the state of the Player ship, at the top of the game window, and plots each game object in the game window. The global variable scale is used to zoom the display in the game window.

The function **InitMac()** initializes the Macintosh application environment. This function was derived from sample programs furnished with the Symantec version 6 C++ compiler. Function **SetupMenu()** initializes the game's Macintosh menus. The menus are built dynamically at runtime, rather than derived from a Macintosh resource file.

The function **HandleMenu()** is called whenever the player selects a game menu item. The standard Macintosh system menu is supported, as well as the ability to zoom the game display, change the manual/automatic playing mode, and change the Player ship's acceleration if in the manual play mode.

The function **HandleMouseDown()** processes mouse events for the Macintosh system menu, the application-specific menus (by calling function **HandleMenu()**), the game window's "go away" icon, and behavior for dragging the game window on the Macintosh desktop.

The function **SetUpWindow()** initializes the game window on the Macintosh desktop. The function **HandleEvent()** checks for an existing Macintosh event, and processes an event if one exists.

The main function initializes the Macintosh application environment, creates the game world objects, and enters into a continuous event loop for handling available Macintosh events, running the spaceship simulation, and updating the display.

Space Game Implemented with 2D Graphics for UNIX X Windows

Chapter 5 contained the design and implementation of a space simulation program with three types of computer-controlled ships. In this chapter, we constrain the spaceship and asteroid positions to lie on a two-dimensional plane, and add control logic so that a human player can take over control of the Player ship from the AI agent.

I developed the UNIX X Windows version of this game using the public domain UNIX implementation Linux. Linux is a great development platform, which I strongly recommend! I would like to thank InfoMagic Corporation (E-mail: info@infomagic.com) for providing a CD-ROM with Linux for the development of the example program listed in this chapter.

Figure 10.1 shows the Harel state transition diagram (Booch, 1994) for the UNIX X Windows version of the two-dimensional sample spaceship game. As you can see in this figure, the UNIX version of the spaceship demonstration game is very similar to

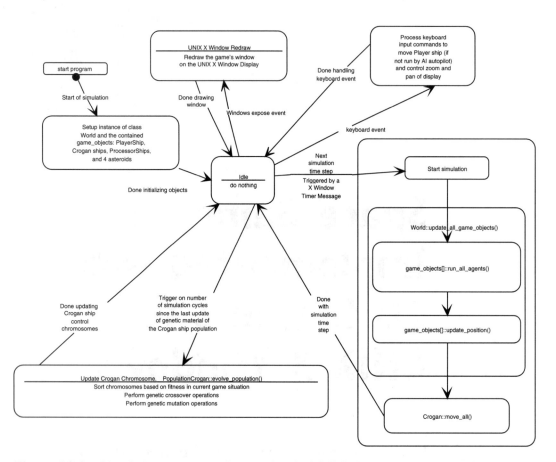

Figure 10.1   Harel state transition diagram for the UNIX X Windows version of the sample space game.

the Windows 3.1 sample program. For X Windows, we will use an X Toolkit work function triggered by a timer event to run the simulation program.

In the game program developed in Listing 10.1, the human player can take control of the Player ship by pressing the p key on the keyboard. When in this manual play mode, the arrow keys can be used to move between asteroids and Processor ships, avoiding Crogan ships if possible. As a game, this example program is not very challenging, but it serves to bring together three important themes in this book:

- Creating C++ VR Agent Toolkit game objects that maintain state (position, velocity, acceleration, quantity of fuel on hand), and that use software agents created with the AI utility classes developed in Chapter 2.

- Real-time graphics display (the X Windows timer is used to update the graphics window).

- Changing the state of the game world by interaction with the game player.

I anticipate that the first thing that many readers of this book will want to try is to retrofit an existing game that they have written using at least the AI C++ classes developed in Chapter 2, and possibly the complete VR Agent Toolkit to manage both the state and behavior of game objects. If this is the reader's first use of the material in this book, then the sample program shown in Listing 10.1 will serve as an example of using the VR Agent Toolkit in game implementations.

The 2D space game developed in this chapter is created by replacing the file TXT_GAME.CPP (file SRC\TXT_GAME\TXT _GAME.CPP on the CD-ROM) with the file TEST_X.CPP (file SRC\LINUX\TEST_X.CPP on the CD-ROM). Listing 10.1 shows the contents of TEST_X.CPP.

Listing 10.1

```
// File: test_X.cpp
//
// Description: An X Windows program to test Intelligent
//              Agent code under X Windows and Linux
//              or any other flavor of UNIX.
//
// Copyright 1995, Mark Watson
//
// This software can be used n compiled form without
// restriction.  All source code rights reserved.
//

// Small kluge: Set the color map entries manually for
// the different ship types:
```

```cpp
const int player_color = 7;
const int pr_ship_color = 14;
const int crogan_color = 9;
const int asteroid_color = 10;

const int FOREGROUND_COLOR = 1;
const int BACKGROUND_COLOR = 2;

#include "world.h"
#include "agent.h"
#include "expert.h"
#include "genetic.h"
#include "game_val.h"
#include "crogan.h"
#include "pr_ship.h"
#include "player.h"

#include "out_log.h"


// For debug output to log file:
//#define GENERATE_LOG

OutputLog *outLog = NULL;



#include <stdlib.h>
#include <string.h>
#include <time.h>


// GLOBAL flag to control automatic/manual mode for player ship:
static int AUTOMATIC_MODE = 1;

// Pointer to game World object:
World *world;

// Pointer to the Crogan genetic population object:
Crogan *crogan;

// Pointer to the player's ship:
PlayerShip *player_ship = NULL;
```

```cpp
// x and y acceleration components for manual mode player ship operation:
static float x_acc;
static float y_acc;

// x and y velocity components for manual
// mode player ship operation:
static float x_vel;
static float y_vel;

static float scale = 1.0;
static int x_offset = 120;
static int y_offset = 90;

// Protoype for single function in setup.cpp:
void world_setup(World *w);


#include <string.h>
#include <stdlib.h>

#include <iostream.h>
#include <fstream.h>

#define FUNCPROTO 1
#define __cplusplus 1
#define NeedFunctionPrototypes 1
#define XTFUNCPROTO 1

extern "C" { void exit(int); };

#define class Xclass
#define type Xtype
#define new Xnew
#define altzone Xaltzone
#define XtMainLoop XXtMainLoop
#define output XXoutput
#define input XXinput

#include <Xlib.h>
#include <StringDefs.h>
#include <Intrinsic.h>
#include <cursorfont.h>
```

```cpp
#include <X.h>
#include <Command.h>
#include <List.h>
#include <Form.h>
#include <Dialog.h>
#include <Shell.h>
#include <Box.h>
#include <Text.h>
#include <Label.h>

#undef class
#undef type
#undef new
#undef altzone
#undef XtMainLoop
#undef input
#undef output

extern "C" {
    void XtMainLoop();
#include <stdio.h>
};

static GC local_gc;
static Widget draw_widget;

void force_redraw()
{
    XClearArea(XtDisplay(draw_widget),
               XtWindow(draw_widget),
               0, 0, 1024, 1024, 1);
}


void draw_circle(int x, int y, int radius, int color)
{
    XSetForeground(XtDisplay(draw_widget),
                   local_gc,
                   color);
    XFillArc(XtDisplay(draw_widget),
             XtWindow(draw_widget),
             local_gc, x - radius, y - radius,
             2 * radius, 2 * radius, 0, 23040);
}
```

```
void draw_rectangle(int x, int y, int x_size, int y_size,
                    int color)
{
    XSetForeground(XtDisplay(draw_widget),
                   local_gc,
                   color);
    XFillRectangle(XtDisplay(draw_widget),
                   XtWindow(draw_widget),
                   local_gc, x - x_size/2, y - y_size/2,
                   x_size, y_size);
}


void handle_keypress(Widget w, caddr_t,  XKeyEvent *keyCode)
{
    char ch[10];
    KeySym ks;
    XComposeStatus status;
    XLookupString(keyCode, ch, 10, &ks, &status);
//  cerr << "k2: " << keyCode->keycode << " "
//       << keyCode->state << " " << ch[0] << "\n";
    // WARNING: the following code may not be portable:
    if (keyCode->state == 1) {  // SHIFT KEY DOWN
        if (keyCode->keycode == 98) {  // SCROLL UP
            y_offset -= 10;
        }
        if (keyCode->keycode == 104) {  // SCROLL DOWN
            y_offset += 10;
        }
        if (keyCode->keycode == 100) {  // SCROLL LEFT
            x_offset -= 10;
        }
        if (keyCode->keycode == 102) {  // SCROLL RIGHT
            x_offset += 10;
        }
    } else {
        if (keyCode->keycode == 98) {  // MOVE UP
            y_acc -= 0.05;
        }
        if (keyCode->keycode == 104) {  // MOVE DOWN
            y_acc += 0.05;
        }
        if (keyCode->keycode == 100) {  // MOVE LEFT
            x_acc -= 0.05;
```

```c
        }
        if (keyCode->keycode == 102) {   // MOVE RIGHT
            x_acc += 0.05;
        }
    }
    if (ch[0] == 'z') {   // ZOOM IN
        scale *= 1.3;
    }
    if (ch[0] == 'o') {   // ZOOM OUT
            scale /= 1.3;
    }
    if (ch[0] == 'p') {   // TOGGLE human player/AI
                         //Assistant mode
        AUTOMATIC_MODE = 1 - AUTOMATIC_MODE;
    }
}

void draw_everything(Widget w, caddr_t, caddr_t)
{

    int num_objects;
    int count_pr_ship;
    int count_crogan;
    int count_asteroid;
    int g;

    static int special_message_count = 0;
    static char special_message[80];

    static char *trade_status[] = {"trade not accepted",
                                   " ",
                                   "trade accepted"};
    static char *mining_status[] = {" ", "mining Magnozate"};
    static char *pilot_status[] = {"Human pilot", "AI pilot"};
    game_object * g_obj;

    // Print out the status line:
    static char status_buf[131], accel_buf[90];
    sprintf(accel_buf,"player vel: (%5.3f,%5.3f)",
            x_vel, y_vel);

    float R4;
    int magnozate;
```

```
int trade_type, mining_type;
if (player_ship != NULL) {
    trade_type = player_ship->get_trading_flag() + 1;
    if (trade_type == 2)   cerr << (char)7;
    mining_type = player_ship->get_mining_flag();
    if (mining_type == 1)   cerr << (char)7;
    R4 = player_ship->get_R4();
    magnozate = player_ship->get_Magnozate();
} else {
    trade_type = 1;
    mining_type = 0;
    R4 = 0;
    magnozate = 0;
}
sprintf(status_buf,
        "Status: %s R4: %6.2f Magnozate: %d  %s %s %s",
        pilot_status[AUTOMATIC_MODE], R4, magnozate,
        trade_status[trade_type],
        mining_status[mining_type], accel_buf);
XSetForeground(XtDisplay(draw_widget),
               local_gc,
               FOREGROUND_COLOR);
XDrawString(XtDisplay(draw_widget),
            XtWindow(draw_widget),
            local_gc,
            15, 10, status_buf, strlen(status_buf));
if (special_message_count < 1) {
    if (trade_type != 1) {
        special_message_count = 15;
        sprintf(special_message,"Trading:  %s",
                trade_status[trade_type]);
    }
    if (mining_type != 0) {
        special_message_count = 15;
        sprintf(special_message,"%s", mining_status[mining_type]);
    }
}
if (special_message_count-- > 0) {
XSetForeground(XtDisplay(draw_widget),
               local_gc,
               FOREGROUND_COLOR);
XDrawString(XtDisplay(draw_widget),
```

```
            XtWindow(draw_widget),
            local_gc,
            15, 25,
            special_message,
            strlen(special_message));
    }
    if (special_message_count < 0) special_message_count = 0;


    // Loop through all instances of game_object in the game world:
    num_objects = world->number_of_game_objects();
    count_pr_ship = 0;
    count_crogan = 0;
    count_asteroid = 0;
    for (g=0; g<num_objects; g++) {
        g_obj = &(world->get_game_object(g));
        int x, y, z;
        g_obj->get_position(x, y, z);
        g_obj->set_position(x, y, 0);
        x += x_offset;
        y += y_offset;
        x *= scale;
        y *= scale;

        OutputLog::write("Moving object ");

        int crogan_scale, pr_ship_scale, player_scale, asteroid_scale;
        crogan_scale = 5 * scale;
        pr_ship_scale = 4 * scale;
        player_scale = 7 * scale;
        asteroid_scale = 20 * scale;

        if (g_obj->get_type() == PROCESSOR) {
            draw_rectangle(x - 2 * pr_ship_scale,
                           y - pr_ship_scale,
                           2 * pr_ship_scale + 1,
                           pr_ship_scale + 1,
                           pr_ship_color);
            OutputLog::write("(processor ship) ");
        }
        if (g_obj->get_type() == PLAYER) {
            draw_circle(x - player_scale,
                        y - player_scale,
```

```
                            player_scale + 1,
                            player_color);
              OutputLog::write("(player ship) ");
              player_ship = (PlayerShip *)g_obj;
        }
        if (g_obj->get_type() == CROGAN) {
              draw_rectangle(x- crogan_scale,
                            y - crogan_scale,
                            crogan_scale + 1,
                            crogan_scale + 1,
                            crogan_color);
              OutputLog::write("(Crogan ship) ");
        }
        if (g_obj->get_type() == ASTEROID) {
              draw_circle(x - asteroid_scale,
                            y - asteroid_scale,
                            asteroid_scale,
                            asteroid_color);
              OutputLog::write("(asteroid) ");
        }
        OutputLog::write(x);
        OutputLog::write(", ");
        OutputLog::write(y);
        OutputLog::write(", ");
        OutputLog::write(z);
        OutputLog::write("\n");
    }
}


int do_one_simulation_time_step()
{
    static float direction = 0.01;
    static float x = 0.0;
    static int count = 0;
    float xa, ya, za, dummy;

    if (player_ship == (PlayerShip *)NULL)  return 0;

    if (AUTOMATIC_MODE == 0) {
      if (player_ship->get_R4() < 1) {
          x_acc = y_acc = 0;
          player_ship->set_velocity(0.0, 0.0, 0.0);
          player_ship->set_acceleration(0.0, 0.0, 0.0);
```

```
      } else {
        player_ship->set_automatic_flag(0);
        player_ship->get_acceleration(xa, ya, za);
        xa += x_acc;
        ya += y_acc;
        x_acc = y_acc = 0.0;
        za = 0.0;
        // modification: it is too difficult for human pilots
        //                to navigate using real physics, so
        //                use the arrow keys as "thrusters"
        //                which have a momentary effect only
        //                (i.e., no conservation of momentum here!):
        xa *= 0.95;
        ya *= 0.95;
        player_ship->set_acceleration(xa, ya, za);
        x_acc = 0;
        y_acc = 0;
        player_ship->get_velocity(x_vel, y_vel, dummy);
        x_vel *= 0.95;
        y_vel *= 0.95;
        player_ship->set_velocity(x_vel, y_vel, 0.0);
      }
    } else {
      player_ship->set_automatic_flag(1);
      player_ship->get_velocity(x_vel, y_vel, dummy);
    }

    // Move the game objects, and periodically
    // update the crogan population:
    world->update_all_game_objects();
    crogan->move_all();

    static int crogan_update_count = 0;
    if (crogan_update_count++ > 100) {
      crogan_update_count = 0;
      crogan->evolve_population();
    }
    // Update the display:
    force_redraw();
}


void main(int argc, char **argv)
{
```

```
    // Set up the simulation model:

#ifdef GENERATE_LOG
    outLog = new OutputLog("game.log");
#endif

    OutputLog::write("Creating instance of C++ class 'World'...\n");

    world = new World();
    OutputLog::write(" ... placing objects in the world...\n");
    world_setup(world);
    // Add in the Crogans
    OutputLog::write("Creating Crogans...\n");
    crogan = new Crogan(world, "crogan.dat");

    OutputLog::write("\nEntering Windows event loop...\n");

    // Set up the X stuff:

    Arg args[10];
    Widget toplevel, canvas;
    toplevel = XtInitialize(argv[0],"VR Agent Demo",
                            NULL, 0, &argc, argv);
    int n = 0;
    XtSetArg(args[n], XtNwidth,  200); n++;
    XtSetArg(args[n], XtNheight, 200); n++;

    canvas = XtCreateManagedWidget("drawingArea",
                                   formWidgetClass,
                                   toplevel, args, n);
    draw_widget = canvas;
    XtAddEventHandler(canvas,
                      ExposureMask,
                      1,
                      (XtEventHandler)draw_everything,
                      (XtPointer)NULL);
    XtAddEventHandler(canvas,
                      KeyPressMask,
                      1,
                      (XtEventHandler)handle_keypress,
                      (XtPointer)NULL);
    XtAddWorkProc((XtWorkProc)do_one_simulation_time_step,
                  NULL);
```

```
XGCValues values;
values.foreground = FOREGROUND_COLOR;
values.background = BACKGROUND_COLOR;
values.line_style = LineSolid;
values.function  = GXcopy;
local_gc = XtGetGC(canvas, GCForeground | GCBackground |
                   GCFunction | GCLineStyle, &values);

XtRealizeWidget(toplevel);

XtMainLoop();
}
```

In Listing 10.1, we use the following include files from the VR Agent Toolkit:

```
world.h
agent.h
expert.h
genetic.h
out_log.h
```

The following include files were defined in Chapter 5 and are specific to the spaceship simulation:

```
game_val.h
crogan.h
pr_ship.h
player.h
```

The C style define statement:

```
#define GENERATE_LOG
```

should usually be commented out. Defining the constant GENER-ATE_LOG turns on debug output to the file GAME.LOG.

The functions **draw_circle()** and **draw_rectangle()** are utility functions used for drawing the game objects in the X Windows game display. The function **handle_keypress()** contains code that may not be portable. The example X Windows game uses the arrow keys on the keyboard for moving the Player ship when in the manual control mode. There are two statements commented out at the beginning of function **handle_keypress()** that print the character codes associated with X Windows keypress events. You may need to uncomment this printout statement, note the character codes for the arrow keys on your keyboard, and modify the constants in the definition of function **handle_keypress()**.

The function **draw_everything()** draws every instance of **game_object** contained in the instance of class **World** in the spaceship simulation. The Xlib function **XDrawString** is used to print the current status of the Player ship at the top of the graphics window. When we plot the game objects, we use the value of the global variable scale to set the size of the objects; the value of the variable scale is modified in function **handle_keypress()** when the z (to zoom in) and o (to zoom out) keys are pressed.

The function **do_one_simulation_time_step()** handles the simulation of all game objects through the public C++ class interfaces of the classes in the VR Agent Toolkit. If the player has turned off the software agent that usually controls the Player ship, function **do_one_simulation_time_step()** uses these global variables:

x_acc // acceleration in the X direction

y_acc // acceleration in the Y direction

x_vel // velocity in the X direction

y_vel // velocity in the Y direction

to update the motion of the Player ship. The global variables x_acc and y_acc are set in function **handle_keypress()**. The variables x_vel and y_vel are set so that function **draw_everything()** can display the velocity of the Player ship in the graphics window.

Function **do_one_simulation_time_step()**, regardless of the mode the Player ship is in, calls the public member function **World::update_all_game_objects()** to move all objects based on their current state (position, velocity, and acceleration). The state of the Crogan ships is updated with a call to the public member function **Crogan::move_all()**. The Crogan chromosome population (for controlling the strategy of the Crogan ships) is updated every 100 simulation cycles by calling the public member function **Crogan::evolve_population()**.

The main function initializes the X Windows application environment, creates the game world objects, and calls X Toolkit function **XtMainLoop** (see Young 1989, Watson 1995), which waits for X events to occur. Keypress events cause the application function **handle_keypress()** to be called, X Windows expose events cause the application function **draw_everything()** to be called, and X Windows timer messages cause the function **do_one_simulation_time_step()** to be called.

Even though the commercial market for UNIX X Windows games is nonexistent, UNIX and X Windows provide a great environment for rapidly prototyping software. Some commercial game developers use UNIX platforms for game development, then port finished games to the DOS platform. If the reader has an extra 100 MB disk partition, I strongly recommend installing the public domain Linux system, with X Windows and the GNU C++ development system.

Ideas for Programming Projects

In writing this programming book, it was a challenge to try to accomplish the following objectives:

- Provide a clear discussion of the requirements that the software utilities are designed and written to meet.

- Provide a useful reusable software design framework, so that the reader can use appropriate parts of the designs specified in this book in his or her own software development efforts.

- Provide useful software libraries that the reader can freely use in his or her own compiled programs.

- Provide easily understood example programs that demonstrate the use of the software libraries.

My E-mail address is listed in this book's Introduction. I would appreciate feedback from my readers regarding both what they like and what they did not like about this book. I would especially appreciate hearing from readers concerning what material in this book most helped them in their own software development efforts, and what material was of less use to them.

This chapter provides some ideas for game programming projects.

Defining New Versions of C++ Classes World and game_object to Support 2D Maze Games

The VR Agent Toolkit can be extended for supporting different types of games and virtual reality simulations. Maze games, like the mega-popular Doom program, are fun to write. Figure 11.1 shows some proposed additions to the VR Agent Toolkit to handle maze-type games.

As seen in Figure 11.1, in order to support maze-type games, we can define a new subclass of **game_object**, class **maze_game_object**, that has class data for weapons and money. The container class **World** is used as a base class for a new class **MazeWorld**, which adds a member function **calculate_best_path()** to return a series of x-y path points for traveling between two specified points in a maze. The new class **MazeWorld** also has class data for storing the locations of walls in the maze. It would be appropriate to store other required environmental data as class data in **MazeWorld**.

Defining New Versions of C++ Classes World and game_object to Support Board Games

The VR Agent Toolkit can also be extended to support board games. For example, if the reader wanted to create a new board game like chess, but played on a larger board with fixed obstacles on the board, the following extensions to the VR Agent Toolkit would be reasonable:

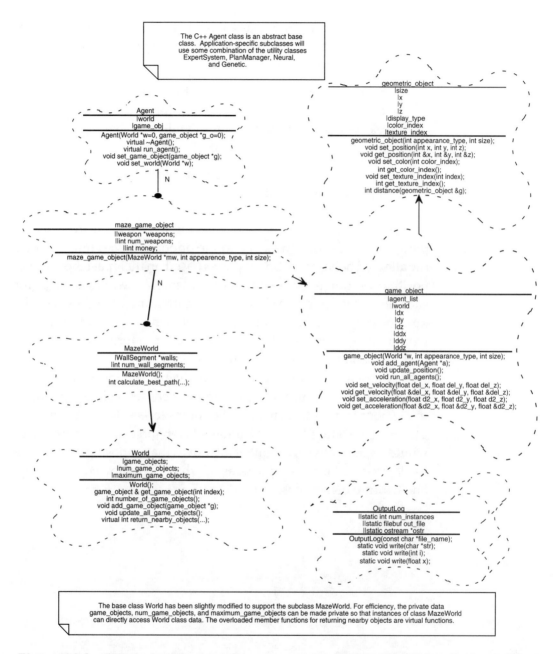

Figure 11.1   Booch class diagrams for new versions of classes **World** and **game_object** for a 2D maze type game.

- Subclass the C++ class **World**, adding class data to store the details of the game environment: board size, locations of fixed obstacles, and so on.

- Subclass the C++ class **game_object**, one subclass for every type of game piece. For a game like chess, subclasses for pieces like bishops and rooks would each have behavior for moving, capturing, and more.

- A subclass of C++ class **genetic** could be used to change strategy control data, for evolving game strategy.

An interesting variation to chess might be a game in which all pieces on a side look the same to the opponent, who must deduce the allowed behavior of board pieces based on their past movement. For the computer-controlled pieces, a template would be kept for each enemy piece on the board for maintaining hypotheses of the kind of piece it is based on past movements. The human player would have to keep track of this same data to form hypotheses as to the capabilities of the computer's pieces.

A similar variation to chess might be a game in which the program assigned pieces with randomly chosen abilities (both for movement and capture) to both the computer's side and the human player's side. Here, both the human player and computer opponent would be required to remember all moves that opposing pieces have made, and make a good guess as to what their allowed movement and capture behavior is.

Non-AI Techniques to Improve Your Games

The main text of this book covered artificial intelligence (AI) techniques for adding character and variety to computer-controlled game agents. This appendix covers a wide variety of non-AI techniques to add excitement to your games and virtual reality worlds.

Constraining the Motion of Game Agents

A main theme of this book is the creation of free-moving game agents that move in reaction to changes in their environment. It is occasionally still necessary in certain circumstances to "hard wire" the motion of autonomous game agents. Three good techniques for specifying specific motion patterns are:

Finite state machines

Movement offset templates

Way points

Finite State Machine for Attacking a Landing Helicopter

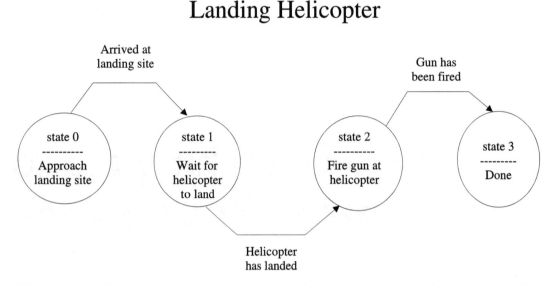

Figure A.1   An example finite state machine. States are represented as labeled circles. Lines between states represent conditions that must be satisfied to transition from a state to the next connected state.

Finite state machines have a specified number of states and conditions required to transition from a state to the next state. Figure A.1 shows an example of a finite state machine for attacking a landing helicopter.

The following C++ code fragment shows how to implement the finite state machine shown in Figure A.1.

```
const int STATE_0 = 0;

const int STATE_1 = 1;
const int STATE_2 = 2;
const int STATE_3 = 3;
const int STATE_4 = 4;

int CurrentState = 0;

while (CurrentState <= STATE_3)
{
    switch (CurrentState)
```

```
{
    case STATE_0:
        if (AtHelicopterSite())
            CurrentState = STATE_1;
        else
            MoveToHelicopterSite();
        break;
    case STATE_1:
        if (HelicopterHasLanded())
            CurrentState = STATE_2;
        break;
    case STATE_2:
        FireGunAtHelicopter();
        CurrentState = STATE_3;
        break;
    case STATE_3:
        MoveInRandomDirection();
        if (RandomInt(0, 5) == 0)
            CurrentState = STATE_4;
        break;
    }
}
```

I recommend using a **PlanManager** object to encapsulate finite state machines. You will probably want to subclass **PlanManager**, adding member variables for current state and other game scenario specific data.

Movement offset templates are occasionally useful to specify a specific series of movements. For example, in a game scenario with many obstacles like a mine field, it is convenient to use a **PlanManager** object that triggers when a game agent is in a specified area at the edge of a minefield. The game designer might plan out the minefield to require the following movements:

Move straight

Turn right

Move straight

Move straight

Turn Left

Move straight

Turn right

Move straight

Move straight

Turn Left

Move straight

Move straight

The following fragment of C++ code shows how this might be implemented (encapsulated inside an instance of class **PlanManager** that is activated when the game agent arrives at the specified spot at the edge of the mine field, and pointed in the correct direction):

```
const int STRAIGHT = 0;
const int LEFT = 1;
const int RIGHT = 2;

contst int NUM_COMMANDS = 12;

int command[NUM_COMMANDS] = {
    STRAIGHT,
    RIGHT,
    STRAIGHT,
    STRAIGHT,
    LEFT
    STRAIGHT,
    RIGHT,
    STRAIGHT,
    STRAIGHT,
    LEFT,
    STRAIGHT,
    STRAIGHT
};

for (int i=0; i<NUM_COMMANDS; i++)
{
    switch (command[i])
    {
        case STRAIGHT:
```

```
            MoveForward(1.0);
            break;
      case LEFT:
            Turn(-90.0);   // 90 degree left turn
            break;
      case RIGHT:
            Turn(90.0);    // 90 degree right turn
            break;
    }
  }
```

Movement offset templates are useful in game scenarios where game objects can move in any direction at will. However, many games now feature physically-simulated objects, which move under the influence of simulated forces like gravity, friction, engine torque on wheels, etc. To deal with this, a different, but related technique to movement offset templates is useful: way points.

Way points are a series of points that a game agent steers towards in a specified order. As the game agent approaches the first point, it will start to steer towards the second point.

Figure A.2 shows a playing area for a robot tank game. Tanks are simulated physical objects that must turn, negotiate rough terrain, etc. A mine field and an ordered set of way points are shown. The curved line indicates how a simulated tank might actually travel between way points.

Interaction with the Player's Field Of View

Placement and actions of game agents in VR simulations and 3D perspective games must be coordinated with the current field of view of the player. For example, in a 3D tank game, the player's view as represented on a computer display might represent the front view out of a tank. In real life, action takes place uniformly around the tank. However, games are meant to be fun! The behavior of game agents should be augmented to be aware of the player's field of view, and to try to stay in front of the human player as much as possible, within the restrictions of game play and game design.

Mine Field

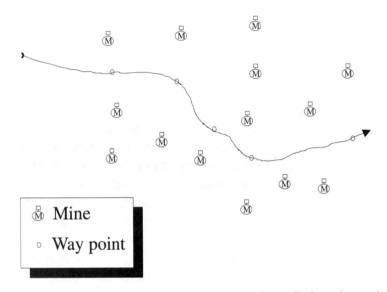

Figure A.2   Using way points to navigate a physically-based, simulated vehicle.

In this example, it is wasted effort for a game agent driven tank to perform a really cool maneuver out of the player's field of view!

One simple technique for concentrating game action in the player's field of view is to have computer-controlled opponents approach the player by first moving to a point in space directly in front of the player, then turning quickly towards the player.

Adjustable Skill Level

The play time of a game can be greatly extended by allowing for multiple skill levels. Intelligent game agents can be designed to use a single numeric skill level parameter. This skill level parameter may be used to adjust many aspects of game play, for example:

Maximum speed that computer-controlled opponents can move.

Maximum rate for changing the heading of computer controlled opponents.

Maximum distance for targeting guns, etc.

Add or remove PlanManager or Expert System components, so the computer-controlled opponents seem to know more tricks for effective game play at higher skill levels.

Increase the number of computer-controlled opponents at higher skill levels.

Coordinate Sound Effects with the Behaviors of Intelligent Game Agents

Great sound effects add excitement to games. In addition to cueing sound effects on collisions, tire skids, guns firing, and so on, consider using special sound effects to show the "emotional state" of intelligent game agents. For example, if you are using genetic algorithms to adjust the strategy parameters of a set of computer controlled adversaries, consider choosing special sound effects that are cued to the distribution of the strategy parameters. For example, if most game agents are being set for aggressive behavior, use harsh sound effects to warn the human player of the "personality change" of the computer-controlled opponents. If the genetic algorithm adjusts most of the computer-controlled opponents in a genetic population for timid behavior, then these opponents might make mild sounds.

Bibliography

Booch, Grady. *Object-Oriented Analysis and Design*. Redwood City, CA: The Benjamin/Cummings Publishing Company, 1994.

Goldberg, David E. *Genetic Algorithms*. Reading, MA: Addison-Wesley, 1989.

Koza, John R. *Genetic Programming*. Cambridge, MA: MIT Press, 1992.

Neider, Jackie, Tom Davis, and Mason Woo. *OpenGL Programming Guide* and *OpenGL Reference Guide*. Reading, MA: Addison-Wesley 1992, 1993.

Watson, Mark. *C++ Power Paradigms*. New York: McGraw-Hill, 1994. This book covers constraint-based programming, neural networks, and genetic algorithms.

Watson, Mark. *Common LISP Modules. Artificial Intelligence in the Era of Neural Networks and Chaos Theory*. New York: Springer-Verlag, 1991. This book provides complete LISP program examples for expert systems, neural networks, natural language processing, and examples dealing with chaos theory.

Watson, Mark. *Portable User Interface Programming in C++*. New York: McGraw-Hill, 1995.

Young, Douglas. *X Windows Systems Programming and Applications with Xt*. Englewood Cliffs, NJ: Prentice Hall, 1989.

Index